What People Are Saying about *Public Speaking for the GENIUS...*

Public Speaking for the GENIUS *is incredibly enlightening to both novice speakers and well-seasoned speaking veterans. Anne Freedman's take on this topic is a breath of fresh air and a must read for anyone who wants to learn and master the art of public speaking.*

> **Antonio Villamil**
> **CEO, The Washington Economics Group**

You have a speaking genius inside of you waiting to bust out! In her groundbreaking book, **Public Speaking for the GENIUS**, *Anne Freedman so eloquently and entertainingly shows us how to tap in to that inner superstar so you can mesmerize the audience with your message and your story. The fun part of all of this is that through her unique and powerful methods, you will not only love the outcome, but you will love this new speaking journey as well.*

> **Allison Maslan**
> **CEO, Allison Maslan International, and Author,** *Blast Off! The Surefire Success Plan to Launch Your Dreams into Reality*

There are several available resources on public speaking. However, if you are looking for one that is well written, offers practical easy-to-apply techniques, and was authored by a consummate professional with more than twenty-five years of experience, **Public Speaking for the GENIUS** *is for you! Anne Freedman has done it again!*

> **Dr. Brian Schriner**
> **Dean, College of Arts and Architecture, Florida International University**

Today, public speaking skills are indispensable life skills! We all need them. Anne Freedman has captured the experience of her many years of helping clients become better speakers in one compelling volume of speaking coaching and rich and relatable anecdotes that makes the reader just want to keep reading—and speaking! Thanks, Anne!

> **Steven Kaplan**
> **CEO, Kaplan Coaching and Consulting**

The book is quite helpful. It's well organized. The content is superb and easy to follow, and it contains great suggestions and reminders. Anne Freedman intertwines interesting anecdotes to keep the reader engaged. I expect to use this book as reference material for my presentations.

> **Carlos J. Martinez**
> **Miami-Dade Public Defender, Law Offic**

D1473328

What People Are Saying about *Public Speaking for the GENIUS*...

Luckily for me, Anne Freedman believes great speakers are made and not born. Molded by her experience, insight, and coaching, I have been able to navigate the public-speaking world in a way I didn't believe possible. Most of the world has some fear about standing in front of audiences and sharing ideas; as an introvert, I was no exception. This book is filled with memorable personal anecdotes and proven tools you will need to overcome natural fears, build on your existing strengths, and find your voice—literally. If you follow the strategies and techniques laid out clearly for you in this book, you will become a genius at building verbal bridges to connect with your audience.

Jen Earle
CEO, National Association of Women Business Owners

Anne Freedman has written a book that is sure to become the "Bible" on communication. She has helped me become a better speaker in my past sessions with her, and through reading her book, she has helped me even more. She can also help you. If you are in a leadership position, hurry up and get a copy and digest it. I assure you that your effectiveness will skyrocket, for communication is the hallmark of effective leadership.

Dr. Mitch Maidique
Alvah Chapman Jr., Professor of Leadership and Former President,
Florida International University

In this compelling and very informative book, **Public Speaking for the GENIUS,** *Anne Freedman shares what she has learned as a journalist, coach, and frequent public speaker. I found her advice on storytelling, the importance of authenticity, methods to increase audience engagement, and how to work a tough room extremely relevant and practical. I highly recommend this book!*

Jennifer Ohl
CEO, Midwest Software Specialists

Anne Freedman weaves informative, real-life stories in with concrete advice on how to be a better presenter. As someone who teaches college freshman public speaking, I can attest to the value of what Anne provides on improving presentation skills. Anyone wanting to enhance any aspect of public speaking skills would do well to read this entertaining book.

Anne Ray Streeter, PhD, APR
Assistant Professor of Communication and Division Chair,
Lindsey Wilson College

Public Speaking

for the GENIUS®

How to present yourself with new confidence, style, and purpose

FOR THE GENIUS IN ALL OF US™

Anne B. Freedman

Public Speaking for the GENIUS™

One of the **For the GENIUS®** books

Published by
For the GENIUS Press, an imprint of CharityChannel LLC
424 Church Street, Suite 2000
Nashville, TN 37219 USA

ForTheGENIUS.com

Copyright © 2017 by CharityChannel LLC

All rights reserved. No part of this book shall be reproduced, stored in a retrieval system, or transmitted by any means, electronic, mechanical, photocopying, recording, or otherwise, without written permission from the publisher.

Limit of Liability/Disclaimer of Warranty: This publication contains the opinions and ideas of its author. It is intended to provide helpful and informative material on the subject matter covered. It is sold with the understanding that the author and publisher are not engaged in rendering professional services in the book. If the reader requires personal assistance or advice, a competent professional should be consulted. The author and publisher specifically disclaim any responsibility for any liability, loss, or risk, personal or otherwise, that is incurred as a consequence, directly or indirectly, of the use and application of any of the contents of this book. Although every precaution has been taken in the preparation of this book, the publisher and author assume no responsibility for errors or omissions. No liability is assumed for damages resulting from the use of information contained herein.

For the GENIUS®, For the GENIUS logo, and book design are trademarks of For the GENIUS Press, an imprint of CharityChannel LLC. WowPitch® and Speaking Studio™ are trademarks of Speak Out, Inc.

Library of Congress Control Number: 2016948084
ISBN Print Book: 978-1-941050-45-3 | ISBN eBook: 978-1-941050-46-0

Printed in the United States of America
10 9 8 7 6 5 4 3 2

This and most For the GENIUS Press books are available at special quantity discounts for bulk purchases for sales promotions, premiums, fundraising, or educational use. For information, contact CharityChannel, 424 Church Street, Suite 2000, Nashville, TN 37219 USA. +1 949-589-5938.

Publisher's Acknowledgments

This book was produced by a team dedicated to excellence; please send your feedback to Editors@ForTheGENIUS.com.

Members of the team who produced this book include:

Editors

Acquisitions: Ellen Bristol

Comprehensive Editing: Kathy Wright

Copy Editing: Stephen Nill

Production

Layout: Jill McLain

Design: Deborah Perdue

Administrative

For the GENIUS Press: Stephen Nill, CEO, CharityChannel LLC

Marketing and Public Relations: John Millen

About the Author

Anne B. Freedman is the founder and president of Speakout, Inc., a Miami-based company established in 1990. She is an internationally recognized leadership communication and presentation consultant, keynote speaker, app developer, and author. Anne works one-on-one with business and community leaders to help them create and deliver key messages in a relaxed, expert speaking style. She also conducts group programs focused on teamwork and leadership communication.

Known for her dynamic, humorous, and memorable speeches, workshops, panels, and training, Anne has engaged, entertained, and educated professionals of all levels. Clients include multinational corporations, Fortune 500 companies, entrepreneurs, nonprofits, and community-based organizations.

Active in her Miami community, Anne served as president of the National Association of Women Business Owners, Miami Chapter, and is a founding member of Go for the Greens Business Conference for Women Entrepreneurs at Disneyworld. She's also a member of the Board of Directors of the Greater Miami Chamber of Commerce and participates in other business and civic groups.

Anne is the author of *Unforgettable Speeches and Sales Presentations in Eight Easy Steps* and a workbook called *Say It! Own It! How to Succeed in Public Speaking*. Her app, *WowPitch*, is available for the iPhone and iPad.

To learn more about Anne's fun, interactive, and innovative speaking and leadership communication programs, please visit *speakoutinc.com*.

To my mother, Natalie B. Lyons, who loved and led by example, never mincing words and always inspiring me with her passion for learning and life.

And to my husband, Ed Fischer, and daughter, Lynne Heather Fischer Seidner, for their patience and support as I keep figuring out how to juggle it all.

A special dedication also goes to all of the men and women who serve our country in many different ways. As a Vietnam veteran, Ed made me aware of the role of our Army and increased my understanding and respect for all branches of the military. His father, Leonard, was in the Navy during World War II, and then became a firefighter in New York City. Lynne was named after Leonard, and in a romantic twist of fate, married Casey, now a firefighter for the City of Miami Beach.

Every day, the men and women in uniform—military, coast guard, firefighters, and police—perform acts of bravery, saving lives and preserving our liberties. With gratitude, I thank you all.

Author's Acknowledgments

Gratitude goes especially to Ellen Bristol for opening up the opportunity to write this book, to the publisher, Stephen Nill, for his confidence in me and patience as I pulled the pieces together, and to editor Kathy Wright for her excellent catches and fortitude. While I previously produced two workbooks, I'd never tackled a project of this magnitude and really did not understand how much work it would turn out to be!

My late husband, Ed, listened patiently as I read chapters to him. Daughter Lynne's unrelenting encouragement to keep going was heartfelt and needed. From afar, I have felt the presence of my dear mother, aunts, and grandparents who always supported my forays, whatever they were. Also, I am indebted to close family members, friends, and coaches who listened to me moan and groan about writing and completing the manuscript. You know who you are.

Subject matter experts Dr. Brian Schriner, Dean of Arts and Architecture at Florida International University, and Dr. Anne Streeter, Assistant Professor of Communication at Lindsey Wilson College, were exceptionally generous in their meticulous review and on-point comments. Karen Payne's above-the-call-of-duty help as an unofficial editor helped me get on the right track and so did Kerry Gruson.

The stories in this book were drawn from the experiences of clients and other speakers I witnessed throughout the country. Names have been changed or omitted in some cases to protect privacy, but it was these individuals' successes along with their less than stellar moments that helped make the broad subject of public speaking more real and relevant. The text is also enriched because of the candor and recommendations from other respected clients and leaders who shared their speaking perspectives as well.

My own evolution as a speaker and consultant would not have happened if associations and clients hadn't taken a chance on me and what I could bring to the table to help their members and executives advance their communication and speaking skills. Looking back, I thank my Nova High journalism advisor, University of Florida professors and editors over the years for taking me to task when I needed it.

Contents

Summary of Chapters

Why are so many of us anxious about speaking to a group when we're fine in regular conversations? What can we do about it?

To reach greatness in speaking, we need to learn how to move past our self-imposed limitations and hurl over the obstacles others may have placed in our path on purpose or by accident. What happened to you as a child or teen matters, but you don't have to let it control you now.

Many exciting avenues open up for those who overcome their reluctance to speak in public—regardless of age—and who become adept at engaging their audiences. You can find yourself doing both planned and unexpected speaking. Each of these platforms can lead to new opportunities for your career, business, and community involvement.

Just because you are an expert or a leader doesn't mean you can stand up with no preparation and present a well-crafted, riveting presentation that an audience is thrilled to hear. Your success depends on how skillfully you sort through your content, build a verbal bridge to connect to your audience, and master the art of reading its signals while you're speaking.

Chapter 4

What Your Audience Really Wants from You 45

The heavy lifting of public speaking actually comes before
you get on stage, that is, the digging into your audience's
background to discover its level of knowledge about your
topic, preferences, and attitudes. This work gives you a solid
foundation for building your message. At the same time, being
able to quickly and concisely introduce yourself in a compelling
way will help you open new doors when networking.

Chapter 5

Overcoming Speaker Reluctance When It's Up to You 55

Looking over our shoulder at the speakers and leaders who have
come before us—and the trials and tribulations they faced—can
give us clues to dealing with our own public speaking demons.
Giants like Abraham Lincoln and King George VI of England
were not overnight speaking sensations, nor did they especially
love the limelight, but their efforts changed history forever.

Part 2—Taking Control of Your Genius Content 69

Chapter 6

Start at the End! What Happens When You're Done? 71

Knowing your goal for speaking guides the entire process
of putting together a powerful, memorable, and convincing
message. You can create both a personal and a professional
objective. A succinct and reengaging summary at the end
reinforces your position as an authority. Most critical: What kind
of action do you want your audience to take when you're done?

Chapter 7

It's Not Really All about You—or Is It? 83

Striking the balance between talking too much about yourself
and not enough to evoke any personal interest in you is one of
the greatest challenges of public speaking. Maneuvering in the

mine fields of language, from "you," to "we," to "I" is another skill that takes practice and dedication to acquire. Certain words and phrases can make persuasion more likely to work while others can turn off your best efforts.

Chapter 8
Organizing Your Content for Optimum Impact......................95

Part of the magic of public speaking is the ability to sift through all the elements you could place into your talk and pull out only the ones that ultimately draw your audience willingly and readily into your world, despite an ever-decreasing attention span. The other key is how you then order your genius content to make your talk easy to follow, leading to the action you're seeking.

Chapter 9
Recycling Your Content for Blogs, Radio, and Webinars.............. 105

Your good content can become a cat with nine lives or more, helping you to expand the impact of your message far beyond its original live speaking purpose. Many online and traditional media await your contributions, in written, audio, and video formats. You'll make Mom proud.

Chapter 10
The Famous Four Parts of the Genius Presentation or Speech........ 117

How do you open your remarks to grab attention from the get-go? How do you set the stage so the audience knows what to expect? What needs to go into the main part of your message? What kinds of closing treatments will enable you to end as strongly as you start?

Chapter 11
Opening Techniques to Avoid Yawns or Worse..................... 129

Those critical first seconds and minutes will either firmly connect you to or disconnect you from your audience.

Fortunately, there are a number of proven methods that can help you come across as a speaker who knows how to attract and keep attention from the start and throughout the presentation.

Chapter 12

The Fabulous Five Formats to Create a Genius Message

What are the different ways you can arrange the content to get your points across in an effective way? Are some ways of organizing your points better for persuasive speeches than others? How can you use these formats for both planned and impromptu speaking? What happens if there's too much information?

Chapter 13

It's a Wrap: Closing with the Right Words

Despite our hard work and planning, audiences can sometimes drift away toward the end of our speaking. You can reengage using strategies that rekindle interest. It's also possible to orchestrate a powerful close that brings about your desired outcomes.

Part 3—Turning Yourself into a Speaking Genius: The Art of Public Speaking

Chapter 14

Curtain Up: Face to Face with the Attention Span Factor

Thanks to smartphones, tablets, television, and movies, today's speakers are up against formidable odds when trying to truly engage with an audience, no matter what the age of those in attendance. By building interactive moments into your talk along with reenergizing phrases and segments to introduce your key ideas, your chances of keeping the room's attention dramatically increase. The right use of visuals will also help you capture and maintain interest.

Chapter 15

While speaking to other personalities who are similar to us is easier than to those who are different, we don't always get to choose, do we? Understanding how people approach their decision-making and relationships gives us the leverage to more successfully persuade and inspire during our important presentations and speeches.

Chapter 16

From our head to our toes, each part of our body can play a critical role in how we present ourselves and our expertise. Seated or standing, the challenge is not only to be aware of what our voice and body parts may be doing while we're speaking but to make them our allies in the pursuit of applause and business results.

Chapter 17

Just as winning athletes, musicians, actors, and card players practice to refine and perfect their skills, speakers who want to come across as confident experts and leaders need to commit time to rewriting and rehearsing their message. Practicing can't be haphazard or lackluster; it requires you to plan both how and where you rehearse and really embrace the effort to get the best outcome.

Chapter 18

Just as car accidents can occur in many ways, without warning, and with varied degrees of dreadfulness and inconvenience, so are the last-minute nightmares that plague public speakers and leaders.

You may or may not be the cause of the unwanted scenario, but how positively you handle the consequences determines how you'll be regarded by your audience and the community. By creating mental and physical checklists and a speaker's emergency kit, you can minimize the impact of these unwelcome events.

Chapter 19
Dealing with Hostile Questions and Technology 239

Whenever you speak to a group—and even one-on-one—it's critical to anticipate what kind of questions you could be asked. By preparing and practicing your responses, especially for potentially negative or disruptive questions from your audience or the media, you will better maintain your leadership position in your office or community.

In a similar vein, even though technology is such a critical part of many presentations and speeches today, it often breaks down, usually at the most inopportune times. To come across as the expert means being able to deliver your message successfully *without* technology if necessary.

Chapter 20
Become a Genius Speaker—and Get Ready for Success! 247

Unlike a movie or video, or even a taped radio show, where you can edit out misspoken lines or snafus in the production, when you're a speaker before a live audience, what you say is not retractable. You may find that things do not go as planned, no matter how carefully you set everything up. However, when you have researched who's attending, developed a well-crafted message, and planned and practiced thoroughly, you deserve the genius speaker title, the applause, and all the good things that will follow.

ike Anne Freedman, I am a full-time communications coach and keynote speaker. For years, I wondered if any of my peers would write a book on public speaking that would meet what I believe are the criteria of excellence. Such a book would be:

🖋 Engaging, entertaining, and easy to read

🖋 Valuable for all levels, from beginners to advanced public speakers

🖋 Authentic feeling, with stories from the author's experience and those of thousands of clients

🖋 Helpful in overcoming fear and anxiety, understanding how to organize content, and ensuring action from our audiences

Anne has written that book and she brings you all of these important lessons and more in *Public Speaking for the GENIUS.*

Anne's engaging writing style and entertaining stories will instantly put you at ease, which is no small feat, as the very thought of public speaking can be anxiety provoking.

Anne is a natural teacher, as she frequently uses real-world stories throughout the book to illustrate her points in a practical way. For example, in urging us not to be ruled by negative experiences from our past, she shares her embarrassment as a seven-year-old with a runaway rabbit, ashamed to speak during "show and tell," as well as a humiliating professional speech early in her career.

In addition to her own experiences, Anne includes relevant stories from many of her clients, as well as relevant historical figures such as Abraham Lincoln, King George VI, and Moses to illustrate how to overcome obstacles.

Anne believes good speakers are made, not born, and she provides a detailed framework for how to become a *Genius* speaker. In these pages you'll learn the most important lessons of effective communications, including how to:

🖋 Avoid the most common mistakes of presentations

🖋 Focus on what your audience really wants and needs from you

- Engage your audience and maintain interest in a world with attention deficit disorder

- Start with the end in mind. What do you want your audience to do?

- Organize a great presentation with a strong opening, body, and conclusion

- Gain extra value by repurposing your content for blogs, radio, and webinars

- Tell stories to engage, inspire, and motivate your listeners

- Use your words, voice, and body language to connect with your listeners and convey a deeper meaning

- Prepare and rehearse in a deliberate, efficient way for maximum impact

- Deal with the unexpected, hostile questions, and technology

All of these issues and more are brought to life in an easy-to-read context. In fact, chapters are formatted much like a good speech: a clear overview of what will be covered, a comprehensive body, and a bullet-point summary of what we learned.

Anne deals squarely with the central concern of most people when she writes:

> *Why is it that so many individuals tell me they are totally comfortable when speaking one-on-one or to a small group, but they freeze, feel sick to their stomachs, or dread the worst when standing before a larger audience?*

> *I believe it's because, at some unconscious level, we think public speaking is a totally natural endeavor and it should not require any preparation. After all, our mouth knows exactly what to do when we open it to talk with our coworkers, fellow club members, store clerks, teachers, or our families. No practice required!*

In *Public Speaking for the GENIUS*, Anne dispels this myth and provides a solution. For those willing to put forth the effort, this **For the GENIUS** book offers a comprehensive guide to making you a better, more confident communicator in business and in life.

John Millen

Introduction

My mother started describing me as a "word merchant" while I was in college, writing feature stories and investigative pieces for the *Florida Alligator*, the campus daily newspaper. It wasn't until years later that I really understood what she was saying, and it especially hit home while I was writing this book on public speaking.

Most of my professional life has been as a writer hired for specific projects. I began with articles and then was asked to write brochures, press releases, biographies, and ultimately speeches and presentations.

You see I never envisioned myself as a speaker. I was shy but curious and dreamed of being an international correspondent, as they called journalists who roamed the world back in the day, working for newspapers and magazines. At the time, I had no desire to be on camera, because of my fear of that way of communicating, along with my limited sense of fashion, and lack of mastery over makeup.

You may not see yourself as a public speaker either. But if you're like many of the men, women, and students I've had the privilege to work with over the past few decades, you are going to be expected to make speeches and presentations—and perhaps a toast or two—as you go forward in your life. Whether you are in sales, government, academia, health care, business, the nonprofit world, or technology, it's not a good idea to hide forever behind social media. Being known on LinkedIn, Facebook, through tweets or blogging, for example, won't help you face to face at a networker or in an interview. It won't help you at a board meeting to get funding approval or for a go-ahead on a new project.

You may find yourself being drawn to speak on video or perhaps traditional or online radio. You'll find that good public speaking tactics are vital here, too. Whatever your mission, you are not mediocre or merely average in the rest of what you do, and there's no reason you can't be outstanding as a speaker, also.

While my first public speaking experience postcollege went off without a hitch—I spoke to a Women in Communication conference about what it was like to be a freelance writer—the next one was an embarrassing disaster. I'd been invited back by the same group, and it was to be moderated by one of South Florida's revered public radio hosts at that time, Audrey Finkelstein.

By this time, my brand new consulting business, providing speeches for business and community leaders, was underway and this was my debut as its founder and president. I was supposed to deliver tips for making an effective presentation, as one of three panelists, each given about fifteen minutes to talk.

But on that morning, I was exceptionally on edge and out of sorts for two reasons. In my test before the workshop started, the slides I'd carefully selected were not advancing. I didn't know why. It had never happened before and I wasn't prepared to present without them. And, no doubt worse, for the first time since my eighth birthday, my parents, long divorced, were both in the same room to hear me, sitting on opposite sides of the auditorium.

Frantically, I hovered over the technician in an adjacent room as he tried to get the slides to work, to no avail. The two other speakers shared their advice and experiences and it was my turn. I waited a few more minutes and then went on stage. Mrs. Finkelstein quietly told me I just had seven minutes as we had to end the session on time.

I stumbled my way through—it was really awful—dreading having to face my mother, an accomplished speaker, and my father, not the most supportive person on a good day. Let alone the shame of allowing this disaster in front of Mrs. Finkelstein, the business people in the audience, and the other members of the association.

Licking my wounds, utterly humiliated, I never spoke there again or even went to another meeting.

What's in This Book?

What you'll find in this book is designed to help prevent you from making the mistakes I made that fateful day, and the many more that I've made since then! You'll be reading about some of my other speaking disasters in the pages ahead, with a goal of giving you a good laugh as well as tasty food for thought.

Public speaking, I have come to realize, is mental, physical, and spiritual and as you turn the pages ahead, you will receive guidance on how to succeed in all three areas. What I've learned from helping thousands of clients as well as my own experiences in the trenches, speaking, and training, is this truism: you can't control everything but you can certainly try!

The mental aspect of speaking requires you to keep at bay the negative demons who will try to knock you off your game. These are the voices from your past suggesting you don't know what you're doing now. You can silence them or, at least, shove them out of the way when it's your turn to present. And once your talk is over, it's over. While you do want to evaluate what worked, and what didn't, as Scarlett said to Rhett in the movie, *Gone with the Wind*, "Tomorrow is another day."

The physicality of speaking may surprise you at first. It still catches me off guard at times. We do have so many body parts to manage at one time, in addition to getting the right words out of our mouth in a timely, coherent manner! Hands, for example, often take on a life of their own on stage, moving as they choose, not following your cues. Hair behaves some days, not others. And you will occasionally get "cold feet" even when you've prepared and planned exceptionally well. It's all normal.

And the spiritual? My grandfather Herman always said, "it is more important to be lucky than beautiful or smart." Others claim you "make your own luck." What I'm talking about here is that realm of the seemingly intangible that surrounds our speaking experiences. Why is it that some days your speaking will go smoothly with enviable ease, and with the exact same preparation, the next time you're dying inwardly because nothing is going the way you intended? I don't have the answer, but I can tell you to expect both scenarios.

As you move into your own public speaking world, I encourage you to remember that these mental, physical, and spiritual dimensions are key to connecting well and consistently with your future audiences and to obtaining the results you want. They will accompany you wherever you go— whether you want them or not.

My goal in writing this book is to give you the strategies, techniques, and inner strength you will need—through my stories, recommendations, and research—to enjoy yourself and thrive as a genius speaker.

ra2studio @ 123RF.com

Getting on Track to Be a Speaking Genius

You have already taken the first big step, by starting to read this book, on your path to being a speaking genius. In this first part of *Public Speaking for the GENIUS*, you'll find an immediately useful set of start-up tools to help you overcome the self-imposed and real-life barriers between you and becoming a speaking genius.

To inspire you to climb aboard and stay the course, I will share the success stories of folks like you who have recently taken their public speaking to a new level. And I'll step back into time to show you how famous speakers faced their own public speaking demons—and emerged as the speaking geniuses I know you can be, also.

Chapter 1

How to Conquer Fear and Loathing in Speaker-land

In This Chapter...

- The "f" words in your life
- You've been public speaking far longer than you realize
- "I'd rather eat glass than speak in public"
- Face to face versus speaking on camera

Probably no single activity induces as much self-imposed terror as public speaking. Tales of woeful consequences abound for speakers who fail before an audience. That failure can range from saying the wrong thing to delivering an utterly boring or off-target message, or not being able to speak at all.

For years, public speaking has remained the number one fear of executives and other leaders, surpassing heights, bugs, deep water, financial loss, and even death, according to many surveys.

In this chapter, I'll lead you through the "f" word exercise to help you begin to eradicate the self-defeating behaviors that result from giving in to fear when you are speaking. I'll also take you on a minitrip back in time to recognize the role public speaking has already played in your life and how a successful client of mine dealt with her own trepidations. With video becoming such a key part of today's communication, I've included a brief introduction to the differences between live and on-camera speaking.

Just remember, now you are in the driver's seat, heading in the opposite direction of fear.

The "F" Words in Your Life

Chances are that the words keeping you up at night, both in a good way and in a negative fashion, begin with the letter "f." Here are some of the usual suspects that my clients and workshop participants have shared with me over the years. The positive "f" words express what they were trying to achieve, how they were described, or what they felt like along the way. The negative "f" words revealed their worries about speaking and its consequences. These concerns included how they might be perceived by others as well as their own turbulent feelings during and afterward.

First, consider the positive "f" words and check off what fits you best:

"When I'm speaking, I will have, get, feel, or can be described as":

❑ Fun	❑ Fabulous	❑ Feisty
❑ Fortune	❑ Fame	❑ Forward thinking
❑ Freedom	❑ Fortuitous	❑ Front and center
❑ Fantastic	❑ Friendly	❑ Favored
❑ Futuristic	❑ Fortunate	❑ Far out

And now, which of these not-so-positive "f" words plague you when you think about public speaking?

❑ Failure	❑ Frivolous	❑ Frightened
❑ Fear	❑ Faint-hearted	❑ Frightful
❑ Frustrated	❑ Flabbergasted	❑ Fanatical
❑ Facetious	❑ Fraud	❑ Far-fetched
❑ Flop	❑ Frigid	❑ Frenetic

You may want to add your own words to either of these "f" lists.

My point here is first to acknowledge that we want *fabulous* things to happen when we speak. At the same time, we almost intuitively sense and can get overwhelmed by the potential for *failure*, the biggest "f" word of them all.

Based on my experience as a communication coach and professional speaker over the past few decades, having worked with thousands of dedicated, passionate, and anxious men and women of all ages, I have found that you *can* have it all. You can experience the fear, the loathing, *and* the successful outcome. They are not mutually exclusive. For many people, the dread never fully departs. With the right tools, attitudes, and experience, however, we gain control over the negative "f" words and begin to manage them, instead of being under their spell.

In your new role as a speaker who exudes confidence and know-how, you will attract what you want and need on the positive "f" list and those negative "f" words will find someone else to haunt. Good riddance, yes?

You've Been Public Speaking Far Longer than You Think

If you are more than four years old, chances are quite high that you've been involved in public speaking for many, many years. Whenever a teacher called upon you to answer a question, from kindergarten on, you were technically doing public speaking. Here are a few other situations that may have constituted your first public speaking experiences:

- Reporting on what you did to earn a badge in Girl Scouts or Boy Scouts at a troop meeting
- Recounting highlights of your summer vacation to your class
- Acting in a school play
- Running for office in student government or another group
- Leading a meeting for your club or a cheer for your team
- Delivering a message to your congregation in a rite of passage ceremony
- Vocally protesting a decision or action
- Presenting an award to a deserving member or friend
- Accepting an award you've been given

It was because of some rabbits that I first developed an aversion to public speaking.

On a Monday morning in second grade, it was my turn for "show and tell," a now nearly extinct form of sanctioned public speaking torture for children in educational settings. Maybe you remember a "show and tell" at your school? Perhaps they called it something else. Regardless, the teacher's purpose was to begin to get us kids ready to stand on our feet for other reports and speaking situations.

Our class pets were a pair of light brown and white rabbits. Every weekend a different child took them home, in two big cages. I was supposed to use my experience with the rabbits for this dreaded oral sharing time of "show and tell," standing before everyone, at the front of the classroom.

Why was I so reluctant to speak?

After school on Friday, my mother and I put the rabbits, in their cages, by the back porch of our home. I grew up in a tiny town in Massachusetts where no one locked their doors. Saturday morning, I went out to feed our guests with carrots and celery and opened the cages. To my horror, both rabbits jumped out and in seconds scurried under the porch, way in the back, unreachable.

I called out to my parents who came running, and no one could entice those rabbits to return to their cages. I was mortified and cried inconsolably for a while, but my parents assured me that they'd soon get hungry and not to worry. Saturday passed into night, and there were no rabbits to pet or feed. By late Sunday afternoon I was a real mess. It was truly a seven-year-old's worst nightmare.

Fortunately, my parents were supportive. They kept going outside to wave carrots and celery stalks under the porch. By Sunday evening, just before I went to bed, the rabbits were safely back in their cages.

But Monday morning, standing in front of my classmates, I started crying when I had to tell about the weekend. And that was all I could do: cry. As you might expect, I was totally ashamed of myself. Looking back, I realize that the runaway rabbit crisis stayed with me for a long, long time.

History repeated itself regarding traumatizing a child when my daughter, Lynne, was about to celebrate her fifth birthday. The custom at her day camp

Trauma in a Blue Tutu

When my daughter was three years old and scheduled for her first ballet recital, I waited too long to get her tutu. Instead of pink, the store only had blue ones left in her size. I really didn't think anything of it and took the blue one home.

But on the day of the recital, my precious Lynne was crushed and adamant. She did not want to go on the stage looking different from the other girls, all in their pink tutus. Although the teacher persuaded her to do the dance, my daughter, now an adult, has never really forgiven me for that incident and claims it is a huge part of why she emerged as a timid person who hates to be center stage alone.

Uninspired

was to call the birthday girl or boy up to the flag pole, where everyone would sing "Happy Birthday." I was there for the special day and she did not want to go to the flagpole. The counselors dragged her to the center, and I did not keep them from doing that. She was terribly bashful and miserable being in the public eye that way.

Her trauma was even worse than my postrabbits weekend appearance. I had stood only before my second grade class when I broke into tears. Little Lynne stood in front of the entire camp and cried her eyes out while they sang to her. It was not a happy day. She tells me that was a turning point—and not a good one—in her ability to feel comfortable before groups.

Maybe deep in your past you were also in the public eye and had a horrible experience like my rabbit saga or Lynne's birthday at camp by the flagpole or her blue tutu calamity (see the sidebar). That painful moment stayed in your psyche, consciously or unconsciously.

Of course, it's even more wrenching and top of mind when we're in our teens or when these awful "in public" episodes happen to us as adults. You're in front of the entire congregation for a religious ceremony or a scouting event and can't get the words out. You forget to say something important while representing your company at an event. A well-known name comes out of your mouth completely wrong. You trip going up the steps in front of everyone. You stumble over words or lose your place, perhaps more than once. These moments are unquestionably excruciating, embarrassing, and etched into our memory almost indelibly.

The question is: how do we get past our fears and trepidations?

"I'd Rather Eat Glass than Speak in Public"

Judie Framan was a savvy public relations business owner from the southwest United States who found herself gaining prominence in her community and on the national stage. We met at a conference of women business owners and she confided, "Anne, I'd rather eat glass than speak in public." I never forgot that way of describing a reaction many people have to public speaking. Judie told me she was sleepless for nights before her speeches and she struggled to really connect with her audiences.

But why? Judie could never tell me why she was so anxious about speaking, only that it was a painful and often humiliating, though necessary, endeavor. Always a pioneer, Judie had been the only one in her high school class to go on to college. She had worked for a Fortune 500 company before launching her own business. Judie became known as a champion of small business and women in the state of New Mexico. She helped fund and start *Enterprising Women* magazine, and she was recognized by the Small

---

Perspiration

Cat Got Your Tongue?

When you get stuck trying to say something, you may hear someone ask unkindly, "Cat got your tongue?" Some historians suggest the phrase originated when criminals were punished by having their tongues and other body parts cut off, which were then fed to the king's cats.

Regardless of whether you have a clear picture of why you're afraid or just an unsettling knot in your stomach when it's your turn to speak, the key task at hand is to move past the fear.

I recommend diligent practice: at least nine complete rehearsals. This commitment usually makes a huge difference in how you feel. You'll find techniques and tips on how to practice in **Chapter 17**.

When you are asked at the last minute to speak, keep the focus on what you know, not what you *don't* know. Be as brief as possible and you'll help keep fear at bay. And the cat won't get *your* tongue!

Business Administration as Advocate of the Year, among many other well-deserved honors.

I helped her craft and practice some of her key presentations over the years, and she got better and better, though never truly enjoying her time in the limelight.

What was Judie's motivation to speak in public?

Judie wanted government to understand the economic role of small business in her community and state, and also wished to advance the efforts of pioneering women. At the same time, she was a practical business woman and knew that by "being out there," she was both supporting causes that she believed in and building her firm's reputation at the same time. Judie died of ovarian cancer, in 1999, leaving a legacy of leadership for women and small business causes.

Which brings us to the question, what is public speaking anyway? What is persuasive speaking? And what are you doing or planning to do?

I believe that one of the main reasons why many people are so fearful or anxious about what is called public speaking is because they are really doing a variation known as *persuasive* speaking. Whenever you are trying to get a "yes," whether you are selling a product, a service, or trying to get others to adopt your recommendations or move in a particular direction, it's a persuasive speaking situation. When you fail to get that "yes" or its equivalent, you can feel demoralized, upset, discouraged, and even downright degraded.

In business and fundraising circles, we gauge our success with persuasive presentations not by the applause we generate, but by the leads, the sales, the go-aheads, the volunteers who step forward, the donations received. Think about it for a moment. What matters is the action that our words generate, right?

When you enjoy success in persuasive speaking, you can expect to produce a ton of money for you or your cause, see career advancement, be invited to participate in new projects, and find new worlds to explore.

In contrast, what is traditionally called public speaking encompasses both persuasive speaking and motivational speaking, and it's often disguised as informative speaking. An expert on health care and weight loss, for example, may appear to be speaking to share vital medical information, the latest research, and other relevant data. But the real goal of the presentation may be

One Talk Can Open Transatlantic Doors

Years ago, I was a speaker at a conference of women business owners in San Antonio, Texas. Unbeknownst to me, the head of an international business organization was in my session.

Afterward, she invited me to be a speaker at her conference in Athens, Greece, the following year—all expenses paid. You never know!

Inspiration

to motivate people to adopt better eating habits, and perhaps to sign up for classes, or buy a special dietary supplement.

Who is asked to do public speaking? Top executives, government officials, elected community leaders, authors, and heads of nonprofits, among others. Why do they do it? A good speech to the right audience can result in traditional media coverage and many social media postings. It can open up amazing doors to you as a person and as a member of an organization or company.

So, in my view, you are already a winner, whether you are doing public speaking or its twin, persuasive speaking. Why? You have chosen to put yourself in the public eye, sharing your expertise, your passion, or your vision. You are making the world a better place with your words. Thank you!

The Worst versus the Best of Times

I thought you might find some encouragement in how other folks like you have dealt with awful speaking situations, either self-created or caused by others. And I've also shared some recollections of pivotal speaking experiences that helped shape my own future in this arena.

She Read and Bombed

Paula Black is an author, coach, and speaker. She specializes in helping lawyers figure out how to have a thriving practice, find what they love doing, and have a life outside of their work.

My first big speech was to a room full of managing partners of law firms, my ideal audience. I prepared my slides and wrote my speech, but when it came to really owning the material, I didn't have the time to prepare for that phase of the process. So I ended up reading the speech and as I was delivering it, I knew I wasn't connecting to my audience members.

They couldn't feel my passion or genuine commitment to helping their lawyers build a thriving practice. I wasn't fully prepared.

I have never again given a speech ill prepared. I don't read my speeches but I don't memorize them either. It's so much better if I speak it. I know the material so well that it flows off my tongue.

He Let His Animosity Show

The late Bill J. Bonnstetter was Founder and Chairman, Target Training International and TTI Success Insights, developers of Communication Style Analysis, Workplace Motivators, Trimex and other reports for companies and their teams.

My worst public speaking experience was influenced by my attitude. When I would be speaking to a group of analytical people—and I tend to dislike analytical people—I discovered that my mindset impacted my presentation. From that day forward regardless of the audience and who's in it, I now go with a positive mindset.

From Stumbling to Super

Howard Shore is Founder and CEO of Activate Group. His business and executive coaches have helped executives and their teams across the country to accelerate business performance.

My most dreadful speaking experience was when I first started my firm and I was asked to speak in front of a hospitality industry association group. I used a canned speech provided to me by an organization and I tried to memorize it. It was not my content and I was not yet familiar enough with the material. I was clearly uncomfortable the entire presentation and my personality did not come out.

Howard has come a long way since that inauspicious start:

My best experience was about nine years later. I was asked to speak in front of seventy-two business owners who were all in the same industry. Prior to the speech I did my homework on what was important to the group and determined their key issues. I also limited the amount of content and told stories. I got my highest survey scores ever. However, the big home run was that I developed a product idea specifically for the audience and my goal was to generate leads. I generated thirty-eight leads!

From Atrocious to Ideal: No Notes—No Net

Dr. Paul R. Ahr is CEO of Camillus House, a program that has provided humanitarian aid to homeless and indigent people for more than fifty years in Miami-Dade County, Florida.

It was a cold, dark, wintry night in Hannibal, Missouri more than thirty years ago. As the director of The Missouri Department of Mental Health, I was often called upon to address civic, consumer, and family groups about the state of affairs in the capitol, especially as they pertained to our department.

After a torturous drive through storm-like snow conditions, with his two young sons in tow, Paul arrived at the venue, the basement of a decommissioned 1920s–1930s era Roman Catholic Church. What had been the "lower church" had been converted into a banquet hall. Its vestibule

---

Uninspired

Technical Details Can Ruin You

One of the first videos I did was to promote my first app, WowPitch. I'd practiced the script and planned where the videographer would tape me. In advance, I'd arranged for a professional makeup and hair stylist to come the day of the shoot. On time, she made me as glamorous as she could, no simple feat! My daughter, with her critical eye for fashion detail, was on hand to act as a production coordinator.

When the video company folks arrived, setup included one lighting fixture. We did several rehearsals. I felt relaxed and ready. They taped and then showed us the preedited version. There were unflattering shadows. Apparently a second lighting apparatus needed for balance had been left behind. When the finished video was delivered via YouTube several days later, despite the hours and dollars that had gone into the production, it was unusable. Moral: You can be undone by circumstances beyond your control.

was a bar which that evening was hosting a popular NFL playoff game, replete with hooting and hollering. The "upper church" had been converted into a bowling alley, which happened to be hosting a tournament at the same time.

> *My speech was atrocious. I had to interrupt it to allow for the bowling balls to reach their marks and the hooters and hollerers to do their thing. At the end, the master of ceremonies, who seemed unfazed by the distractions, asked for questions, and receiving none, thanked us for coming and wished us a safe journey home.*

When Paul and his sons returned to their car, the snow was piling up, as was his anxiety.

As the boys were buckling up for the ride home, Tom, then ten, tried to console him, saying, "Dad, that was the best speech you ever gave."

"How can you say that?" barked Paul. "That was the worst speech of my life."

Tom replied, "Because when the man asked if anyone had any questions, no one did. That's because you answered all their questions in your speech."

Years later, Paul was to hear a speaker that forever changed how he prepared the most significant presentations he would give.

> *About twenty years ago I attended a Mass at the St. Louis Cathedral celebrating the retirement of the longtime Director of Catholic Charities in that city. The honoree, a close personal friend of mine named Jack, was suffering from late-stage cancer and was given a short time to live. During the Mass, Jack got up to speak, and gave the most eloquent speech I had ever heard, all without a written note. While he was speaking, I turned to another friend and said, 'What a privilege it must be to deliver your own eulogy.'*

> *Ever since that day I have striven to emulate Jack's spellbinding "no notes—no net" performance. Thankfully, I have accomplished the "no notes—no net" goal twice, each time in remarks lasting about a dozen minutes. In each case my feat was meant as a silent tribute to my friend, Jack.*

Face to Face versus Speaking on Camera

Until relatively recently, the only people who interacted with video and TV cameras were actors, actresses, broadcasters, and professional athletes. When top executives found themselves in the spotlight, it was usually to deal with a crisis such as a natural disaster, security leak, embezzlement, or some other issue they'd really rather not talk about but had no choice.

Today, your ability to "shine" on camera has become as important as your success in live, traditional public speaking. Websites look dated with no video elements. More and more emails are including links to video. YouTube and TED presentations are the norm. People can create their own YouTube channels and post their videos on any topic, anytime.

Apps such as Periscope, owned by Twitter, and Meerkat, allow anyone to do live streaming to their social media followers from their mobile devices. Once only the domain of traditional media, with these apps, everyone can immediately share on video what's happening in their neighborhood, business, school, or personal life.

With the ease now of creating a simple video on your computer, tablet, or smartphone in minutes, the challenge remains: "What do I say?" and "How can I look and sound good on camera?"

What you'll find in **Chapters 9–14** of *Public Speaking for the GENIUS* will also help you craft your message for your videos.

At the same time, take some comfort in the fact that most people are not great *at everything*. I've worked with TV personalities who were excellent on camera, but really uncomfortable speaking to a live audience with people looking right at them! They also were only accustomed to delivering a message that lasted one to two minutes at the most—known as a sound bite. Being able to keep an audience's attention for ten to twelve minutes—your standard breakfast-lunch-or-dinner talk—let alone a forty-five-minute keynote address is truly a different skill set than maintaining interest in a video for only a few minutes.

Your mission, should you choose to accept it—as that old spy show once challenged—is to give yourself the time and commitment needed to master both face to face and on camera public speaking.

Over the years, I've grown increasingly at ease before audiences of all sizes. Of course, I continue to prepare extensively, every time, and I'll be sharing with you some proven techniques for you to try in the pages ahead. When it comes to on-camera performance, I want you to know that I, too, have had to learn to appear more natural and effective. It hasn't been easy, but if I can do it, as a teenager several times over, it's going to be a piece of cake for you!

So, let's get started!

To Summarize...

✏ Acknowledge the negative "f" words but embrace the positive ones that influence your public speaking and your life.

✏ Unlike other skills like driving a car or doing taxes, the foundation for your successful public speaking has been in place since childhood.

✏ While the fear of public speaking is real and prevalent, an equal truth is that nearly everyone is actively engaged in its sister form, persuasive speaking, every day.

✏ Speaking before a group and on camera have similarities and also big differences.

Chapter 2

Opportunities for Speaking Geniuses

In This Chapter...

- So you don't want to run for office, but...
- The tale of an Internet underdog
- How a banker expanded her reputation and influence
- From shy teen to professional speaking consultant

"**T**he squeaky wheel gets the grease."

You may not appreciate being called "squeaky" as a speaker, but the adage points out that you get what you want by being heard. In a world increasingly filled with noise of all kinds—digital, traffic, industrial, music, and more—having your voice recognized above the din is increasingly difficult.

If you watch any of the election debates or the countless political ads, you may conclude that frank, open dialogue about important issues is secondary to accusations and attacks. Yet, candidates who speak well before the cameras and also on stage to their live audiences definitely continue to hold an edge.

As clients I have worked with over the years and news stories consistently demonstrate, the power of the spoken word remains a major factor in today's business and community endeavors. Leaders continue to come up from the ranks when they can convey ideas in ways that promote teamwork, generate worthwhile solutions, and otherwise guide their organization and community to new and better places. My own life has followed this path, too.

So You Don't Want to Run for Office, but...

It's sad to say but generally true, winning or losing in elections is not related to the candidates' experience, resume, or grasp of the issues. A win is due to a combination of how well they speak before groups, how they appear on camera, and their fundraising power. The latter also depends on public speaking and networking capabilities.

I contend that just like political candidates, everyone is in the same position in their professional and community roles. We are running for office even when we are not running for *elected* office. Aren't you and I frequently trying to get people to do things we want or feel are important? While we're not necessarily going after a vote in a booth, we are seeking approval, support, or some other kind of action.

The gift of gab, or a lack of it, determines if a candidate gets elected or reelected. Most candidates, and those now serving in elected positions, rely on so-called "talking points" to carry on their public conversations, their speeches to audiences, and their presentations to prospective donors. These talking points—usually thoroughly critiqued and reviewed by staff and close supporters—are what they intend to say on any given topic, including potentially disruptive or negative questions.

Recently I got a call to help the incoming president of an industry group who wanted to serve but who was miserable at the thought of having to speak before the entire association. He was at home in the board meetings but had never addressed the large gatherings throughout the year, nor had he participated in any of the lobbying the position was going to require.

The same day, I was also approached to work with the owner of a pest control company who found himself with less than adequate visuals and uninspiring content to share at the weekly meeting of one of his business leads groups.

In both cases, these business professionals had accomplishments and stature that made others assume they would be good speakers as well. Their own lack of familiarity with key speaking basics, however, was interfering with their ability to take advantage of the exposure their respective leadership opportunities posed.

The takeaway here is to think of your own reason for public speaking and to begin to identify what your talking points may be. What is important to you? What are you passionate about? Why? And why would anyone else care? What's in it for them to listen to you?

Talking points serve two primary purposes: (1) They help clarify what is most critical for you to be prepared to discuss. (2) They force you to identify worst-case scenarios that could arise from potentially negative questions or embarrassing revelations.

Pure Genius!

How Her Talking Points Hit Home

To build a local chapter, the national chairperson of an organization I've belonged to for several decades offered her wisdom:

◆ Go beyond social media and personally invite people to attend your events. Her Indianapolis chapter increased from less than forty members to more than three hundred in two years because "I went through my Rolodex and invited people to come." (She acknowledged that certain younger members may not know what a Rolodex is, and explained that it's a personal database, a collection of business cards of people she has met networking.)

◆ You are not alone! She advised those attending to take advantage of the leadership and mentoring programs being offered at the national level.

Guest speaking at a Miami chapter was Billie Dragoo, founder and CEO of RepuCare, Inc., then serving as interim Chairperson of the National Association of Women Business Owners (*nawbo.org*). She shared the same pointers in speeches across the country.

I'll be expanding on these ideas with you in upcoming chapters. The exercise, for now, is just to begin looking at yourself and your expertise as a set of talking points, as if you, too, were running for office. You want to be ready for every opportunity that presents itself, yes? This exercise can definitely help!

The Tale of an Internet Underdog

A few years ago, at what some might call the dawn of the changing Internet world, an upstart technology company decided to take on the long-revered web address—the .com ending for most sites. After successfully persuading the government of Colombia in South America to let it market the country's domain extension—.co—as a product others could buy, the entire executive team went to work speaking to targeted groups and select media. Their mission was to spread the word about this exciting new way for companies to market themselves on the Internet.

Chief Communication Officer Lori Anne Wardi was charged with speaking to a group of start-up companies at a national technology conference in the United States.

Although she had been a corporate lawyer and business consultant before joining .CO Internet S.A.S., Lori Anne was feeling quite anxious about this particular speaking engagement. She would be facing a room filled with several hundred entrepreneurs—known for their notoriously short attention spans and willingness to ask pointed questions. Compounding the stress was the fact that her speech would be streamed live on the Internet to other entrepreneurs around the world.

In crafting her message, she carefully chose words that would resonate with these start-up business owners. She was among the first to use the term "disruptor" to describe what technology companies were doing in the marketplace. She highlighted the example of companies like Google, Facebook, and Apple that had used the Internet to grow hugely successful enterprises, and told how they had started with a simple idea that accelerated into a global business.

To overcome her own nervousness, she practiced extensively, aloud, in front of her fellow executives and with me as her presentation coach. And as she rehearsed, she continued to refine the message, eliminating chunks and adding places where she could interact with the audience.

What earned Lori Anne heartfelt and vigorous applause at the end of her presentation was the way she connected the audience's own experience with start-up ventures to the idea of successfully bucking the established norm. In her company's case, it was recognizing that while .CO Internet S.A.S. was an Internet underdog, its aggressive and original platform offered domain owners an unprecedented marketing opportunity to promote their businesses that existed nowhere else on the Internet.

Fast forward to the spring of 2014, when .CO Internet S.A.S. was bought for $109 million by giant technology company Neustar. The speaking efforts of Lori Anne and the entire start-up's executive team clearly had attracted the right kind of attention.

It Begins with Putting Yourself Out There

Whether you speak at a weekly meeting or you only have an occasional request to be in front of a group, I encourage you to seize or create as many opportunities as you can to stretch your capabilities going forward. Why?

Similar to exercise or pursuing excellence in a sport or the arts, most people need consistent practice and some dedicated coaching to reach their full potential. It all begins, however, with identifying what you want to achieve in the world of speaking and then putting yourself out there, preferably smack in the middle of making it happen.

IMPORTANT!

From Local Banker to Senior Vice President and Community Leader

Griselda Martin (name changed for privacy purposes), a branch manager for a large community bank, loved people and felt totally at ease in one-on-one meetings and in small groups. She was selected to participate in the public speaking and leadership development program I conducted for her bank a few years ago.

In her role as branch manager, she was expected to build relationships with nearby businesses and residents that could lead to new customers.

She was also tasked with encouraging existing customers to expand their use of the bank's services.

As part of my leadership program and to foster business development for the bank, Griselda agreed to accept speaking engagements at local groups. The bank also budgeted to sponsor special events at her branch.

Convinced that talking about financial issues would not be exciting to most of the folks who would attend, she delved into the history of the area of town where her branch was located, identifying business pioneers, popular landmarks, and other aspects of life in her community that were distinctive and memorable. She gathered old photographs and interviewed surviving family members and those who had worked for longtime companies.

Griselda rehearsed in front of bank employees first, in the training sessions I was leading, changing certain parts as her colleagues and I suggested. She quickly grew more confident, and her sunny personality was able to emerge in front of a group, just as it did in more private circumstances.

The result was a fun, fast-paced look at the neighborhood that accomplished a business goal—promotion of the bank—without feeling like a commercial. Griselda had many promotions after that and is now a senior vice president at her bank and a recognized high-level leader in the local chamber of commerce. She attributes the public speaking skills she acquired along the way as a big key to her career success.

From Introverted Teen to Professional Speaking Consultant

I was a shy teenager who was also curious. In high school, I started out playing clarinet in the band, and later found my true passion, writing for the school paper, the *Nova Vue*. After attending journalism summer camp at the University of Florida in Gainesville (home of the Gators) the summer before my senior year, I came back to the campus of Nova High, in Fort Lauderdale, Florida, brimming with ideas. As editor and armed with my new expertise, I was able to convince the advisor that we needed to transform from an "8½ x 11" paper to a tabloid size, like a real newspaper. Having to interview teachers and fellow students to write stories, as well as work with the other student journalists, helped bring me out of my shell.

I Asked the *Miami Herald* to Add a Teen Section

To this day I don't remember how I pulled it off, but at age seventeen, just after high school graduation in the summer before going off to college, I got an appointment with the managing editor of the *Miami Herald.* Larry Jinks was a kind man who patiently listened as I tried to convince him that the *Herald* needed a teen section. In hindsight, I see this was really my first-ever formal presentation. Flush with my recent success as editor of my high school paper, I had come ready to persuade. What I showed Larry were two sample teen pages on which I pasted stories and the types of ads I thought would support such a section.

Well, Larry did not hire me but he did send me to the editor of a local, respected suburban newspaper group, the *Coral Gables Times* and *The Guide*, where I was brought on to create pages for teens, at twenty dollars a week, a twenty-hour a week commitment. The other twenty hours I spent at the Burger Castle, making shakes and French fries. That summer began a process of forcing me out of familiar behind-the-scene zones and into more face-to-face encounters with strangers than I had ever experienced before.

Overcoming a Fear of Flunking Out

Afraid I might flunk out during my first few months at the University of Florida if I came out of my dorm room too much, I waited until the second term to seek out writing assignments on *The Alligator*, then a daily on-campus newspaper. It was a glorious time for a young reporter in the late 1960s! Every day it seemed there was a different kind of protest—against the War in Viet Nam, ending curfew for female students, changing the drinking age, for marijuana legalization, you name it. I got to write about panty raids (seems so quaint now, yes?) and state secrets, about frat parties, the advent of computers, and the disappearance of the Bicycle Man, an iconic figure in Gainesville.

All of this reporting meant I had to call up to make appointments, show up and ask questions, and then write up the results.

After graduation, I worked for two local newspapers and then struck out as a freelance writer, providing articles for magazines and newspapers and services to public relations firms. It was in this role that clients began to ask me to write their speeches.

How a Machete Helped Me Speak

My own speaking career began in my late twenties when Women in Communication, a local industry group, asked me to do a speech on being a freelance or independent writer at their annual conference. I had not given a speech since my public speaking class at the University of Florida. In that course I had only earned a grade of B, and it was a pivotal experience for me. I realized that despite my skill and training as a feature writer and news reporter—writing for the eye—I didn't think I was cut out for what broadcast journalists and public speakers had to do. Since I was also still an introvert in college, I opted to stay the course in print journalism rather than step up to the emerging TV world.

Fast forward to my talk before one hundred communication experts. My time slot was one of the worst imaginable for a conference, right after lunch.

Before the conference I did a little research on the origin of the word "freelance," and based on what I found, decided to borrow my husband's three-foot-long machete, sheathed in light brown leather, which he had brought back after living several years in Puerto Rico.

I started by waving the machete over my head and then explained the origin of the word freelance. I discovered that the term freelance came from medieval times when knights sold their "lance" or sword to the highest bidder. Their services weren't free, but these knights were free to be hired by different castles for a particular duration.

Then, I shifted into a more personal mode, sharing some of the trials and tribulations I'd experienced with deadlines, getting sources to cooperate, and dealing with editors, all of which are different when you're independent, not employed by an established newspaper. This part I did in first person, using "I" to describe the special challenges I'd faced.

To ward off my own nervousness about speaking and in a concerted effort to keep awake a midafternoon audience, I decided to use a collection of "toys" to help make my points. I figured that if I had "toys" to distract myself, I wouldn't be so anxious. It's a strategy I continue to use and recommend to you.

Every few minutes I remember holding up a different large and colorful prop—a big feather pen, a toy clock, and a mirror. Somehow I got through the talk, they applauded, and I remember being relieved when it was all over.

How I Started Coaching

As a freelance writer for speeches, I had a routine. First, I'd do the research. Then I'd say the speech aloud. Finally, I would turn it over to the client. No one ever gave it back, so I had no reason to suspect anything was wrong.

Every so often, clients would invite me to hear them deliver the speech. After a few times attending these speeches and wanting to crawl under the closest table because they were so awful, I began to change my tactics. I insisted that a client say the speech to me at least once, so that I had the opportunity to help adjust it.

From this one-on-one consulting work and requests for training an entire team, our specialized workshops and the Speaking Studio programs evolved. I also began to get invitations to speak at conferences and meetings.

In the early days, I did quite a bit of "free" speaking to Rotary Clubs, university classes, and other local groups. My purpose was both to drum up business and to gain more confidence myself.

Letting Yourself Fly

In the beginning, I can tell you that I was not light-hearted about these appearances. I'd really get uptight and anxious and threatened to divorce my

Start Your Own or Join a Speakers Bureau

In the early years of my company, we launched a Community Speakers Bureau promoting the clients I had helped with presentations to land speaking engagements. They weren't paid for speaking but benefitted from publicity and the chance to appear in front of anywhere from twenty-five to fifty plus people at breakfast, lunch, and dinner meetings. Both new and experienced professionals and business people were trying to expand their sphere of influence, attracting new patients and clients in a genteel way.

You can strengthen your speaking skills and help your cause at the same time—whether it's cancer research, the arts, your child's school, or the environment—by participating in a speakers bureau or creating one.

Inspiration

Hanging Crepe

The origin of the expression "hanging crepe" comes from medieval times when families hung a black cloth over their outside front door to signify that a loved one had died. Over time, the phrase became associated with a discouraging or doom-filled medical prognosis and other truly disappointing news.

Definition

husband every time I had a new speaking challenge. So if you feel a bit overwhelmed and fraught with anxiety, too, I believe it's totally normal.

At the same time, it's helpful to remember that if people want to hear you speak, it's usually because they believe—rightly or wrongly—that you are an expert with something valuable to say. It's not just because you are gorgeous or someone's daughter or son, although those factors may help. Your speaking engagement is imminent because you have developed a reputation in your field, or because you are the in-house go-to person on the project, or because your opinions and information are valued.

The challenge is to allow yourself to bring the passion you have for your topic, your project, your product—whatever you're talking about—into your voice, your words, your entire body. To truly connect with an audience means temporarily taking off the mask that hides your emotions and giving yourself the okay to be your true self on stage.

I don't mean you want to "hang crepe" in front of a group, that is, show everyone how depressed or down you are, if that's the way you are feeling before your speaking engagement. That's not only unfair, it's unprofessional and selfish. Those kinds of negative emotions are real, but they don't belong in your speech or presentation.

To Summarize...

🖋 Even if you don't see yourself as a candidate for elected office trying to capture votes, whenever you open your mouth to speak you're seeking some kind of result from others.

🖋 Trotting out the spot-on message to the right audience at the ideal time is both art and science.

🖋 Speakers of any age can face challenging audiences and things don't always go as expected.

🖋 You can transform yourself into a speaking genius with commitment, persistence, and a bit of guts—as I did!

Chapter 3

Four Common Mistakes Speakers Make and How to Avoid Them

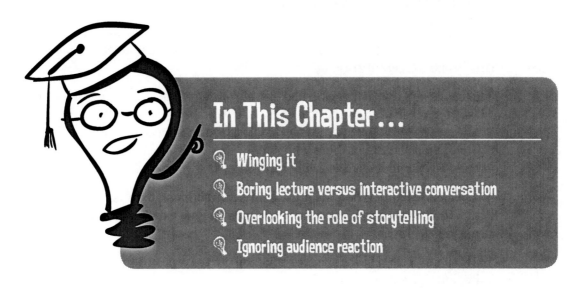

In This Chapter...

- Winging it
- Boring lecture versus interactive conversation
- Overlooking the role of storytelling
- Ignoring audience reaction

One of the best ways I've found to reduce anxiety when undertaking anything new is to ask a ton of questions before diving into the task. Maybe it's my journalistic training. Or it could be a wish not to appear helpless or dumb in a new arena, especially technology.

In this chapter, to help you continue to minimize the impact of any negative "F" words on your genius speaking, I will give you a rundown of the most common mistakes that speakers make and tell you how to avoid them.

First, I'll explain why a lack of preparation dooms most speakers. On the flip side, I'll reveal why having to do impromptu speaking doesn't mean you can't do a good job. You will analyze how a presentation that maintains the interest of those in your audience differs from a deadly lecture.

Next, you will also gain an understanding of the need to delete more content than you expect, strategically, before you speak. And I'll give you pointers on storytelling and reading your audience that will keep you on top of your speaking game.

Speaker Mistake Number One: Winging It

What Do You Mean by "Wing It?"

Where did this English-only expression come from, and why is it not a recommended tactic for most speakers?

The phrase "winging it" seems to have several different late nineteenth and early twentieth-century origins.

One theory says that actors who had trouble remembering their lines in the late 1800s often relied on prompts from men and women off stage *in the wings* of the theater, those adjacent areas not visible to the audience. The performances of ill-prepared actors—or those who had to carry on when the prompter wasn't on hand—became known as "winging it."

Another explanation is that the phrase simply describes a baby bird taking flight from the nest for the first time, a wonderful image that applies to fledgling speakers as well, yes?

I had been told early in my speaking that the phrase was attributed to Orville and Wilbur Wright, the Indiana brothers who invented the airplane. They did an extensive amount of testing on gliders before advancing to what we think of as an airplane today. On the gliders, a man would stand up and literally walk up and down on the wings of the aircraft to help balance it during flight, a feat that gained the name, "winging it." I confess that in writing this book, I could not find any substantiation for this origin, but I still like the mental image it evokes.

How to Tell If a Speaker Is "Winging It"

Here are some clues that let you know when a speaker is not ready for prime time:

🔖 The speaker is obviously unprepared for the situation or question and looks uncomfortable or nervous.

🔖 You hear many verbal fillers such as "er," "uh," "um," and "you know," between sentences because the speaker doesn't know what to say next.

🔖 The message is disorganized, hard to follow, and not particularly impressive.

🔖 The speaker asks the audience or person who made the introduction how long the speech is supposed to last and is clueless about the expectations of the organization that invited them.

You've no doubt seen speakers exhibiting the behaviors in the examples above. It's painful for everyone in the room and especially painful for the person in front of the group.

Experienced speakers are not actually winging it when they get up to speak extemporaneously. They are pulling up content that has previously worked from their experience bag. They know how to pace themselves, how to interact with the audience, and how to make their points. Public speaking is an acquired skill that you can develop with practice and commitment.

Why not wing it? No one in an audience appreciates sitting through an awkward, poorly-crafted message, which is what

Think Rubber Chicken

I wave a rubber chicken in the air during my workshops to illustrate "winging it" and discourage its practice. When you try to wing it, I contend, your presentation or speech will have as much flavor, as much substance, and as much lasting appeal as Charlie, my much beloved and long-suffering rubber chicken.

Not having a clear plan or the opportunity to practice can mean you accidentally leave out critical points, stumble when pronouncing words, or muddle through with irrelevant or inaccurate statements.

By the way, I've done some work in Spanish and discovered there is no equivalent expression for "wing it." So I have adapted the phrase into Spanish, which roughly translates as "don't fly without all of your feathers."

Inspiration

happens most often when someone wings it. If you are the speaker, not having a definite plan or the opportunity to practice can mean you accidentally leave out critical points, stumble when pronouncing words, or muddle through with irrelevant or inaccurate statements.

What Are Some Anti-Winging-It Solutions?

Give yourself ample time to clearly identify the two or three main points you want to get across in your remarks and build your message around them. Even if you receive a last-minute request to speak, write down the two or three most critical ideas you want to get across, on a napkin if necessary.

For best results, always practice aloud, out of order, in pieces; and time each element to be sure you're not exceeding your scheduled allotment. For last-minute winging-it situations, assume control *as if* you'd practiced. No one knows unless you tell them otherwise!

In coming chapters, I'll introduce more tactics and techniques you can use to help avoid winging it even when you are asked to give an impromptu presentation or speech, a last-minute request with absolutely no time to prepare.

Speaker Mistake Number Two: Lecture versus Interaction

If you think about a classic sermon by a member of the clergy, or a typical university lecture, the majority are one-sided affairs. Somebody talks. You listen. It's often dry and dull, or worse, dreary and draining.

Sometimes we're lucky, yes? The speaker is riveting. Thoughtful. Inspirational. Full of valuable ideas and data. After all, there are clergy who know how to connect to their congregation, and there are also a few wonderful professors and teachers out there. Additionally, every once in a while, we're thrilled when corporate or nonprofit leaders, coaches, or entrepreneurs can make us feel glad we were on hand when they spoke.

What Kind of Speaker Do You Want to Be?

Today's audiences are demanding and expecting cinema-like experiences when they sit before a speaker in a live situation—whether it's a staff meeting, sales presentation, speech, fundraising effort, or webinar. Instead of patiently and politely listening to a speaker drone on and on about a particular area of expertise or point of view, audiences can and do whip out their cell phones or tablets and lose themselves on the Internet.

For you to counteract the chance of coming across as boring or otherwise not connecting well with your audience, I recommend you incorporate what I call The Speaker's Three E's:

🖘 *Entertain them.* First, strive to create *entertainment* value in your message. Examples of this first Speaker E are a relevant and preferably humorous story or set of delicious, smile-evoking comments. You can also use a funny sign, prop, or video clip, or a combination of elements.

(I'll talk more about storytelling in **Chapters 14** and **17**.)

🖘 *Educate a bit.* The second Speaker E is to plan the *educational* value you are including. What practical takeaways are you giving in your message? No one wants to waste time these days. Are you sharing your expertise and experiences in such a way that your audience feels lucky to have been listening to you? What tips, pointers, references, visual examples, or other content can you impart so that the message does not seem like a dull lecture or sermon?

How can you organize what you know so the audience can absorb it as painlessly and completely as possible? We'll explore more about organizing your content in **Chapter 8**, but go there now if you're curious and need the information right away.

🖘 *Energize with inspiration.* The third Speaker E is *energizing inspiration*. What can you impart that will help people overcome the feeling of being overwhelmed, stressed, pulled in too many directions at the same time, and needing inner strength? When you're the speaker—no matter what your role or objective—I believe you have a much better chance of accomplishing your goal when you tune into the motivations of your listeners and charge up the atmosphere with your own brand of energy.

While each of us is motivated by different things, I believe it's our obligation as a speaker and leader to build into messages a genuine taste of your passion for the topic as well as why you believe in its importance.

When you build the Three Speaker E's into your message, you'll be the kind of speaker we all want to hear.

What Does Your Cup Say about You?

I was asked to do a motivational speech for a local charity event and my first reaction was to say no. While I have helped many speakers to be motivational and tried to be motivational in my training and keynotes, I'd never before given a speech with a purpose of inspiring a group to do something other than as president of my chapter of the National Association of Women Business Owners!

The brilliant solution came from some wise folks in a mastermind group to which I belonged. Why not combine how I teach people to communicate with a motivational approach, they suggested? Armed with that vision, I accepted the invitation to speak.

Since the theme was a tea party, and Starbucks was a sponsor serving both coffees and teas, I called my talk "What Does Your Cup Say about You?" In it, I compared the ways we typically drink our morning beverage with the kind of behavior we usually display in our conversations and interactions with others.

For example, I described the direct personality types as those who tend to want to experience a different kind of coffee or tea every day, seeking adventure and dominance over this part their morning ritual. The outgoing and socially-minded influencers prefer to enjoy their coffee in the company of others. The introverted steadies may avoid breakfast entirely, or have the same exact tea or coffee every day. And the data-prone check-listers are known for following a precise schedule and set of procedures in the morning, assuring that their coffee comes out correctly and they are on time for the day. (Look for more on these styles and their role in your genius speaking in **Chapter 15.**)

In the presentation, I went on to guide the audience through how to take advantage of these differences to make their community volunteering and fundraising endeavors more successful.

I was grateful to my friends who helped me see how to add inspirational overtones to a how-to message. You can, too.

Speaker Mistake Number Three—Overlooking Storytelling

Ever since we were children, stories have delighted us, scared us, and motivated us to action. It's been my experience that your audience will not remember the facts you so diligently gathered and organized, no matter how impressive. What they will value and repeat to others are the relevant and well-told stories you share about your expertise, your trip, your project, or whatever has led you to be in front of them that day.

My early professional years were working as a journalist, and my training was focused on writing about other people's stories. As I mentioned earlier, I was expected to be neutral, to find and report on information and points of view on both sides of an issue. I loved interviewing all kinds of folks—musicians, artists, entrepreneurs, community leaders, teachers, and even ex-cons—because they often revealed fascinating encounters and observations.

As a journalist, I was expected to create vivid descriptions and, equally important, to select the most compelling words the person I was interviewing had said and capture them on paper, inside quotation marks.

You Might Find Yourself on the Dark Side

I remember writing about a drug treatment program that claimed to have a high success rate for its graduates. Some of the parents I spoke to raved about how the program had saved their kids' lives. The police thought it was a stellar example of how to get kids off drugs. The mayor and elected officials who helped fund it were happy to be quoted on the program's positive impact.

But there was a dark side, I also discovered. Some of the teens and other parents told me off the record that the whole experience felt like brainwashing, the leader was mean and two-faced, and the staff followed directions explicitly with no regard to how individuals responded to the so-called treatments. The teens told me that sometimes they got sick to their stomach, cried for hours, and were not allowed to talk to their parents or anyone else for days on end.

As a young reporter, not many years older than those troubled teenagers, I was inclined to believe their stories. I grew angrier and angrier as I interviewed parents and teens who gave me example after example of mistreatment, callous disregard for the rights of children, and near-torturous behavior. But I could not write what I thought or felt. I had to write the story so that it appeared even-handed, balanced with the positive and negative findings I had discovered.

When the story appeared in the newspaper, I did get angry calls on both sides of the issue, which meant I did my job as a journalist. But that is *not* your job! You do not need to be neutral or even-handed in what you describe, as I was expected to be as a journalist.

When you are the speaker, I urge you to *own* the stories you present and tell them in as personal and as convincing a way as possible. These are your stories, told from your perspective, revealing your own feelings and reactions to whatever happened.

Your Storytelling Has No Limits

Ideally, when you present a story, you take us with you on your adventure so that we can reexperience it with you and sample the full range of emotions, colors, sounds, tastes, and conversations that left their mark on you.

In the beginning of my speaking career, I deliberately kept myself out of the story equation—staying true to my journalism roots. With experience, though, I realized my responsibility was to really connect with my audience. I started to share my relevant life and professional experiences with my audiences and individual clients. You've already read some of them in the first few chapters and you'll encounter more throughout the rest of the book.

Good storytelling is a form of live theater, and the top actors always practice extensively before appearing on stage. The award-winning movie actors also rehearse

Words Are Not Enough

Another important thing to remember about storytelling is that the words are only half of the equation. The other half is how you *tell* the story. Ask yourself these questions:

◆ Are you racing through, or pausing for dramatic effect here and there?

◆ Are you varying your vocal variety, getting quieter at key points, and raising the volume at others?

◆ What about your eye contact? Are you looking at the audience or only at your notes? Where are you adding appropriate gestures, moving your body and your hands to make a point?

◆ How is your posture? Are you standing erectly or slouching? Are your movements reinforcing the story or are they awkward?

IMPORTANT!

their roles for hours and hours before filming. The actors' job is to make you believe that they are actually the characters you are seeing.

While the stories you tell may be a part of your personal or professional life experiences, it's one thing to describe to your friends or family members what happened, and a whole different challenge to present it to an audience of strangers. Take your cue from the world of fine actors and allow yourself ample time to fine-tune the pieces of your stories with spoken-out-loud practice, so that you come across as natural and credible.

One technique that actors use to elevate the energy level in their delivery is to attach a certain emotion or set of emotions to a particular group of lines, or an individual line, i.e., angry, happy, frustrated, satisfied, or light-hearted.

Go through your story and highlight critical parts in different color markers, and then assign an emotion to each color. What you don't want to do is tell the story in only one tone, in only one color, a sure-fire way to lose your audience's attention.

You can embrace your nervousness as an ally. You can also deliberately look for opportunities to use storytelling to interact with your audiences.

One of my favorite former newspaper editors, David Lawrence, Jr., shared his approach to public speaking with me:

> *I like to be nervous before every speech. Really.*
>
> *A speaker always knows—or at least I do—when it has gone well, and when it has not. There have been occasions when I've approached the podium and thought to myself: 'Piece of cake. I've got this one knocked.' In every one of those occasions I've not done my best. Being a bit uptight makes me think harder, perform better.*
>
> *Every chance I get, in starting a speech, I play off something the introducer said, or something happening in the room, and I almost always do it with humor. I do that to loosen up myself, and the audience.*

David is a retired publisher of the *Miami Herald* and now president of a pioneering nonpartisan grassroots organization that supports the need for increased investment in the first five years of a child's life, The Children's Movement of Florida. He is also Community Leadership Scholar at the University of Miami School of Education and Human Development.

I do a lot of speaking around Florida and around the country. Almost all my speaking is about matters of 'school readiness' and investment in early learning. Before I speak anywhere, I do a bunch of research—much of it on the Internet—about the real world for the children of that community or state. People know when you're really prepared, and when you aren't. They appreciate that you've really worked to know their community.

In just about every speech, I insert the personal. That frequently includes stories about my own life, including my growing-up years, and my family. People are hungry for people of values—people who inspire them—and for just plain, straight talk.

And I really love the Q&A portion. The interchange forces you to rise to the occasion and share some real wisdom, frequently in the form of personal experience.

To connect—to create the kind of relationship you want with an audience—avoid hiding emotionally or personally, even if that is a more comfortable route to take.

Speaker Mistake Number Four— Ignoring Audience Reaction

If two-thirds or more of your audience are fully engaged with their cell phones, tablets, or laptops during your presentation, chances are you're not connecting the way you expected to do. Other clues include an excessive amount of yawning and coughing, and nose blowing not attributable to a sudden flu epidemic. A sea of knees that look like they are inching toward the door and widespread slumping in the seats is also not a good sign.

What do you do if you find yourself with an audience that is not paying attention to you and your message?

Sample Questions to Reengage Your Audience

What have you done when you've been faced with this kind of situation?

What worked best and why?

Would you share what you tried that didn't work well, and why you thought that happened?

When do you think is the best time to change the direction of what your group is doing?

How do you introduce a new concept like this at your office?

What use do you see for this kind of approach in your world/office/community/personal life?

Example

First, I do not recommend that you ignore their reaction, no matter how painful. It's not necessary to get on your knees and grovel in apology. It's also not a good idea to take off your clothes, whistle loudly, or stomp your feet. You do need to change course and move away from the tone and direction you planned or risk things turning even sourer.

It takes guts, practice, and a true knowledge of your subject—and the audience's interests—but you *can* reengage an audience that has drifted away.

One tactic is to have ready, in advance, a set of purposely stimulating questions that can easily provoke interaction with the audience members. Why? If things start going south, you won't need to make up questions on the spot.

Another way to salvage a presentation that is failing is to switch tracks and move to an area of your message that you know has worked well before. If you're covering three points, for instance, and the first one is falling flat, give yourself the okay to jump to the third and most compelling part of your message. Then, strive to create an interactive environment where you are not the only one speaking.

Remember, most audiences *want* the speaker to succeed. No one likes to be bored or feel as though their meeting is a waste of time. By recognizing you're off track and then getting yourself back on, everyone wins.

To Summarize...

🖋 The expression, "fake it 'til you make it," does not bring about the optimal results in public speaking.

🖋 Designing a presentation that strategically involves your audience and gets them to respond periodically helps assure that you keep people engaged throughout.

🖋 You can convey both emotion and valuable information through carefully planned and practiced storytelling.

🖋 Good speakers learn to listen to an audience with their eyes and react with strategies to rekindle interest. Be on the alert for telltale signals that attention may be waning: too much texting, looking at watches, unexplained coughing, paper shuffling, and multiple private conversations around the room.

Chapter 4

What Your Audience Really Wants from You

In This Chapter...

- Knowing your audience—and why it matters
- How to figure out what they care about
- The role of your elevator speech
- What works and what usually doesn't

Although dating has changed dramatically over the years—from personal introductions to online sites and variations in between—I suggest that once two potential lovers meet, a timeless dance begins with its own special music. Those who are wise and successful in dating have figured out how to recognize and respond to what their dating partner wants and to adjust their steps accordingly.

When you are face to face with an audience, you're in a similar dance. There are expectations on both sides. Figuring out what an audience wants can be just as challenging as the dating game, if not more so!

In this chapter, to help you choreograph the words and ideas of your presentation, I'll take you through the process of getting to know who is in your audience before you actually speak to them. To make a positive impression when networking, an activity with many similarities to dating, I have also included the key basics of crafting a self-introduction known as an Elevator Pitch. You'll also find some recommendations of what *not* to include in your messages.

Knowing Your Audience—and Why It Matters

If you have ever gone to a networker or any kind of meeting or social event where you didn't know anyone, chances are high that your first few moments weren't that comfortable. If you're on the shy side, you pray that someone will step forward and introduce himself or herself to you. If you're somewhat outgoing, you look around for a person who seems a bit welcoming and forge ahead to introduce yourself. In either case, you are often painfully aware of an invisible barrier between you and the others in the room, and your goal is to cross it into the land of friendliness and familiarity.

When you are face to face with an audience of any kind there is always an invisible barrier at the outset—be it an industry group, the parent-teacher association, a city commission meeting, or your own team. I call this invisible barrier in speaking and in networking your *credibility fence*. The folks on the other side are sizing you up even before

Flash but No Real Connection

I was at a chamber of commerce luncheon where a major car company had spent thousands of dollars on sponsorship. At the last minute, the high-ranking executive who was supposed to speak canceled. Instead, a beautiful young woman who appeared to have no stage fright greeted everyone warmly in a comfortable manner.

Right away, however, the speaker began to lose the audience, because she talked about the new vehicles shown in her slides as if she were at a car show. It was painfully obvious that the substitute did not do her homework on the audience of business leaders and that whoever should have briefed her for the last-minute assignment was nowhere to be found.

Uninspired

you say a word, but especially as you begin to try to connect with them. They want assurance that you will not waste their time, that you know what you're talking about, and that you are worth the attention you're asking for.

How well and how quickly you can climb over the credibility fence and what happens once you're on the other side will determine much of your success as a speaker.

Think back to a recent time when you were in an audience and the speaker was so awful that everyone around you was cringing and cranky. What happened? The speaker never found the latch that opens the credibility fence. Despite struggling to locate a way to climb over the fence, the efforts clearly failed.

For good role models, you need go no further than remembering your best teachers or professors, a motivating coach, or captain in sports or dance. Perhaps it was a member of the clergy whose sermons inspired you to do the right thing and did not put you to sleep! Why were these speakers able to keep your attention and focus you on a course of action? From experience and based on familiarity with their audiences, they knew what the students in their classes, the athletes, and the congregation wanted and needed to hear. Further, they understood that adding the right quotient of emotion to their conversations was vital for a true connection.

How to Figure out What They Know about Your Topic

The popular adage about what happens when we assume—you make an "ass of u and me"—definitely applies to preparing for a speech or presentation. To avoid assuming anything about your audience, I encourage you to play journalist by asking the basic five *who-what-when-where-why* questions, along with the *how/how much* questions, and directing them to the person who invites you to speak or with whom you have made the arrangements to be on the agenda.

If the person you're consulting for this vital preperformance information doesn't have access to what you need to know, or lacks some of the answers, don't be afraid to ask for another source to call or visit. The more complete the answers you get, the better you can prepare for a successful presentation and prevent avoidable discomfort or worse.

Here are questions I recommend you ask in advance of your speaking:

- "Who will be in attendance?" Get as many particulars as you can, by age range, job title, experience with your topic, and any prevailing attitudes it would be helpful to know.

- "What is the purpose of the group/meeting/project?" It's not enough to hear that the group meets once a month for dinner, or that the project is part of an ongoing series. Dig as deeply as you can to be clear on what *their* mission is and how *your* words and experience can be helpful.

- "When do the group members meet and when did they decide this topic was of interest?" A breakfast talk may need a different energy or content than a keynote after dinner and cocktails. Additionally, you want to know as much about the group and its decision-making as possible.

- "Where will the presentation be and where do you think the audience stands on the topic?" Again, your goal is to capture as much relevant background information as possible, to help you best craft your message and break down that invisible barrier.

To Wait or Not to Wait

An international media executive I was coaching tried for weeks to get key details about his role in an upcoming panel at a local university conference designed to help get out the Hispanic vote. His email invitation had only contained *where* and *when*, nothing more.

With fewer than two weeks until the event, Raul (name changed for privacy purposes) and I shifted gears. Instead of waiting for the moderator's response, we developed a set of five questions that could be asked. After practicing answering them, he forwarded the best to the university.

The moderator did incorporate Raul's questions into the panel discussion. Bottom line: when in doubt, take charge of your own speaking destiny.

Perspiration

🖋 "Why do you think there is interest in my topic? Why do you want me to speak on it?" You may or may not get complete or even totally honest answers to your questions. Ask anyway!

🖋 "How would you approach this presentation if you were doing it?" Ideally, the person in the group is an insider who will reveal some valuable hints that you can incorporate into your approach. You do not have to follow the recommendations exactly, but it's a good idea to listen carefully and apply what works best.

What are their chief interests?

From my experience, most people pay attention to a speaker for one of three main reasons:

🖋 They believe you're going to *help them look good* in some way by sharing your secrets, insights, relevant experiences, or other beneficial and timely advice.

🖋 They're expecting you to *show them how to save* money, time, mistakes, frustration, or some other important success-garnering technique.

🖋 You're fun, engaging, a problem-solver, and entertaining, and they *want* to listen to you.

When you help a group or an individual look good, help save them from wasting time or resources, and keep them entertained, you are bound to hit your mark!

What's in Your Elevator Pitch?

There's an additional step that will bring you closer to the results you are anticipating. That's to have a set of natural-sounding self-introductions ready, also known as Elevator Pitches or, as I call them, your WowPitch introduction. I named it so because of an app I developed for the iPhone a few years ago.

They Are Wearing Invisible Hats

When I am asked to speak about creating an elevator pitch—a memorable thirty-second self-introduction or a personal branding statement—I always bear in mind that most of the people in my audience are wearing several invisible hats at the same time. To connect with people and reach your goal,

What's an Elevator Pitch, a WowPitch Introduction, a.k.a. Elevator Speech?

The name comes from city skyscraper experiences. When salespersons or executives entered an elevator and found someone significant inside they wanted to impress, they had about thirty to sixty seconds as the elevator climbed, or descended, to introduce themselves and secure a meeting.

These quick business introductions became known as elevator pitches or elevator speeches, and the term also applies to presentations designed to secure investors. Television shows like *Shark Tank* have further popularized the idea of getting your ideas across quickly and succinctly.

A newer name for this self-introduction that has become popular is your personal branding statement. Similar to the efforts of classic advertising where products compete in the marketplace, how do you differentiate yourself from others, especially those who do similar work?

Definition

you may need to devise several different elevator pitches.

One hat is usually their day job—the business or professional role they play. They need an elevator pitch or self-introduction that inspires further conversation in a networking situation or stimulates an action, such as securing an appointment, meeting over coffee, or a lunch date.

A second hat is often their role as a volunteer or leader in a nonprofit group that supports a cause or institution. It could be a school or religious project, an environmental program, or a foundation that funds research into breast cancer, autism, or Alzheimer's and dementia. These community-minded folks tune into my presentation or webinar to get tactics for crafting messages that help them get others involved as volunteers or as donors to the groups that are a major part of their lives.

A third hat is the personal one worn by an individual who is looking for something new. It could be a new career opportunity or a way to come across well in the dating arena. Maybe the outcome desired is simply a new friend. Or perhaps, the quest is for a referral to a caregiver or even as a sitter for a child or dog.

Regardless of which hats the people in your audience may be wearing, you will win their hearts, minds, and dollars by matching what you plan to say to the benefits and problem-solving advice they want.

Some of My Networking Self-Introductions

◆ "I work with business and community leaders, and aspiring leaders, who want to come across as nonboring, confident experts whenever they speak, whether to a group or one-on-one, every day. My name is Anne Freedman and I'm the CEO of Speakout, Inc."

◆ "I help executives and community leaders to not be boring and to get the results they need when speaking to their teams, and to industry and community groups as well. My name is Anne Freedman and I'm CEO of Speakout, Inc."

◆ "I help executives, business owners, and community leaders who are concerned about having the right content when they speak and who want to deliver their message with confidence and style every time. I am Anne Freedman, founder and CEO of Speakout."

Example

It's Not Really About You

When we click with someone new, it's always somewhat magical. I'm not only talking about a romantic attraction, I'm referring to those times when you talk with a prospective client, or a new member of an organization you're involved with, or someone you happen to meet networking.

The other day I connected by phone with a woman who was building an online jewelry business. We had what turned out to be a long and fun conversation and while she did not become a client, I invited her to attend one of the groups in which I am active. We both felt as though we were old friends picking up a conversation where it had left off.

What did I do? I asked her questions about her goals, her business, her background, and what had prompted her to call me in the first place. She was unquestionably the star of the conversation and the initial barrier of talking to a stranger had definitely vanished.

As a speaker, your goal is similar to the goal of a networker. You want to establish rapport and find a way to easily scale that credibility fence between you and the audience. When you select the right stories, facts, and solutions, and make your delivery as real and stimulating as possible, the opening in the fence readily appears.

A proven method to eliminate the invisible barrier in the room is to enable the audience itself to become a key part of your performance. You strategically ask, for instance, a series of questions that you invite audience members to answer, and then incorporate their responses into your next set of remarks. The technique is not for the faint-hearted because you really don't have any control over the answers you receive. But with today's increasingly limited attention span, this approach can be a winning way to gain audience acceptance and appreciation.

How to Dig for More Information

When it comes to gathering background on your audience to prepare for your presentation or speech, I believe more information, not less, is better. The more you know about your audience and its interests, the better you can tailor your remarks to get the outcome you want, be it applause, a recommendation, a sale, or simply a go-ahead for your project.

While asking questions of whoever invited you to speak can reveal valuable insights, I recommend you push yourself further to gain a broader perspective. Doing research is much easier than it has ever been, but don't limit yourself too early in your fact-finding and analysis. You can always discard stuff later. While Google remains a king for gathering all kinds of data, there are dozens of other web-based sources, like Bing, Yahoo, and DuckDuckGo, that can give you visual information and another set of sources to check.

Avoid the potential for embarrassing assumptions about your audience or the group you'll be addressing by giving yourself time to do a thorough review of its website and bios of key leaders. Before I began working with an energy company, I assumed it was involved with the sale of oil or maybe natural gas. After perusing the website, however, I realized that was not the case at all!

Gain more perspective by watching any videos posted online and seeking out digital and print versions of related industry publications. A visit to the local library can be worth the effort since the professionals there can help you discover valuable resources you didn't know were available.

If possible, check out the backgrounds and topics of previous speakers who have addressed the organization or group to which you're scheduled to speak. Find out who was well received and why, as well as who failed to fascinate or succeed.

What Usually Doesn't Work

In popular movies and TV shows, the old-time detective would interrupt a crime witness who was blathering on and on about what she had seen with this pointed request: "Just the facts, ma'am." When it comes to connecting optimally with an audience, however, "just the facts" is generally not enough.

Here's a rundown of what else spells doom for a speaker.

✒ *Too much information (TMI).* Certain personality types feel as though they are cheating an audience or appearing unprofessional if they don't pile up a ton of facts and supporting data to include in their presentation. If you find yourself overwhelmed with TMI, I recommend you give yourself time to step away for a few hours, then step back with a red pen or scissors in hand and start cutting!

✒ *One size does not fit all.* I admit to being what my dear late mother called "greedy for life." I don't really like to say "no" to anything. To save time so I can go do something I haven't done before, I try to convince myself that I can take a presentation that I've worked very hard to perfect and reuse it for a new speaking engagement. But I always wind up tweaking and adjusting the message to line up carefully with the new audience. That's because every audience deserves and expects my message to be especially created and geared for them. Yours does, too.

✒ *Only stories.* A pet peeve of mine is having to listen to what are billed as "success stories." Typically, these speakers give a blow-by-blow rendition of how they built their business, became a star athlete, or achieved some kind of celebrity status. While the stories themselves may be entertaining, if they are not followed by what the speaker learned from the experience or by recommendations and ideas I can use, I find myself hoping for a quick end to what I call verbal diarrhea.

✒ *Only a video.* While videos can be a terrific way to quickly and expertly show an audience what your organization, product, or service is all about, I don't recommend that they substitute for you as the expert speaker or leader. Some people hide behind a video, putting it up for viewing and then asking for questions or comments afterward. Remember, the video is not what enlists the volunteers, makes a sale, or convinces the group. That's your job.

To Summarize...

- Crafting your message without a good understanding of who will be in your audience and what they care about can be a disaster waiting to happen.

- You can become a good detective to acquire what you need to know before you speak.

- The art of developing a solid elevator speech or self-introduction, and identifying questions to ask in networking situations, help prepare you for dealing with more formal audiences as a speaker.

- Extremes in either providing too much information or not enough of the right kind can ruin your relationship with your audience.

Chapter 5

When It's Up to You: Overcoming Speaker Reluctance

In This Chapter...

- No room for being selfish
- Good speakers are made, not born
- Overcoming odds: Abraham Lincoln
- What Moses, King George VI, and Elmer Fudd did

Developing new speaking skills is similar to mastering other challenges such as training for a marathon, learning to play golf, tennis, or a musical instrument, writing a book, taking language lessons, or even tackling a new software program.

At first, it can be overwhelming and seem impossible. There are new terms to absorb, rules to follow, goals to reach. To advance, it usually means we have to let go of habits, certain attitudes, and preconceived notions. When we do that, we open ourselves up for a new kind of success.

You are not alone in your quest to be regarded as an articulate and commanding presence. In this chapter, you'll read about the travails and successes of some well-known historical figures. I've included President Lincoln's speaking challenges and victories to inspire you to celebrate your own progress.

Knowing what Moses and King George VI of England went through—long before they were popularized in the movies—will also help you understand that public speaking is not a sport to "win." Instead, it's a chance to showcase yourself with dignity, power, and grace.

No Room for Being Selfish

A question I ask my self-described "nervous Nelly" or "nervous Ned" clients, when we start to work together, is this: "Would you say you are a selfish person?" Surprisingly, some folks do tell me straight up that they do see themselves as selfish! But most of them quickly answer that they are *not* selfish.

I go on to explain that when we allow nerves to get in the way of sharing our expertise and passion, when we fail to practice sufficiently to become totally at ease with the material, or when we don't bother to prepare at all, we are, in fact, being selfish.

What happens when we allow our nerves to rule is that we are thinking only of ourselves and our feelings, instead of the value of what we are sharing with others. If you believe that you are, indeed, an expert, or that the direction you want to take an organization is right, or the cause you are supporting is worth it, then you have the right—the obligation—to get out of your own way!

In a similar vein, I believe people are being self-centered when they attend a networking event and don't make an effort to talk with people they don't know. One of the exercises I recommend to help new speakers overcome their initial reluctance to appearing before an audience or a group is to practice being the first to speak at these events, that is, to approach strangers and initiate the conversation. For folks involved in supporting causes, this effort can expand your recruiting of volunteers and even potential donors. For singles, this skill set can help you transform the dating scene as well.

Always have a question ready to ask the new contacts about their business or interests in addition to being ready to share a little about your position and organization. Why? You make a better impression when you appear interested in them rather than simply being interesting yourself.

Good Speakers Are Made, Not Born

Why is it that so many individuals tell me they are totally comfortable when speaking one-on-one or to a small group, but they freeze, feel sick to their stomach, or dread the worst when standing before a larger audience?

I believe it's because at some unconscious level, we think public speaking is a totally natural endeavor and it should not require any preparation. After all, our mouth knows exactly what to do when we open it to talk with our coworkers, fellow club members, store clerks, teachers, or our families. No practice required!

From my experience, for public speaking to be truly effective, it takes a series of thoughtful steps to ready your message and then a ton of disciplined practice.

Now, I agree that some people seem born with certain gifts. My daughter, Lynne, for example, has always had a keen eye for color. When she was five, a friend of mine was deciding which outfit in her closet to wear for a party. Without hesitation, Lynne pointed at one dress and announced, "That color is much better for you." She was absolutely right.

Some people you know seem to be natural dancers, artists, athletes, and cooks, while others are completely at home with and excel on computers, with numbers, in the garden, when asking people for money, and as leaders. And yes, there are folks who have what we call "the gift of gab." They seem to be able to get up, unrehearsed, and mesmerize everyone. The truth is, they are a very rare breed. If you listen closely, they may be eloquent or fun, but there's often not much substance in their words.

What Is Natural?

An entrepreneur who built his business from selling phones from his car into a billion dollar technology enterprise was asked about his path to success at a breakfast panel. "Be yourself," he encouraged. To my surprise, he then launched into a tirade against what he called "that public speaking b.s.," adding that he did not believe in extensive preparation for speeches or presentations.

Unlike that technology guru, I believe most people truly benefit from a solid grounding in public speaking, which is why I wrote this book. Think about makeup and its power for women. Or what the right clothes can do for a man. Neither route is natural but they can be essential to making the overall impact you're seeking.

Perspiration

Think about the most successful and highest-paid athletes. They spend hours and hours practicing to make their passes and moves look effortless. Similarly, professional actors and actresses rehearse every line and related movement for hours and hours to appear entirely natural—in live theater and on camera.

To become outstanding speakers, it takes dedication to honing your craft, in the same way that the highly touted athletes, movie stars, musicians, and other artists you admire have done.

The off-stage, behind-the-scenes work endured by a great speaker is not glamorous. It is often tedious and time-consuming. But the rewards that come with well-beyond-the-ordinary public speaking can make it all worthwhile.

What Abraham Lincoln Did and Didn't Do

Best known for delivering one of the most famous of all speeches, the Gettysburg Address, and for abolishing slavery, during his tenure, United States President Abraham Lincoln was placed under the microscope by journalists and other observers as a speaker and as a leader. His speaking abilities did not develop overnight and they did not seem to come to him easily. He spent many years polishing his ability to connect and relate to audiences during the hundreds of speaking opportunities that came his way throughout his life, in his youth, in politics, in his twenty-five-year law career, and as president.

Here's a brief rundown of some of what he did and did not do that helped earn his enduring fame as one of America's most notable orators.

President Lincoln did these things:

Believe in Brevity, Most of the Time

I asked a number of people how long they thought the Gettysburg Address actually was. Most said ten-fifteen minutes or they didn't know. Although I had been required to memorize the speech in high school, long ago, I didn't remember its length. Amazingly to me, the Gettysburg Address lasted just over two minutes and was only 300 words. Mr. Lincoln delivered his remarks during the American Civil War, on Thursday, November 19, 1863, at the dedication of the Soldiers' National Cemetery in Gettysburg, Pennsylvania.

The Gettysburg Address: Not Just for Students

Below is the entire Gettysburg Address. Try saying it aloud, pausing for effect, and relive the vitality and motivational impact of this historic message.

Take each section one at a time. Deliver the words slowly and emphasize those you believe could carry more power if you raised the volume of your voice a bit.

Go back a second time and determine where you could pause to stir even more interest. Where does it make sense to speak a little faster?

Think about President Lincoln's state of mind as he prepared and practiced this address. What would yours have been? What was he trying to accomplish with this message? What are you expecting the outcome to be for yours?

These are the kinds of questions and the process I encourage you to consider when you are developing your own Gettysburg Address.

Four score and seven years ago our fathers brought forth on this continent, a new nation, conceived in Liberty, and dedicated to the proposition that all men are created equal.

Now we are engaged in a great civil war, testing whether that nation, or any nation so conceived and so dedicated, can long endure. We are met on a great battle-field of that war. We have come to dedicate a portion of that field, as a final resting place for those who here gave their lives that that nation might live. It is altogether fitting and proper that we should do this.

But, in a larger sense, we cannot dedicate—we cannot consecrate—we cannot hallow—this ground. The brave men, living and dead, who struggled here, have consecrated it, far above our poor power to add or detract. The world will little note, nor long remember what we say here, but it can never forget what they did here. It is for us the living, rather, to be dedicated here to the unfinished work which they who fought here have thus far so nobly advanced. It is rather for us to be here dedicated to the great task remaining before us—that from these honored dead we take increased devotion to that cause for which they gave the last full measure of devotion—that we here highly resolve that these dead shall not have died in vain—that this nation, under God, shall have a new birth of freedom—and that government of the people, by the people, for the people, shall not perish from the earth.

The speaker before President Lincoln on that historic day gave a two-hour address and no one remembers his name. President Lincoln's place on the agenda was considered an afterthought—and look what happened! In the sidebar you'll find his entire, remarkable speech.

Choose Words that Anybody Could Understand

Mr. Lincoln was known to show respect for people of all stations in life. This attitude was reflected in how he selected the words and phrases he used in his speeches. You didn't find thousand-dollar words or ones only the supereducated would understand. I encourage you to review the words you've chosen for your message to see if there's a simpler, better way to get your ideas across.

Always Prepare

Historical accounts tell us that Mr. Lincoln did not leave much to chance. He was known to devote many hours to practicing aloud before delivering political speeches and his presentations as a lawyer.

From a lecture by William H. Herndon, January 24, 1866:

Mr. Lincoln thought his speeches out on his feet walking in the streets: he penned them in small

Practice Was Good for Lincoln, But for You?

I frequently encounter executives and certain community leaders who challenge me about the need to practice. They contend that being familiar with the material is what matters and that they'd rather be "natural" than come across as rehearsed.

In more than three decades of speaking and coaching, I have observed that the speakers who seem the most natural are usually the folks who have rehearsed the most thoroughly. Part of rehearsing is revising your message in tiny chunks, if needed, to make your words and emotions simpler to convey.

As I like to say, there's nothing natural about makeup or public speaking. When done properly, the techniques are supposed to disappear so listeners concentrate only on the person before them, not the shade of lipstick nor the individual words themselves.

Pure Genius!

scraps—sentences, and paragraphs, depositing them in his hat for safety. When fully finished, he would recopy, and could always repeat easily by heart.

President Lincoln did not do these things:

Let His Appearance Be an Interference

Joshua Speed, in *Reminiscences of Abraham Lincoln*, wrote as follows:

Mr. Lincoln's person was ungainly. He was six feet four inches in height; a little stooped in the shoulders; his legs and arms were long; his feet and hands large; his forehead was high. His head was over the average size. His eyes were gray. His face and forehead were wrinkled even in his youth. They deepened with age, "as streams their channels deeper wear."

Generally he was a very sad man, and his countenance indicated it. But when he warmed up all sadness vanished, his face was radiant and glowing, and almost gave expression to his thoughts before his tongue would utter them.

Have the Best Voice Quality

From a letter of William H. Herndon, July 19, 1887:

Lincoln's voice was, when he first began speaking, shrill, squeaking, piping, and unpleasant... everything seemed to be against him, but he soon recovered.

It's fair to say that we were not all handed equal gifts at birth when it comes to the quality and appeal of our voice or personal appearance. However, when you take time to organize your information and ideas, when you imbue your words with passion and energy, you can gain the upper hand in any speaking situation.

How They Overcame the Odds

Many of us are familiar with the Biblical story of the shy Moses and his destiny to become the spokesperson for his people and their reluctant leader. When faced with the demand by the Almighty to confront the Egyptian king to extract freedom for the Jews in slavery, he replied: "Why me? I cannot speak well!"

Moses Could Not, but You Can

In modern times we have options that were not available to Moses, including antidepressants and antianxiety drugs that can help severe cases where social anxiety and public speaking phobias interfere with an individual's life. I know speakers who take half of an antianxiety pill before getting on stage for an important presentation. While I am not endorsing such a routine, I do encourage you to find an approach that calms your nerves and bolsters your spirit, such as a massage, going for a long walk or run, a new hair style, watching a funny movie, or other similar activities. Additionally, there are speech therapists and psychotherapists with special training in these arenas.

You can also find support groups and educational programs that focus specifically on public speaking, including debate clubs, Toastmasters (*toastmasters.org*), Dale Carnegie, acting and voice coaches, and other services like the one my company, Speakout, Inc. (*speakoutinc.com*), provides.

Pure Genius!

The background story is that as a child, Moses burned his mouth, developed a lisp, and suffered from a social anxiety that made him extremely quiet and withdrawn. He probably thought he was the only one on the planet who suffered from the heart-pounding, sweat-inducing dread of public speaking. Many people today run away from public speaking and leadership roles because of the same social anxiety that plagued Moses.

Despite his shyness, however, it was ultimately Moses himself who found the inner courage to say aloud the words of the Almighty. He had to speak to convince the Egyptian king to free his people from slavery. Later, Moses' role was to inspire thousands of ancient Hebrews throughout their long journey to the land of Israel after their Exodus from Egypt. Moses overcame his fear of public speaking and his own limitations to become one of the most important and often quoted men in history.

You may not have to go head-to-head with an Egyptian king anytime soon, but your words and ideas—and you—deserve the opportunity to be heard, and you *can* do it.

The King of England's Private Public Speaking War

You may have seen the trials and tribulations of another reluctant leader who dreaded public speaking: King George VI of England. His story about transforming his stammering and paralyzing fear into successful speeches was popularized in the award-winning historical drama film *The King's Speech.*

In a similar way to the Bible's Moses, Prince Albert, the man who would become King George VI, was thrust into the monarchy against his will and in an unexpected way. His older brother, a gregarious, articulate, and favored son, was supposed to be the king. But just four months before his coronation, Edward ducked out to marry a newly divorced woman who was not accepted as meeting the standards for a queen in that time.

Fate intervened, and the man who would be king was encouraged to seek out the help of Lionel Logue, a former actor who had recently moved to London from Australia. Using methods from acting, including breathing and diction exercises, along with heavy doses of positive reinforcement, Logue guided the future king away from his fearful, awkward delivery style into a more confident, forceful, and natural-sounding leadership voice.

The former actor turned public speaking advisor is credited with saving the reputation of the King of England and the entire United Kingdom just before World War II.

Among the sounds that were especially difficult for Prince Albert to pronounce were the letters K and Q, particularly troublesome for someone who lived in a world of kings and queens. It took countless hours of practice, weird-sounding word repetition, and careful editing of speeches to substitute phrases that were easier to say. That commitment to rehearse along with sheer determination transformed the once horrific public speaker into the leader he needed to be, uniting his country as World War II descended on Europe.

What the Movie Did Not Reveal

What you did not find out in the movie was that Prince Albert ("Bertie") had worked with nine other speech specialists before Logue, with no improvement.

It omitted the frequency of therapy sessions, reportedly eighty-two in a four-month period and a seven-day-a-week commitment to practicing.

It omitted the backup plan that was in place should the king freak out at the coronation and freeze at the last minute: A recording compiled and pieced together of the prince saying the various parts of the coronation speech. It was not used.

IMPORTANT!

Trying to Hide an Accent

At age seventeen, when my mother began to study at the University of Michigan in Ann Arbor, each freshman was required to undergo a voice and accent analysis. After an hour of testing, the professor said confidently to her, "You were not born in the United States." The way she pronounced words was too clear, her grammar was too correct, and she lacked any identifiable regional overtones.

He was uncannily right. My grandparents were Americans who lived in Havana, where mother was born, for thirty years. She was bilingual, learning to speak English and Spanish fluently. But in Spanish, although unfailingly grammatical, Mom inevitably slid into the Cuban style of speaking, making her roots obvious.

Uninspired

His coronation speech on May 12, 1937, was the first to be delivered by radio to the entire Commonwealth. By all accounts, the new king did a spectacular job, exceeding everyone's expectations.

My point here is that good public speaking is no accident. And it does take courage.

"Courage is doing what you're afraid to do. There can be no courage unless you're scared." —Eddie Rickenbacker, World War I fighter pilot ace, race car driver, and former head of Eastern Airlines

What Can We Learn about Accents from Elmer Fudd?

Be vewwy vewwy quiet; I'm hunting wabbits. —Elmer Fudd

Elmer Fudd, the bald-headed, baggy-pants Looney Tunes character who hated and incessantly hunted Bugs Bunny, always pronounced the letters "v" and "r" as "w." His trademark style of speaking has been imitated by show business giants like the late and much beloved Robin Williams. It was the model for one of the recurring characters in *The Big Bang Theory* television show, with Barry Kripke talking like Elmer.

The way Elmer Fudd spoke—with so many w's in his sentences—was entirely understandable and funny to most ears. He was cast in dozens of notable cartoons including "A Corny Concerto" and "What's Opera, Doc?"

A key point to consider is that Elmer was undaunted by how he sounded to others. His focus was entirely on where the "wabbit" was and what he was doing in his tireless pursuit of Bugs Bunny, his sworn enemy.

In Miami, where I've lived since I was seventeen, we say *everyone* has an accent because so many people have moved to South Florida from elsewhere, are on vacation, or are visiting with family. From the northeast United States, we hear the word talk pronounced as "tawk." From the midwest, the broad a's become ChiCAHHHHgo. From the deep south, the "y'all come back now" drawl remains common. There are the clipped sounds of the Caribbean and the fast-paced pronunciation of the Latin Americans. Not to mention the range of language sounds made by tourists coming here from all over the world.

As a community leader and businesswoman, my Cuban-born mother was an excellent public speaker in English and Spanish and prided herself on a crisp, clear, and engaging delivery. She was always correcting others on their grammar and she instilled proper use of language in my sister and me, and the grandchildren as well. No doubt it was her influence and example that led me to do public speaking.

As a speaking coach in South Florida for many years, I've worked with countless executives for whom English is a second language, along with an equal number of native-born English speakers. I have found that some of my clients are fearful and uncomfortable as public speakers because they believe their accent is interfering with understandability or their credibility as an expert.

In some cases, these fears have been justified. The clients were difficult to understand when speaking English, so I referred them to experts in accent reduction. These patient specialists focus on pronunciation and retraining the mind and the mouth to make the demanding sounds of spoken English.

Similarly, I have encountered native English speakers who are ungrammatical, mispronounce words, use racially charged or inappropriate language, or who have a particularly strong regional accent. I was able to help these individuals as long as they were willing to rephrase or reframe their message, and practice the new version until it flowed smoothly.

I do believe that if your accent or pronunciation is interfering with your understandability, it is critical to get professional help. Just as with any other exercise program, it's just wishful thinking to expect overnight results. With commitment and practice over time, improvement is definitely possible, as I've seen in dozens of clients over the years.

The good news is that the richness of English as a language can be a lifesaver for both foreign-born and native speakers. For example, over the years I have found that most Hispanic speakers educated overseas are best to avoid the word "focus" when speaking in English. It comes out as a variation of a bad four-letter word. Instead, I guide these folks to say their "objective" is, or "goal" or "direction."

If a native English speaker is tripping over certain words consistently, it's nearly always possible to find alternatives that are easier to say.

To me, the most important things to remember about accents are these truths: if you have a terrific message, if your diction is clear and pronunciation accurate, most audiences will love, appreciate, and accept your accent—and you!

While none of my clients has yet achieved the fame of Abraham Lincoln, many have faced similar hurdles regarding a sense of awkwardness and the necessity of working hard to say the right words at the right time.

My takeaway from these stories of President Lincoln, Moses, King George VI, and the cartoon character Elmer Fudd is that everyone has some kind of speaking challenge to overcome. It may be physical like Lincoln's height, appearance, and sad countenance. It could be a speech defect like Moses had or a psychologically induced stammer such as King George VI suffered. Or the inability to pronounce words properly like poor Elmer Fudd who simply couldn't say certain words in a normal manner and who always sounded funny when he spoke.

I encourage you to accept and embrace your distinctive way of speaking. It would be very boring if everyone sounded the same, yes?

To Summarize...

- Your know-how and opinions are valuable. Allowing nervousness to keep you from sharing them is selfish.

- Great speakers don't start life that way; the skill set is developed and built with ongoing learning and practice.

- Historical giants like Moses and President Lincoln were also ordinary people with public speaking challenges they were able to overcome.

- Each of us has gifts and qualities that make us different and special when we're committed to genius speaking.

lightwise @ 123RF.com

Taking Control of Your Genius Content

In this part of *Public Speaking for the GENIUS*, we explore what it takes to reach your speaking goal, what content you're going to need to make it happen, and how to brainstorm and organize your genius content for best results. You'll think about the language you're choosing and be introduced to ways to use your content to extend your ideas beyond your immediate audience to those you can reach in written formats. Additionally, you'll learn cool techniques to open your talk and capture attention from the moment you start speaking.

Chapter 6

Start at the End! What Happens When It's Over?

In This Chapter...

- What success and your hidden agenda mean to you
- Summaries that pop
- Don't go past the Close
- To thank or not to thank the audience

When European explorers set sail to claim the North and South Poles, they had a good idea where they wanted to wind up. They just didn't really know what would be encountered on the way, how long the journey would take, or the quantity of supplies they would need. Despite the odds, some captains were able to plant their flags, receiving recognition and riches and landing their names forever in the history books. Others, though brave, perished in their pursuit.

As a speaker, your mission is to chart a course that leads us, your listeners, to the destination you have established. That end place can be to volunteer for or donate to your cause, buy something from you, enroll in a course, put down a deposit, or give you a go-ahead on your project.

In this chapter, you will find strategies to help you reach your destination. Identifying what you personally aspire to accomplish in your speaking journey—including how you end your message—will help assure your return as a hero, whether you are seeking fame, fortune, or something else.

What Does Speaking Success Mean to You?

You can measure success in many different ways as a speaker. The most obvious and traditional is a standing ovation accompanied by a ton of heartfelt applause when you're done. But is that what *you* want? Is that *all* you want?

For success in persuasive speaking, I believe you need to have the end goal of your message in plain sight from the moment you start working on it. Most of us tend to jot down content as it bubbles up from our brain's inner recesses. While that strategy can work, without recognition of our ultimate target we tend to ramble and not reach our true destination.

Knowing what we want to accomplish when we speak is much clearer for some individuals than others. A salesperson seeks a sale. A teacher looks for students to raise their hands and answer questions. A candidate is after votes.

So what do you truly seek when your presentation or speech is said and done? On the next page, you'll find a set of motivations that I have found drive many people—perhaps you, too—to do public speaking. Please check off whatever applies to you and fill in the "other" spaces as you see fit.

When your speech or presentation is over, success for you can mean. Check off what applies:

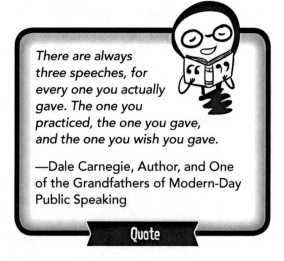

There are always three speeches, for every one you actually gave. The one you practiced, the one you gave, and the one you wish you gave.

—Dale Carnegie, Author, and One of the Grandfathers of Modern-Day Public Speaking

Quote

Money-Related Outcome...

- ❑ Increase in salary
- ❑ Get a new job
- ❑ Land a new client
- ❑ Raise capital for my business
- ❑ Other (write in yours) _____

- ❑ Close a deal
- ❑ Obtain a contribution for charity
- ❑ Be recognized as an expert

You Supported a Cause To...

- ❑ Get pets adopted
- ❑ Increase voter registration
- ❑ Obtain a vote for you or your candidate
- ❑ Other (write in yours) _____

- ❑ Sign up volunteers
- ❑ Enact water conservation practices
- ❑ Seek out alternative fuel systems

You Helped...

- ❑ Inspire students to read, study, get good grades
- ❑ Encourage new habits, practices
- ❑ Take care of an elderly relative or neighbor
- ❑ Other (write in yours) _____

- ❑ Bring food to a sick person
- ❑ Feed a poor family
- ❑ Rescue a dog or cat
- ❑ Guide in the learning of new skills

You Obtained...

- ❑ Go-ahead for a key project
- ❑ Commitment to form strategic alliances
- ❑ Other (write in yours) _____

- ❑ Recognition as a front-runner
- ❑ A leadership role

You Created...

- ❑ A green haven of plants, trees, and décor in the garden
- ❑ A willingness to try new spices, flavors, and foods
- ❑ Other (write in yours) _____

- ❑ A new look for a home or office
- ❑ Interest to try out new makeup, clothes, or hairstyle

Looking Good and Feeling On Top

The consul of a European country was responsible for introducing a renowned boys' choir that was ending its American tour with a summer concert at a large local church. His overt goal was to set the stage for the audience and to create curiosity and anticipation for what they were about to hear and see, in much the same way as a good speaker introduction is done.

Though dreading public speaking, the consul wanted this important opportunity in front of key players in the community to be successful, and to come across as charming and knowledgeable.

In further discussion, however, the consul told me that he realized that the true objective for his message introducing the boys' choir was to stir interest in visiting the small country he represented by quickly painting a picture of the many other art and cultural offerings one could find there. It was also to establish himself as the go-to person for questions about both tourism and economic investment.

After weeks of intense practice, the night of the concert arrived. "I didn't sweat and I did a good job," he shared with me, adding that he got many positive comments from folks in the audience.

The next day, in an interview with a local radio station, the consul said he was relaxed answering questions about the boys' choir and the country he represented. "The interviewer asked me if I do this all the time," he told me, feeling good about himself and his public speaking progress.

Once you've identified your true goal for the presentation or speech, you can begin to map out how you'll ask the audience to provide whatever you are seeking. I recommend that you write out at least three or four different versions of what you could say at the end, as your call for action, and then say them each aloud. Give yourself a chance to hear your own voice and decide which option best captures your passion.

Wake Up to Your Hidden Agenda

While the visible or tangible result of your public speaking matters to you as a business person or as a community leader, I have found that your *hidden agenda* can be equally critical and sometimes even more important.

Your hidden agenda is what you personally and emotionally care about that happens when you're finished speaking. Often, no one except you knows or cares what this hidden agenda may be.

I always ask my clients at the outset of our work together what they would really like to accomplish for themselves, as well as for the company or organization they represent.

Their hidden agenda can be as simple as "not to look stupid," "to get through without crying," "to make a fantastic impression," or more positively, "to knock their socks off!" It can also be "to get someone to notice and hire me away."

Here are some other examples I've heard over the years about the hidden agenda for a particular speaking engagement that clients were willing to admit.

"Make it through without wetting my pants."

"Make sure they ask me the next time."

"Come across as the expert."

"Appear in control even though I'm not."

"Get them to ask me for a proposal."

The executive director of a foundation that issued grants in the community once confided to me that his hidden agenda for staff presentations to nonprofits was to scare off poorly run agencies. By emphasizing the foundation's rigid requirements for reporting how funds were spent and the results achieved, only the well-managed entities dared to apply for grants.

Don't Let Emotions Cloud Your Big Ending

I've helped a number of clients ask for big sums of money from potential investors. I'm happy to report that in quite a few cases, they got what they asked for! Pitching with a goal to obtain what seemed like a huge amount of cash was new for many of these individuals. In the beginning of our work together, the investor-seekers would often lowball the amount they were trying to get, afraid they would turn off the money source or alienate the person who had set up the meeting.

As the clients gained a sharper picture of the outcome they wanted in terms of capital coming in, when they thought about the value they were bringing to the table, and the hard work and money they'd already put into their business, the fear and timidity about asking for a grand sum went away.

Perspiration

A technology start-up executive recognized that her hidden agenda was to create a buzz about her product that would extend far beyond those present at the venture capital conference.

A chamber of commerce leader wanted to change the perception of his being a somewhat rigid speaker who was challenged to pronounce names correctly to a more relaxed, approachable, and in control persona.

How Not to Summarize at the End

And so, ladies and gentlemen, it should be obvious by now what you need to do to attract the highest-paying buyer for your property. Don't procrastinate. Start today to get rid of the x^&& in your home so it looks bigger than it really is. Take down all of your personal photographs and hide them away in a drawer or closet. You want the buyer to visualize themselves in your home, not you or your family. And accept that you need a professional on hand to talk to the prospective buyer, because most homeowners blow the deals without even realizing it.*

While the summary followed the flow of the message, its tone was patronizing and even a bit offensive. The good information was outweighed by the not-so-hidden arrogance of the speaker.

WATCH OUT!

Be honest as you identify your hidden agenda, along with the overt goal you set for yourself. It's so much easier to pull together the right content when you are truly clear about where you're headed and what you want the outcome to be.

Summaries That Pop

If the last few minutes of your talk are boring, you can kill the good impression you worked so hard to make.

Briefly summarizing the main points you covered as part of your conclusion is one of the most recommended ways to end, but your goal is not simply an academic recap. The right summary can nail down the audience's opinion of you and whatever you're out to accomplish.

Although it may seem obvious, an effective summary recaps the presentation in the same order the content was delivered:

- Point One
- Point Two
- Point Three

Going out of order can confuse and undermine your closing statements and call for action.

The Secret to an Audience-Satisfying Summary

A good summary is more than a recap of the facts and figures you covered, in the order you presented them. To summarize like the pros, it helps to go back to each of your main points and reiterate the pain or problem you resolved in your message, ideally with a reference back to a particularly relevant example or reference. Funny or exceptionally memorable anecdotes work best.

You aren't limited to simply recapping your main points if there's another element that is worth repeating or reminding your audience about in your closing summary.

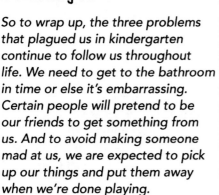

What the Speaker Learned from Kindergarten— A Summary Close

So to wrap up, the three problems that plagued us in kindergarten continue to follow us throughout life. We need to get to the bathroom in time or else it's embarrassing. Certain people will pretend to be our friends to get something from us. And to avoid making someone mad at us, we are expected to pick up our things and put them away when we're done playing.

This ending leaves your audience members in an upbeat mood, giving them a chance to reflect once again on the humorous and timeless points you raised.

Example

I was working with a senior executive of an international environmental organization who was making a presentation to Asian companies considering major investments in Latin America. Her goal was to gain their commitment to pay attention to the environmental and social impact of big construction projects in the region before they started the bulldozers.

Leonora (name changed for privacy purposes) began by showing a newspaper headline reporting $5 million a day in fines being paid by one foreign company for six months because it had failed to meet with local leaders before launching a major dam construction project. So strong was the example that I encouraged her to remind her listeners in the summary at the end of what had happened to the foreign company because it did not comply with the nation's environmental laws.

One of the bonuses that comes from thoroughly thinking through your close when you are just beginning to develop your message is that you can discover an important point you might have left out otherwise. You may be making assumptions or trying to convince through logic only when you haven't adequately proved your position or attached enough emotion to drive your message home.

Let's say you envisioned including two main points in your message, A and B, with supporting facts and examples. You've spent time researching what stories and data you need to make these points come alive. When you do a mock close, however, incorporating a summary of A and B, you may find that you're missing a third point that could make your argument much more convincing and far likelier to evoke the reaction that you want.

When you do the heavy lifting, that is, plan exactly what to say in your close early in the process of crafting your message, you save time in the long run and increase the odds of hitting a home run.

But having the right text is not enough. To make the impact you want, your summary needs to convey your belief in what you're summarizing, what you have recommended as solutions, what your experiences have demonstrated, and what this information can do for the audience. Your summary cannot simply come from your brain to your mouth. Your feelings, your passion for the topic, and for the question at hand, also need to be strongly evident at the close.

How Not to Race at the End

As you approach the close, there's a natural tendency to begin speaking faster and faster since you're likely to be anxious to finish. When you speak too fast, especially in a multicultural environment, you make it harder to be understood. You undercut the value of what you're saying by speeding through your message. It's called racing to the end.

To counteract this behavior, I recommend that you deliberately slow yourself down as you approach your final few minutes. Put a sticky note, for example, on your speech with a happy face to remind you to both smile and keep your pace steady. Listen to the volume of your voice, too. Sometimes deliberately softening it can be effective, before a louder crescendo. Most often, a solid, reasonably loud, and enthusiastic close works the best.

IMPORTANT!

Don't Go Past the Close

One of the first things my late husband, Ed Fischer, taught me about selling was the adage, "Don't say 'bah bah,' when 'bah' will do." That is, don't talk too much and especially don't talk your way past the close, the time when the prospective buyer is ready to say, "Yes!"

The same holds true when you're winding down your speech. Don't keep talking so you go past the close.

You've probably seen what happens when speakers appear to have ended their talk and the audience starts to applaud. But it really wasn't the true end, just a deep pause. Oops! The audience is disappointed because it thought the speaker was done. The speaker is caught off guard and feels awkward because there wasn't an opportunity to make a final point and end the message properly.

For most persuasive speaking situations, a close has two parts. I wrote about them in the previous section:

1. The reenergizing summary highlights what you've talked about.

2. The clear call for action motivates the audience, your board of directors, your department, or a group of volunteers to *do* something, ideally by a certain time or date.

The success you wanted from your public speaking engagement and satisfaction of your hidden agenda are dependent on how well you articulate and execute the close.

Overcoming Call-for-Action Reluctance

While some folks appear to be—or are—natural salespeople, fearless when it comes time to ask us to buy whatever they are selling, many of us are uncomfortable doing that. Why? We don't want to be seen as too aggressive, pushy, in your face, or any of a number of other unflattering words that promoters are often given.

What happens, though, when we do not let our audience know what we expect at the end of our message in a clear, concise, and convincing manner? Alas, nothing. All that time and effort we've invested in developing our proposal, our message, or the new plan can be a total waste.

I attended a three-day conference for business owners which was to be an opportunity to focus on what I was doing to build my own enterprise. While packed with thought-provoking and practical exercises which definitely helped me plot and plan out ideas and timelines, by the end of the second day it became apparent that another agenda was underway, too. Offered by a serial entrepreneur, Allison Maslan, CEO of Allison Maslan International, the conference was actually a novel way for her to recruit clients for her annual coaching program for entrepreneurs, The Pinnacle.

During the event, Allison sprinkled testimonials from clients who had gone through her program with hints about what was going to be offered. By the time she actually revealed the details of what was included and invited us to enroll, no one was surprised and quite a few were ready to sign up. Her call for action was direct, unabashed, and convincing: if you were ready to make a serious change in your business and financial future, if you wanted a holistic approach that took into consideration what else you wanted from life, if you wanted to become a part of a group where the members helped each other, this was the program for you.

As you've probably gathered, I did sign up, with some urging from my daughter, who had accompanied me to the conference. "You can't not do this," she said firmly.

Your close needs to compel action from your listeners. When it works, you can celebrate the victory of moving your audience members from passive to active participants, whether they be buyers, team members, donors, fans, or formerly disinterested citizens.

Signal When You're Done

After you've uttered your last words, whether you thank the audience or not, if you are standing, smile and take a few small steps backward and tilt your head into a slight bow. Depending on the setup, look toward the person who introduced you to hand back control of the meeting or event. If the topic is sad or serious, a big grin might not be the best approach and a more neutral expression would probably work better.

If you're seated, smile at the audience, do a slight tilt of your head into a tiny bow, and then turn to the moderator or person who introduced you to take over once again.

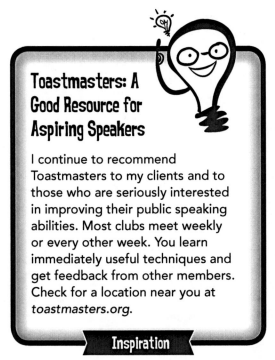

Toastmasters: A Good Resource for Aspiring Speakers

I continue to recommend Toastmasters to my clients and to those who are seriously interested in improving their public speaking abilities. Most clubs meet weekly or every other week. You learn immediately useful techniques and get feedback from other members. Check for a location near you at *toastmasters.org*.

Inspiration

What about when you have introduced yourself and you are running the meeting? It's nearly the same. Finish your message. Smile. And tilt your head slightly to the group or the audience. If you're responsible for adjourning the meeting or event, thank everyone for coming.

To Thank or Not Thank the Audience

As a member and past president of a Toastmasters International Club many years ago, the question of whether or not to thank the audience when you were done speaking was a frequent source of conversation. The prevailing wisdom was that a speaker did not thank the audience at the end, as it was, instead, the people in the room who ought to thank the speaker for the speaker's time and expertise.

And while I thought that Toastmasters' policy was a noble sentiment, I observed that the majority of professional speakers—men and women often paid thousands of dollars for their time on stage—*always* thanked the audience. It wasn't a long, drawn-out thank-you after their close, but the words were unquestionably spoken aloud.

Determining What Is Best for You

It depends, in part, on what is customary in your circles. If you're addressing your board of directors, it's probably a good idea to thank board members for listening to you. The same is true for a group of elected officials, a Rotary Club, and prospective investors.

Within your own department, maybe a thank-you is not needed at the end of remarks. It can even sound contrived or as if you are trying too hard to be liked or accepted. At the same time, every office and business culture is different. Observe what those you admire do, and follow suit.

If you're invited to address a school, an association, or your church, synagogue, or mosque, I believe a little thank-you at the end can go a long way.

My mother always taught me to err on the side of being polite and using good manners, whenever possible. Speaker protocol is not universal, and manners do change from one culture to the next.

When in doubt, ask what is customary and take your cue accordingly.

Thank you!

To Summarize...

🖐 Identifying your hidden agenda as well as your overt mission can increase the odds of your success and save you time in the long run.

🖐 Summaries look simple, but they need to recap emotional as well as factual content.

🖐 Make sure your audience knows you are really finished.

🖐 Saying *thank you* at the end is recommended, but optional.

Chapter 7

It's Not Really All about You—or Is It?

Most people don't wake up with visions of buying a life insurance policy or a cemetery plot. Neither do they usually see themselves signing up to volunteer to get the vote out or feed the homeless. Closer to home, it's rare that anyone willingly wants to spend the day cleaning out the garage or closets.

Usually, we need a bit of a push to do something that we really don't want to do or would not have envisioned on our own, right? Knowing whether that push needs to be gentle or strong, and how to word the conversation, is the heart of being a persuasive communicator. What can get in the way is our fear of rejection or discomfort with having to ask for what we want. From my experience it is entirely possible to move past these self-imposed barriers.

In some cases, the balancing act is how much or how little to share about yourself and your own experiences. Sometimes, it's a question of choosing certain words over others. That's what you will discover how to do in this chapter.

Match Your Mission to Theirs

When you're making a persuasive presentation, when you're trying to get a group to move ahead on something that matters to you, the challenge is to figure out how to match your goal to theirs.

Think about a parent and a teenager and the perpetual tug-of-war that relationship entails. You want Susan to grow up and be a responsible adult, to make the right decisions and to do the right thing. She wants to have a boyfriend, be able to stay out late doing what you'd rather not know, and be popular.

How skillfully you maneuver in the land of goals, as a speaker, can make or break the connection you want to establish with your audience.

Let's imagine that your goal for your presentation may be to sell me something or get me to move in a direction you'd like me to go. But my interest may lie in keeping the status quo—in not changing my website host or not joining in your efforts to put new procedures in place at work. I may like, or be willing to put up with, what's now the norm. What you want and what I want may not coincide.

How can we avoid that clash and emerge on top?

Before you go too far into your message crafting, it's critical to get as accurate a

Creating the Illusion of a Shared Goal

Over the years, I've had the privilege to consult with many financial planners as clients, helping them to craft messages targeted to both individuals and groups.

Melanie (name changed for privacy purposes) was a senior vice president with a large bank. Like most financial planners, she was expected to sell certain sanctioned products while maintaining a solid working relationship with her clients. They believed her role was to help them earn the best possible return in their portfolios. And it was, but her own earnings were higher when she could add the company's special promotions into the equation.

If this illusion of a shared goal is legal, moral, and you can sleep, go ahead.

Perspiration

picture as possible of what the pains, concerns, issues, and hopes are for the audience you are addressing. The best way is to ask questions of decision-makers, the rank-and-file, and anyone else who will be affected by what you intend to propose or the issues you plan to raise.

Below are some sample questions you can ask, pulled from the journalism training I got as a young news reporter many years ago. Generate information by asking these beginning words:

- Who?
- Where?
- What?
- Why?
- When?
- How/How much?

Here are some *who* questions:

- "Who do you see as being most impacted by (your topic)?"
- "Who has presented on (your topic) before?"

Here are some *what and when* questions:

- "What do you know about (your topic)?"
- "What has been your experience before with (your topic)?"
- "What would you like to know about (your topic)?"
- "What is getting in your way with respect to (your topic)?"
- "What would keep you from going ahead with (your topic)?"
- "What are some of your concerns with (your topic)?"
- "What has frustrated you about (your topic) in the past?"
- "When do you see your organization applying (your topic)?"
- "When have you heard something similar previously?"

Here are some *where* and *why* questions:

- "Where have you found (your topic) relevant in the past?"
- "Where do your solutions with respect to (your topic) usually come from?"
- "Why do you believe there's interest in (your topic)?"
- "Why do you think (your topic) hasn't been approved or adopted before?"

Here are some *how* questions:

- "How much do you think your group knows about (your topic)?"

- "How would you like (your topic) handled differently than it's been treated in the past?"

Weave in Your Own Stories and Views

As a young newspaper reporter, I was taught to leave myself out of the story. What the people I interviewed told me and what the research and facts revealed all were acceptable and expected to be included in the article. A reporter was supposed to be neutral, nearly invisible. When you were reporting, it was all about what she said, or he said. What I personally saw, felt, or believed was not allowed to be expressed in a news story.

If you watch most regular television news programs today, the neutral, impartial, third-person voice remains the preferred delivery approach. Unless the reporter is relaying a request from the police for "you" to contact them with a crime tip, for example, you won't hear much "you" during a broadcast.

Outside of traditional newscasts, today's media (including the Internet versions) is much more "I" focused and reporter-centric. You can readily see the "I" focus in blogs, podcasts, reality television, and celebrity interview shows. These media

James Bond Helped Me Break the Ice

One of the first workshops I led was for an insurance company, with ten men in attendance. I was nervous as I'd never before worked with an all-male group or conducted a session where I had to keep group members engaged four hours. Of course, they did not know that!

I put up an image of Agent 007, James Bond. Instead of saying, "Every eight minutes, our hero was in a different adventure," what came out was, "Every eight minutes, our hero, James Bond, was in a different *bed.*" While the men laughed heartily, I felt myself turning deep red. The unintentional result was a thawing in the room, forging the trainer/audience connection.

Inspiration

hosts can be good models for you to mirror, depending on your profession, industry, and goals.

Striking a balance between how much you want to reveal about yourself and how much the audience wants or needs to know remains a dilemma for most speakers.

When I began public speaking as a professional consultant and doing workshops as a trainer, I was still not comfortable talking about my own experiences. Instead, I used examples drawn from the clients I was working with—disguised to protect their privacy. Additionally, I incorporated references from books and articles and described first-hand observations of politicians, business leaders, and others in the limelight.

As time went by, I found that the groups I was training seemed to value my own personal experiences related to public speaking—especially when they were delivered with humor and poking fun at myself on occasion—as much as the how-to techniques and instruction I was providing.

Disasters Can Be Valuable

At an afternoon workshop I was conducting before the National Association of Women Business Owners many years ago in San Antonio, Texas, I suddenly became aware of a large mass in the back of my pants. The Mexican influence on the Texas menu meant I had consumed quite a bit of delicious refried beans, and I was immediately afraid that nature had taken its course. In the room were about one hundred women leaders, and in the extreme back of the audience were my mother and young daughter, who had come along to enjoy the sights.

I was talking about what I call the law of averages in public speaking, those times when things happen that are beyond your control, and that need to be anticipated as the "what-ifs." How you handle those what-ifs when they do occur can preserve or destroy your reputation as a professional and as a leader. Here I was thinking, "What if I did go in my pants? How can I get past all these women to the bathroom and what should I say? And what shall I do next?"

After a few more excruciating minutes, I realized what had happened. The microphone support unit had fallen into the back of my pants.

What did I do? In front of the audience, I grabbed the unit from inside the back of my pants, held it up for all to see, and quickly explained what happened. We all laughed and I used it as a real-life, real-time example of the what-ifs and law of averages at play.

While making an embarrassing mistake is not a recommended tactic to endear yourself to an audience, talking about the incident is something you can use to your advantage and weave into a future presentation to help you make a specific point. My worst experiences as a speaker, shared with others, help them think about what they can do to avoid the same thing and how to deal with their emotions in seemingly out-of-control situations.

How can *you* use your own stories to advance your message and help you better connect to what the audience wants and needs?

Balancing the Use of I, We, and You

A pet peeve of mine is speakers who spend their entire message telling me how they did something, such as how they built their company, or what's important to them about the topic, without ever inviting me and the rest of the audience to be a part of the conversation. That is taking the "I" use to an extreme, and I encourage you not to fall into that trap!

Look through your outline and speaker notes. How often do you see an "I" listed? If you have far more "I's" than "you's," you may want to recalibrate a bit.

Here are some related issues that can throw you a curve, if you're not careful:

When Is It Best to Refer to Yourself as "We"?

I recommend that if you're part of an elected group, or a board of directors, a nonprofit, or a company, depending on the topic, you'll be received better using the collective "we" to describe your point of view. For example, a vote to go ahead with a new stadium has gained a majority of the council. Or management has decided to launch a new line of products or services. Similarly, if you're a part of a research team or a sports team, employing the pronoun "we" will keep you from appearing too egotistical.

As the president of an association, you speak for the decisions of the board of directors, so a "we" is appropriate.

Answering a question posed by a reporter—especially a broad one like, "Why did you decide to do ...?"—gives you a platform quite similar to starting a speech or a presentation. You also need to decide whether to use "we" or "I" in your answer.

When Is It Best to Use "I"?

I believe it's the optimal pronoun when you're describing your own, personal experience with the topic, with a product, service, or problem. When you relate incidents from your childhood or travels, your own caretaking experiences, on-the-job happenings with coworkers, or client problems, the conversation will be more credible and three-dimensional when told from your own vantage as an "I."

When and How Is It Best to Use "You"?

It's fine to tell a story in first person, saying "I" to disclose what happened and what you felt, saw, tasted, or experienced. But to maintain interest and especially to lead your listeners toward an action you want them to take in a persuasive presentation, it's vital to strategically sprinkle "you" throughout your remarks. Here are some examples of phrases that you can try out:

- "You may agree that…"
- "Your experience may be different and…"
- "You may find that…"
- "You may know that…"
- "Your doctor might have…"
- "You might have heard that…"

Often, the difference between a great professor and an ordinary one, a go-to expert versus a knowledgeable but dull source, is how they reach out to the students or audience, how they convey the information.

Too Far Away to Connect

A visiting rabbi at my synagogue gave a sermon about how dangerous certain holy and historic places are in Israel now due to the unrest in the Middle East. He described how years ago he'd gone to pray at one of these ancient sites and how frustrated he was that he could no longer safely go there, closing with a wish that he might one day be able to visit there peacefully again.

A simple reach out to the audience with a phrase like, "If you'd been in that cave with me, you would have seen…" was all that he needed to help us relate to his loss. It would have removed the invisible wall he'd erected between himself and the congregation. Too much "I" or "we" by a speaker can result in an unintentional disconnect.

Uninspired

Recently a university professor was invited to speak to one of my business groups to update us on the global economy regarding promising emerging markets. He reported that the impact of the once-thriving BRIC countries— Brazil, Russia, India, and China—was waning. Taking over are the MINT nations which include Mexico, Indonesia, Nigeria, and Turkey.

His message was neutral, factual, and reporter-like, but there was no personal warmth or wit in his remarks. If only he had simply added, "If you were to go to Mexico today, compared to just a few years ago, you would see..." or a statement that seems more personal: "Despite what you're hearing about in the media, Turkey is..."

Extracting the Stories Within

Some people seem to bubble over with personal stories and experiences to punctuate their presentations or speeches. They either mesmerize or bore you with tales about their dog, cat, kids, or in-laws, a recent vacation or the new love in their life. You are either stuck listening or happily hearing the tale unfold, depending on what has happened, how well the story is revealed, and its relevance to you.

When you craft a message, it's always helpful to plot out your main ideas or your singular issue early in the process. At the same time, to help assure that you won't fail to connect with your listeners, reach within to find a relevant personal anecdote that will reinforce at least one of your points. Then, climb back into your memory bank and capture still another episode from your past experience that will help drive home what you're trying to get across. You can use an example of how well a program or product worked or describe a disaster or near-disaster that others can learn to avoid.

Words to Avoid When Persuading

From my experience, certain words can alienate your audience almost as soon as they are uttered. Others can take away from your stature as an expert. The two at the top of the list are these: *should* and *must*. Closely following are the words *ought to*, *never*, and *always*. And in its own class, I encourage you not to say the word "hope" aloud in business circles. More on that ahead.

Only mother can tell me what I *should* and *must* do. Or *ought* to do. When you tell me that I *should* do something, or worse, that I *must* follow a certain procedure, my natural tendency is to rebel, to do the exact opposite. These

Think Cocktail Conversation

My roommate, Deana, was a hospitality major who got to take the most popular course on campus at the time: Beverage 101. She and her classmates were required to sample different beers in one class, wines in another, and spirits in the others, as part of their training about the role of liquor in restaurants and hotels. My friends and I were jealous that she actually got credit for taking this course.

Every time Deana came home to the apartment after one of these classes, she was brimming with a different story about the brewing, production, and history of these popular drinks. It was from her that I learned the phrase "cocktail conversation."

When you've put the right story into your message, it's going to be repeated to others informally as cocktail conversation as well as in business settings, helping to establish your expertise and name in the influential circles in which you travel.

Inspiration

words are like pointing a finger in my face and demanding a certain behavior.

Instead, I recommend a few alternatives to persuade people to follow your directions.

- A more neutral set of words to use includes these openers: "It's company policy that...," "The rules state...," or "We are required to..." Even an emphatic statement like, "It's necessary that we..." can be better received than telling someone or a group that they should or must carry out your order.

- Related words that can be off-putting are solidly stating either "We never do that" or, conversely, "We always follow Plan A." You sound unbending and unapproachable when your statements are so emphatically one-sided. A more open stance will foster dialogue and increase the probability of acceptance. Instead, try: "It's been our experience that..."

Here's another batch of words I strongly encourage you to replace with some more respectful vocabulary.

- "What were you thinking?" versus "Would you please help me understand what led you that conclusion?"

- "Really?" versus "I'm surprised to hear you say that. What is your expectation for this?"

This next group I call the wimpy words. Using them too frequently, especially in a truly persuasive situation, indicates that you are wishy-washy and not truly convinced about what you're stating or seeking.

🖋 "I would like to…" or "I want to…" implies doubt. Instead, try a stronger "I am going to…" or "I recommend that…"

🖋 "I hope you will agree with me…" implies uncertainty in your position. Instead, "I expect you'll agree with me." Or, "I anticipate that you'll accept my recommendation."

🖋 In the same category is the doubt-inspiring word "maybe." "Maybe you'd agree that Plan B is the way to go." Instead, you could say, "It's worth considering that we follow Plan B, wouldn't you agree?"

Too Much "I" and Not Enough "You"

When all is said and done, the key question remains: Is your message crafted to make you look good and get the outcome you're seeking, or is its purpose to give members of the audience what they want? The magic, with hard work, of course, is to meet both objectives at the same time—to get what *you* want by giving them what *they* want.

Part of the strategy to achieve this win-win outcome is to do your homework about the motivations, challenges, pain points, and desires of the group or prospect you are trying to persuade to do what you'd like them to do.

Once you're clear on what you are up against, which can be real opposition—or simple ignorance about you, your project, your organization, product, or service—you're in a better position to think about what content to use or not use.

It's critical to keep in mind that most decision-making is really not logical, so bring out in full force whatever emotional examples or relevant stories that you can share in the time frame you're given.

Keep asking yourself, "What's the worst thing that can happen?" And at the same time, "What's the best thing that can come out of this speaking opportunity?" By getting ready for both possibilities, you'll emerge as the confident, together communicator you want to be.

One last clue lets you know that you are lacking enough "you." Evaluate your use of gestures, those seemingly natural but often contrived strategic movements of your hands, body, and eyes. If there's no place for you to reach out toward the audience with either one hand, palm up, or both hands, you're probably saying too many "I's" or "we's" and not enough "you's."

To Summarize...

- True connection and speaking success come when you match your goal to what your audience wants.

- When you share your own experiences and outlook, you strengthen your message and its impact.

- Balancing when to say "I," "we," or "you" takes practice and planning.

- Language is powerful, and choosing the wrong words can interfere with your ability to persuade.

Chapter 8

Organizing Your Content for Optimum Impact

In This Chapter...

- How your genes affect your decision-making
- The value of the quick outline
- Why less is more
- Keep your mind open for more good stuff!

When I go to an event, unless I'm there to provide critique to the speaker, I'm listening for what new facts, stories, techniques, or points of view I can learn. I confess the content does not need to be practical to grab my attention, just really interesting. But my passion for learning is not universal. Remember that not everyone in your audience will be as excited as you are about the content you are presenting.

While I love helping others develop their voice as a speaker and leader, I also find the back end of speaking fun and satisfying. Like a detective, I enjoy unearthing new ideas and diving into the history, challenges, discoveries, and personalities of a topic, company, or team. This curiosity applies to both developing content for my own messages and for creating client presentations.

The next most enjoyable step to me is pulling the pieces of content together like a jigsaw puzzle, finding how they interconnect, and locating the best position for them in the presentation. This chapter will give you tactics for organizing the wonderful material you have assembled.

The Hidden Role of Your Genes

I'm convinced that two kinds of genes, neither of which is acknowledged by scientists and doctors, secretly dominate our lives. Whichever one *you* were born with can determine your fate when it comes to organizing content—and, most likely, many other elements in your life.

The first gene is what I call the *throwaway gene.* My sister, Sara, has always had the philosophy that if you haven't worn it or used it in the past three months, you don't really need it. When my nephews were young, she readily tossed out games and toys if a part got broken or the boys simply lost interest in playing with them. Her home and her closets continue to reflect this powerful gene's presence in her life. There is no clutter.

A client who once was in the real estate business, buying, fixing up, and reselling properties, was even more of an anti-saving-stuff extremist than my sister. She called her style of decorating and living "minimalist." Everything was beautiful and purposeful. There just wasn't much of it.

If you've inherited the throwaway gene, you probably find chopping out the lesser elements of content a fairly simple and painless task. You're then able to focus on the major points that will drive your message home.

I was blessed—or cursed—with the other kind of gene, what I've dubbed the *keep-it* gene. The brain says, "But I may need this

From the Many to the Best

Let's say you've got a list of thirty possible talking points you could include in your message, ranging from key facts and statistics and supporting data to personal anecdotes—and they are in no particular order.

One simple way to begin to narrow the field down is to circle what you see as the two or three most important ideas. Try saying them aloud. Ask yourself: "If I shared only these points, would I get across the gist of what I wanted to say?" If not, keep going and try circling some of the other points until you discover what your core ideas truly are.

Example

_____ one day!" I admit it pains me to throw away almost anything and I've had to work really hard at staying ahead of stuff taking over my drawers, files, garage, and life in general. Sometimes, with concerted effort and usually aided by my daughter's determination, I make strides in lightening ship—in shedding, indeed, shredding, stuff.

When it comes to putting together your presentation, if you've been afflicted with the *keep-it* gene, chances are you have identified entirely too much information to include and will no doubt struggle to narrow it down.

How many ideas, ideally, work best for most presentations or speeches? From my experience, a maximum of two to three main points gives you the best chance of accomplishing your speaking goal, no matter whether you're on for ten minutes or two hours. For a message of fewer than ten minutes, a maximum of two main ideas is recommended so you can fully develop the ideas.

Main Points for the Cup Talk

After gathering a ton of information on coffee and tea, and integrating it into my customary presentation on communication styles and motivators, here's how I set up the core points in my message entitled, "What Does Your Cup Say about You?"

Point 1—What your morning rituals say about you

Point 2—How to persuade the four different morning personalities

Point 3—The role of motivation in getting what you want from others

Example

Most people will embrace having to pay attention to two or three themes or tracks at a time, but no more. Why? You're not the only thing going on in their lives, professionally or personally. Your competition is all of the other efforts to command and keep their attention, from the Internet to TV, from ads to music, from work to leisure pursuits, from family to community causes.

If you've been around teens or kids who know you well enough to be somewhat rude, a prevailing putdown for someone who rambles on and on is this: TMI—too much information!

This admonition applies not only to your actual comments, but to your visuals, brochures, handouts, and other materials as well.

How do you know which two or three main points to use in your message? Try saying the final draft of your two or three main points aloud. Do they sound compelling? Would you want to listen? Would your friends, coworkers, or customers? If not, maybe you need to keep pruning.

That's where overcoming the keep-it tendencies and being judicious with the quick throwaway behaviors can result in a clear and viable set of choices. It's not a straight path, but once you've identified these main points, and you're confident in your selection, the rest of the writing falls into place much faster.

The Quick Outline Reward

Let's call the three main ideas you intend to present Apple, Banana, and Cherry.

What do you want us to know about Apple? About Banana? And about Cherry? Ideally, you'll list one to three subpoints under your main points. These subpoints are the stories, facts, and examples related to the main point. While you want to give similar weight to each of your main points, you don't need to treat each exactly the same way.

For example, Apple can reveal the statistical or research support for your position. Banana can review the problems or issues. Cherry can disclose the options you see to resolve the situation.

I've found that a quick outline using the Apple-Banana-Cherry

To Tea or Not to Tea, That Is the Question

As I started to brainstorm my ideas for the motivational message a local charity had requested, I dove off the deep end into its tea party theme. I wrote down everything I knew and could find out about tea, including reading tea leaves, the ways people drink tea, the traditions of the tea ceremony, what tea had to do with the American Revolution, the healing properties of tea, the new tea stores that had opened up in area malls, and on and on.

I was having a ball with the research, but I soon realized that nobody would really care about most of what I'd learned! I was able to take only one or two of what I considered the fascinating facts and weave them into my actual first point, which explored the different ways we communicate.

Perspiration

headings helps me clear my head of competing demands by my data to "choose me." It helps me overcome guilt at leaving stuff out because I can readily see that the anecdote, while amusing, doesn't really advance my message. Or the research finding, though time-consuming to gather and substantiate, doesn't really make the impact I had hoped it would.

Your finished outline may be one page only, or less, depending on how much you write about your version of Apple, Banana, and Cherry, your main points, and how detailed your subpoints are.

I was invited to do a one-hour workshop for a group of international bankers downtown, but the day before the meeting, they called asking me to shorten my session to forty minutes. Turns out the event was coinciding with the televised World Cup and the nearby Miami Heat game. The organizers were concerned that the traffic they were expected to generate would mean quite a few late arrivals and delay the start of our program.

Since I already had a clear outline, in Apple, Banana, and Cherry points, and my PowerPoints were done, I thought it would take just a few minutes to cut out content and get the timing down. Instead, it took two and a half hours to whittle down the slides and outline into the forty-minute program that I was scheduled to present the next day.

My Apple point covered what you needed to do before arriving at a networking event. My Banana point introduced the techniques to use when you're face to face, to get the best possible results. And my Cherry point explored the postnetworking activities to undertake that can lead to new relationships, business, and contributions.

While the outline was clear, I found myself attached to the subpoints, the stories, and exercises I'd wanted to present to the group. I confess it was hard to let go of my carefully assembled content and colorful, sometimes funny slides. However, if I had not gone through the quick outline process initially, then fleshed out the details as I did for the actual presentation, it would have been a nightmare to alter a sixty-minute message into a forty-minute one, less than a day away.

Keep It versus Throw Away?

You may find yourself fighting yourself, too, as you go through your material to assign it to the best place on your quick outline.

What do you want to avoid when putting together a quick outline?

❧ Avoid focusing on the order of your main points as you craft the quick outline. At this point, it really doesn't matter. Just concentrate on what needs to be included, and what you can discard.

❧ Avoid reverting to the *keep everything* position. Why? A quick outline with too much detail, with too many points and subpoints, can thwart your ability to identify the most tantalizing and memorable elements you've gathered. Think, as the kids say, TMI. Too much information.

❧ If your tendency is to activate your *throwaway* gene and cut, cut, cut, remember that you'll need those subpoints to help make your main points come alive.

Finding the Ideal Order

While alphabetical order is a comforting and familiar way to organize ideas, sometimes your best ideas show up later in your creative or brainstorming process. It takes a little while for your creativity and thought processes to catch up with each other and that's entirely normal! That said, your quick outline— Apple, Banana, Cherry—may not be the best order for you to achieve your speaking goal.

How do you know what the optimal order may be?

One strategy is to begin to recite aloud what you've written on your outline as if you were telling your best friend the two or three main points you intend to present. If the Apple, Banana, Cherry order seems to work—great! But, it's entirely possible that you'll go further, faster, by beginning with Cherry, then going to Apple and winding up with Banana.

When you create your main points as independently as possible, you gain the flexibility to reorder them or even eliminate one, depending on the speaking situation requirements.

When I deliver a public speaking presentation, my content usually revolves around three main points:

❧ The science of strategic speaking, which includes how to match what the audience wants with your own goal, and how to organize your content to do that

Modules: Magic Building Blocks for the Longer Message

When you are expected to deliver a message anywhere from thirty minutes to a few hours or more, the speaker's best friend is called the module. A module is a twelve- to fourteen-minute chunk of your presentation or speech. In a half hour, you'll have two modules. In an hour, four, and in two hours, eight modules.

Each module will have from one to three main points—actually subpoints of your main ideas. What's cool about employing modules is that if you find it necessary to shorten your talk or you want to stay in one area longer, you can simply cut out an entire module and no one—except you—will know what you've left out.

Definition

🔍 The art or theater of speaking, which showcases how to use your body, voice, and personality to capture and keep attention

🔍 The law of averages, which helps you identify and prepare for the potential pitfalls as well as the honors that speakers may experience

To keep my workshops and keynotes fresh, I'm constantly listening for new stories and techniques to share, by attending meetings, reading, taking webinars, and connecting with new people. Once you have designed a quick outline for your message, you'll find you can easily use it again and again, simply updating the stats or adding different examples.

Another way to determine which order for your content might be best is to leave out one of your main points entirely as you try your ideas aloud. If the flow of what remains sounds right and natural, your remaining point may work best at the beginning or at the end of the presentation. You may find that what you thought was a main idea was actually more of an engaging opening statement, or it could be helpful to make your conclusion stick.

If you find yourself getting frustrated in determining the optimal order for your content, I recommend you spend time developing each of the main points as independently as you can. Choose the most intriguing story, examples, facts, and images you can to help you convey this portion of your message as a stand-alone entity for now. As you continue your efforts, the right order will become evident to you.

I can't emphasize enough the importance of reciting aloud what you are writing or planning, as you go along in this process. Saying your written words aloud will save you time in the long run and increase the likelihood of producing an outstanding spoken message. Why? If you have written something that you can't pronounce or talk about in a natural way, it's a good idea to know that early in the development of your message, when you can still change things around.

Why Less Is More

Most people are too busy and too preoccupied with their own lives and issues to pay as much attention to your message as you would like (and no doubt deserve). How do we combat this universal and growing attention deficit disorder that plagues young and old alike?

President Theodore Roosevelt once said, "Speak softly and carry a big stick; you will go far." He was quoting an African proverb and used the phrase in a number of his foreign policy speeches. While I don't think President Roosevelt's approach will make you too popular or effective as a persuasive speaker, I do recommend that you get in the habit of carrying a big pair of invisible scissors.

It used to be that an elevator speech was a minute or two, the time it took to ride an elevator up or down with someone and engage in a quick but impressive conversation to set up a meeting or lunch. Today, popular wisdom says you need to introduce yourself exceptionally in ten to twelve seconds.

In a similar vein, it's hard to imagine a time before the TV remote clicker was invented. In those prehistoric days, you were forced to watch the seven or eight minutes of programming between commercials or you had to get up out of your chair to go turn the knob to another channel. The only way to avoid the commercials was to leave the room to go to the kitchen, restroom, or outside.

With the power of the remote, you can skip commercials, record any show you want, and zip around to watch pieces of as many different channels as you can absorb. However, for speakers, the remote has continued to erode the world's attention span even further. Depending on what's on TV, the average time is three or four seconds between clicks. As a consequence, you may lose your audience members' interest after three or four seconds because they are mentally clicking away from you. While you may be able to ask members of an audience to turn off their phones or at least put them on vibrate, you can't truly control their actions.

Trends Still Favor Good Speakers

What we're seeing as a result of social media's widely accepted word and character limits—Twitter's 140 characters and Facebook's similar abbreviated posts—is the use of fewer and fewer words in everyday communication. Instead of using the phone, a whole generation is writing texts and losing the art of conversation.

Take heart, though, in this counter-Internet reality: thousands and thousands and thousands of people worldwide are still going to conferences to learn from experts and connect with others in their fields, face to face. Breakfast, lunch, and dinner speakers remain in demand—especially when they include memorable stories as part of the conversation. Many companies continue to insist on weekly meetings that are a combination of live and online video.

So, how do all of these trends impact your speaking?

For years I've used the adage, "when in doubt, cut it out." Using those invisible scissors I mentioned earlier can be painful and it's definitely not fun. But your audience, your team, your

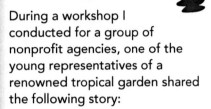

Fear of the Butterfly

During a workshop I conducted for a group of nonprofit agencies, one of the young representatives of a renowned tropical garden shared the following story:

A little girl on a field trip from her kindergarten started crying and screaming the minute she entered the butterfly exhibit. "What's wrong?" he asked. "The butterflies are going to bite me!" she answered, and her crying intensified.

The garden employee told us he quickly reached out and grabbed a butterfly, and put it in the palm of his hand.

"See this black part? It's called the proboscis. It's the mouth of the butterfly and as you see, he has no teeth. He cannot bite you."

According to the garden employee, the little girl immediately stopped crying, broke into a huge smile, and skipped around for the rest of her school's visit to the butterfly exhibit.

"This is what we do at David Fairchild Gardens," he said proudly, in closing.

Inspiration

boss, or whatever community you are addressing will be much happier, more inclined to listen and go along with your request when you've made your remarks as brief as possible.

Stay Alert for More Good Stuff!

Even though you've carefully organized your content and your Apple-Banana-Cherry order seems to be the way to go, don't close the door too soon on what could be a deal-making addition to your message.

🖋 It could be that tidbit you heard on National Public Radio on your drive to work, or saw on your friend's Facebook page.

🖋 It could be that comment in passing that your boss shared at the coffee machine.

🖋 It could be a new law the legislature just passed that changes everything.

🖋 It could be the draft of the best player in the league was just announced.

🖋 It could be a sudden changing of the guard and you know what it means.

You get the idea.

Being a successful speaker means you're the person of the moment, and you are the expert of the hour. Although it's a constant battle for attention these days, given the lure of smartphones, the remote clicker, and other technologies, staying on top of what's happening in your industry, your office, and your community can make a world of difference in being seen as merely adequate—or a public-speaking genius.

To Summarize...

🖋 Your keep-it or throwaway genes can influence your message's content.

🖋 Devising the quick outline keeps your ideas on track.

🖋 Today's audience won't listen too long.

🖋 Be alert for new material when you least expect it.

Chapter 9

Recycling Your Content for Blogs, Radio, and Webinars

In This Chapter...

- Turn your brilliance into a blog, newsletter, and tweets.
- YouTube, here you come!
- Take to the air: Use radio and webinars.

If you imagine yourself painting a rainbow across the sky as the content-gathering part of public speaking, the legendary pot of gold at the end is filled with something far more valuable to you as a speaker. In it you will find a rich, personal gold mine of pertinent data, reusable stories, and practical examples.

Regardless of whether your goal for genius speaking is business-focused, community-minded, or even personal, chances are good that you gathered considerably more information than you needed or were able to present in the time you were given to speak.

I admit cutting out certain stories or statistics can be painful, especially when you invested a ton of time and energy to harvest them. Truth is, your thoughtful editing will make your message stronger. At the same time, don't despair that those pieces of gold you found in your personal gold mine will never see the light of day.

In this chapter, you'll see how your golden words can be transformed into social media posts, articles for traditional media, webinars, radio shows, and other speaking opportunities.

Words Go Far Beyond Your Mouth

What can you do with your personal content gold mine? I recommend that you recycle your treasures into other formats such as a newsletter or blog that can help you promote your expertise, cause, or organization. A blog, by the way, is simply a written piece that you post online, tied to your own name or company website, or as a guest posting on someone else's blog.

One of the motivators for me in writing this genius book, for example, was a chance to create content that I could excerpt and use for my own blogs and newsletters.

Another option is to contribute your brilliance as a guest blogger to the more established blogs, depending on the topic. To find established bloggers in your field, just Google "bloggers." For instance, if you search for "bloggers, public speaking," a list of more than two hundred will come up, each offering tips and insights to help you continue to master this critical skill.

If you produce a newsletter, articles with photos or illustrations can go a bit longer than three hundred words, but the shorter lengths help assure more readership. There are a variety of low-cost online newsletter services, with colorful templates you can easily adapt to your own logo,

Use Your Gold in a Blog and More

I've been told by experts that 200 to 300 words is the maximum recommended for a blog, but the rule is not in stone.

You can post your own blog using free websites such as *wordpress. com* or *blogger.com*. You can also send out a weekly or biweekly email to a special list you develop, highlighting a few teaser lines from your blog, and a link to it on your website. I've been doing weekly email blasts with good results.

Be sure to check out what formats work best for your style and the readership you're trying to build.

Inspiration

color scheme, and content. They make it simple for you to email out your public speaking recycled content in written format. Among them are Constant Contact, iContact, and MailChimp. For more robust mailing programs, you may want to consider InfusionSoft.

Traditional media, including your local newspaper and magazines, is still open to guest articles and columns that match its editorial criteria. If you're speaking at an event, the media may include the topic, location, time, date, and cost in a calendar listing if you upload it or send your notice ahead to meet their deadline.

If you speak at an organization that produces a newsletter itself, such as a Rotary Club or a women's group, you can submit a short recap of your comments along with your photo, which could then appear in the next edition. Since these groups are mostly volunteer-driven, they'll appreciate your providing a ready-made article for their newsletter.

Facebook, Google Hangouts, and LinkedIn, among other social media sites, are quite speaker-friendly. You can simply extract a one- or two-line set of comments from your speech or presentation and post it, ideally along with a photo of you in action or a link to a video if one was shot. People can then "like" or "comment" on your message and share it on their own pages, giving you additional material to incorporate into future public speaking engagements.

Social media continues to evolve and become more sophisticated regarding capturing the preferences and interests of those who frequent the various sites. You can match your brilliance to those seeking it to further your business and community goals.

Present Your Content in a Google Hangouts

You can send your content to up to one hundred people or talk with up to fifteen via video, in a free service called Google Hangouts. Capabilities continue to change so double-check before you start your outreach program this way.

In a similar way to Facebook, you invite friends, family, and business contacts into your Google circle, and you can then use this digital platform as a way to share your fantastic ideas and information. By the way, the video feature is a convenient and no-cost method for trying out new material or refining your existing message. Schedule a meeting or dress rehearsal with a trusted few. Neither you nor your audience members need to leave their home or office!

Inspiration

Turn It into Tweets

If transforming your content into two hundred or three hundred words for a blog or article is not your cup of tea, reducing an idea, fact, or position to 140 characters for a tweet to post on Twitter, online, may be more to your liking. While it's hard work to condense anything meaningful this way, you'll be in good company. Everyone from the president of the United States to celebrities to corporations is using Twitter to send out their briefest messages or tweets online.

Words Fly as a Blog, Too

In my workshops and keynotes, I talk about why not being prepared when you present can ruin your reputation, kill a deal, or worse. People will forgive a bit of nervousness if you forge ahead with well-organized, worthwhile content, and if you appear passionate about your topic.

I was able to take the first part of **Chapter 3** in this book and transform it into a blog, entitled "Why Winging It Only Works for Chickens and Other Feathered Creatures." I shortened the content to three hundred words and kept the main points intact. To illustrate the blog, I posted a color photo of a rubber chicken, similar to the one I used in my live presentations. The blog was well received. Yours will be, too!

Inspiration

Some people tweet daily or even more often from an event. For example, if you are the speaker at a meeting, you can invite your listeners to send out a tweet describing one aspect of your presentation to their followers. When I speak, I post my Twitter name on a slide: @AnneMiami and invite folks to tweet. I've seen this request more and more at conferences, too.

The goal of social media is to generate interest in what you are saying and to help you develop a following. A benefit of these online formats is that you can use this forum to get feedback on your ideas and proposals, and later incorporate comments and opinions into your future live and video presentations as well.

YouTube (and Beyond), Here You Come!

In that rainbow of content you have developed, there will be some elements that are almost begging to be caught on camera. The expression, a picture is worth a thousand words, is especially true for the right video treatment of your topic.

What criteria can you use to decide if something is worth creating a video about and then posting on YouTube or in another online program?

🖋 First and foremost, can you successfully convey the idea or information in one to two minutes maximum? YouTube and other online viewers have an attention span that is notoriously short and getting shorter all the time. On the other hand, the popular TED talks (*ted.com*) average up to about seven minutes, so my point is that nothing is yet set in stone about the ideal length.

🖋 Your video can feature information from your PowerPoint or Keynote (on a Mac or iPad) presentation, for example, and not necessarily show you in person on camera. How can you take one of your main points in a PowerPoint format and make it come alive in video?

🖋 Dos and don'ts with related examples drawn from your speech or presentation can become snappy and appreciated videos.

🖋 A brief step-by-step approach with video demonstration of the techniques taken from your speaking content, followed by a specific call to action, can be another avenue for your efforts.

🖋 Tell one of the more memorable stories or personal anecdotes you like to present to an audience in a video, as a "teaser" to encourage others to buy your book, to support your project or cause, to attend your event, or even to check out your website.

After I became more comfortable doing webinars that ran about forty-five minutes and experimenting with short online courses, I was ready to try other video ventures. My next step was to start producing and posting one to two minute videos with tips on public speaking and executive communication. In my weekly email blog posts, I provided a link to these videos as well, enabling me to continue to give value to my readers and expand awareness about my coaching, programs, and this book.

Get Invited or Do Your Own Radio Show

When I've been invited onto radio shows and webinars, a question I've often been asked is this: "Why are people so afraid of public speaking?"

Being allowed to answer that question gives me a platform with thousands of radio listeners to introduce myself and my services, without appearing to be advertising directly.

For webinars, which are online events that can be educational, the number of those who register may be smaller than your reach through radio, but it's usually a more qualified, targeted list with interest in your topic.

Look through your content and pull out the questions you could be asked—and answer—in a short, upbeat manner. Write those questions down and provide them to your host, whether you're asked for them or not. Why? You have a better chance of being asked what will help you get remembered and sought-after when the questions are relevant and you're on your game with the answers.

How can being on radio help you?

If you're representing another business or your own, you have the opportunity to be showcased as an expert, sharing the same kind of content you normally do with an audience or client.

If you are involved with a nonprofit organization, a radio appearance lets you promote your cause and events in a way that lets you appeal personally to listeners, many more than you can usually address at one time.

Part of my expertise is helping teams and boards interact in a way that produces less drama and more results. To help its leaders better manage their volunteer board of directors, I was invited several times to participate as a guest presenter in a webinar conducted for more than seventy chapters of a national association of business owners. My segment was about twenty-five minutes and I showed humorous slides as well as practical pointers to reinforce the advice I was sharing. I also had sent the host questions ahead of time for her to ask me.

From that webinar appearance came invitations to speak at their national conference as well as new business.

As I mentioned earlier, I've been hosting my own webinars since the summer of 2014, experimenting with topics and formats. Part of the reward has been building my email list and the other has been attracting new clients and speaking engagements.

From Consultant to Radio Producer

Marcy Rosenbaum was increasingly frustrated with her successful management consulting practice. She knew she wanted to reinvent herself but wasn't sure what to do or how. "I hate to be on stage," she admitted. "I hate to have my picture taken. And I'm an introvert." During her long commute to consulting jobs, she says she listened to more than ten thousand hours of National Public Radio, and as a fan, knew every show and host by name and style. After volunteering to read for the blind on air to fulfill her passion for helping others, and being told she had a great voice, she decided to transform herself into a radio producer.

Her first program, The Livelihood Show (*livelihoodshow.com*), began in 2011 and since then she's hosted more than fifty one-hour segments. The common theme is to give listeners insights into how others have reinvented themselves, along with access to experts who help change lives, professionally and personally. It started by submitting her idea to one of the online radio networks, Radio Ear Network. The network accepted her proposal and charged thirty dollars an episode to upload and broadcast her show in a weekly designated time slot. Not knowing anything about producing a radio show, Marcy shadowed a local NPR host, volunteering to help book guests, make calls, and learning the ins and outs of the technology and production details. She also, through networking, found a coach to help her master the equipment, technology, and software.

Being a guest or a host of a podcast—an online broadcast—gives you the chance to "create, purpose, and repurpose" your valuable content, Marcy said.

"When you give a talk, you talk, and it's gone," she pointed out. "But when you are recorded, you can make yourself heard again and again. When you add the finishing touches of postproduction, such as editing format and sound quality, you create an audio business card that represents you doing what you do best."

What can you do with a podcast after its initial play on an Internet station?

🖋 It can be uploaded to play on your website as a customized message or introduction. Imagine saying to a potential client, "Have you heard my show?"

🖋 People can download your podcast from iTunes and other similar aggregators who market their library to interested people who are looking for great ideas and stories. Potential listeners can find you and when they like what they hear, they can sign up for a subscription to hear more of your genius podcasts.

Your podcast can be transcribed and you can sell it as an e-book to generate some revenue or additional followers. The easiest way to publish your first book is to create an edited e-book from a presentation transcript. Put together an engaging title with good cover art and you can offer a Kindle book that captures your style and message.

Marcy's latest effort, *entrepreneurradio.org*, has her teamed up with real estate investor and founder of The Strategic Forum for entrepreneurs, Seth Warner. She's conducting interviews with business owners on the psychology behind what they're doing, talking about their mindset and what it's like to take risks. They are monetizing the effort by securing sponsorships.

From Despair to Podcast Network Owner

Looking for a way to climb out of debt and the loss of her limousine business in the aftermath of Hurricane Ivan, Joanne Quinn Smith discovered "Talk Shoe" (*talkshoe.com*), an online site that provided podcast recording and hosting. Armed with her two main assets, great extemporaneous speaking skills and extensive contacts, she told me she started podcasting.

"I had long been disappointed with the local news axiom, 'If It Bleeds, It Leads,' she said, "so in 2007 I started a podcast, PositivelyPittsburghLive, which immediately caught attention. But it was new technology and at that time not easy for guests to get on the talkcast/podcast live."

Online Radio with You as the Host?

Type in "free online radio shows" in Google or some other search engine and you're going to find a diverse set of options for you to explore.

Some of the hosts of these online shows have developed significant followers, not just in their own cities, but nationally and even internationally.

One of the key advantages of online radio is that you record your shows in advance at a time that's convenient for you. They are aired at scheduled times which you can promote as well.

Check out these leading sites where you can explore your own possibilities:

◆ *blogtalkradio.com*

◆ *radioearnetwork.com*

◆ *voiceamerica.com*

Perspiration

The TechnoGrannyShow was born to teach people how to be a guest over the phone on this multimedia platform. She told me:

> *I was then inundated by listeners who wanted to know about Internet technology. My brand name became TechnoGranny. A business associate suggested that being the owner of a full-service marketing company that helped clients with low-cost marketing tools, qualified me to produce a show called MondayMorningMarketeer. This program offers fifteen minutes of gorilla marketing tips. The niche following on this show enabled me to turn eight blog posts from one of the series on Marketing Plans into my first book, Folly of Marketing Plan in Your Head, 101 Compelling Reasons to Write One, in June 2013.*

Other books followed.

Two years after her first podcast's launch, Joanne had quadruple bypass surgery and did not work for nine months, except for her shows. On returning to work in the midst of the recession, both her marketing business and speaking career took off. She attributes her success to the podcasting/Internet radio and winning the Small Business Association Journalist of the Year Award, having been nominated by the National Association of Women Business Owners, Greater Pittsburgh Chapter. She was the first journalist to receive the award without a newspaper byline and without being associated with a conventional radio station.

"I won it totally for new media," she said. "Today, *positivelypittsburghlive magazine.com* enjoys over two million visitors a year with seventy channels (audio and video podcasts) and syndicated pages (blogs). So one flagship podcast turned into an entire network."

Joanne has recorded over a thousand podcasts which have accumulated over a million Internet listeners.

What has that done for her business?

> *Now when I get calls to speak, I have myriad speaking samples and topics online that my prospects can choose from. The vast amount of content makes me extremely visible, so that when I interview with prospective clients, they are already convinced to hire me and now are just discussing price, which by the way goes up accordingly with one's credibility.*

For both consultants and speakers, consistent effort as a podcaster can be the key to getting quality bookings, great referrals, prequalified business prospects, and setting the price that you deserve—not just the one that clients want to pay, but the one they WILL pay.

Don't Overlook the Webinar

Webinar has become a widely understood term for an online seminar or educational program. Many are free, often used as a sales hook to get you to sign up for a longer, fee-based program or to sell you a specific product or service. As a speaker, you can build your reputation and revenues for your business or your cause, by hosting or being a guest on a webinar or webinar series.

Every day a new webinar hosting company seems to come online, offering a new range of features. Some are completely free and others charge a monthly subscription, based on the number of attendees you expect to sign up.

Here are some pointers to help you host your own webinar, based on my own experiences and those of some clients:

🖎 *Read the instructions!* More specifically, be sure you complete all of the training that comes with the software well before your planned date. Every platform is slightly different. Double-check that your equipment will work with the webinar software.

🖎 *Do a dress rehearsal and record it.* Plan a practice session with everyone who will be on the webinar and record it. During the playback, analyze how you sound and what you could fix. It helps to have talking points or even a script to follow.

🖎 *Invite a partner.* When the leader of another business or organization joins you, you not only double the range of information you also get backup help in case something goes wrong, and you can take turns answering questions or responding to chat questions.

🖎 *Don't rush.* You sound more in control with a slower pace. Talk too fast and the audience may miss what you're trying to say or show them because the presentation software doesn't always flow in real time; it can lag and leave your audience behind you a bit.

🖐 *Fake, if necessary, being cool, calm, and collected.* The reality is that something will go wrong; some won't be able to hear you, their screen will freeze, or the slides won't show up. All of these things have happened to me and to folks I know who do webinars all the time. Apologize if you can't fix something and keep going, or you may lose the rest of the attendees. If all else fails, consider offering a free item and the opportunity to attend another session.

🖐 *Narrow your focus.* We have a tendency to want to tell them everything! Just as any other speaking situation, the hard part is choosing what really needs to be presented, and what can be cut depending on your time frame. Decide how many points you can present and stick to it.

🖐 *Honor the question-and-answer time.* People want to be able to ask questions in a live webinar, so if it's an hour, be sure and leave at least ten to twenty minutes for this option. You cultivate fans and potential clients by giving them direct access to your expertise this way.

My learning curve was more than a bit painful when I started offering webinars. It took me several months and countless embarrassing moments to eventually master the ability to look and sound at ease on the camera. I've embraced this new way of speaking. You can, too.

To Summarize...

🖐 You can self-publish online in many popular ways.

🖐 You can turn your presentation into a video to expand your reach.

🖐 You can be a guest or host your own radio show or webinar.

Chapter 10

The Famous Four Parts of the Genius Presentation or Speech

In This Chapter...

- Opening strong, so they can't wait for more
- Setting the stage with your prebody summary
- Organizing the body, managing your content
- How to close, achieving your purpose

"Oh, she's a natural!" A good speaker can get that reaction from an admiring and perhaps somewhat jealous audience. From my vantage, natural talent in sports, the arts, and even technology is an accident of birth, an unasked for gift that helps some folks excel.

But I believe that *genius* public speaking—being an outstanding, memorable communicator—is absolutely no accident. To speak so that people listen and act takes both know-how and much practice.

What you say in your opening moments can determine whether anyone listens to you or drifts off into their own world. How you set up the critical overview of your remarks can continue the initial interest or shut it down completely. Putting your important material into an easy to follow format requires deciding what to cut out as well as what to keep and how to say it. And your success is directly tied into how you end your message to bring about the outcome you need.

What's ahead in this chapter gives you practical guidance on how to transform yourself into a well-organized, respected speaker.

Opening with Style and Determination

One of the questions I'm often asked is this: "How much personal information should you share, if any, and where does it go in your talk?" My response is usually: "What are you trying to accomplish with this public speaking situation?" Your goal for your talk helps determine what you need to say at the beginning, and how you move into the rest of your message.

The new CEO of a cruise line company, only five months in the position and also new to Miami, was the keynote speaker at the local chamber of commerce. The company, with more than 115,000 employees worldwide, had suffered some awful press of late due to a series of regrettable accidents on its ships overseas and close to home.

Instead of a corporate approach or a remotely defensive posture, the CEO started by telling the audience of three hundred plus business leaders how he had been born and raised in a poor section of New Orleans by hardworking and dedicated parents. Sitting in the audience, I could see how those around me started almost immediately shifting from polite interest to genuine attention.

The speaker continued, describing how he had advanced in his career and his surprising selection by the founder of the company to head the global cruising industry giant. He made us laugh by revealing how he and his wife had just purchased a condo on Miami Beach at the height of the real estate market boom and he hoped he'd be around long enough to make it worthwhile.

He was engaging, real, and kept the interest of a diverse and often hard-to-please crowd. His message expanded into the company's new plans for cruising, the changing nature of its ships and programming, and what he saw as the biggest challenge ahead.

For his opening, he used one of the techniques you'll find in **Chapter 11**, called *Tell a story*. By doing so, he established a personal connection with every member of the audience.

At the same time, such personal disclosure is not always appropriate and it doesn't always work to be so forthcoming!

I still remember the shocking installation speech of the new president of a women's business group to which I belonged. Here's how she began:

"I'm a bitch."

The newly installed leader went on to say that she considered the label a tribute to being gutsy and not willing to take poor excuses from employees or family members. She suggested that others in the room could proudly share her title, too.

While her opening commanded attention and the technique is one of the methods I'll go over with you in **Chapter 11**, her treatment turned out to be offensive and off-putting. She lost respect and failed to motivate many attending to get involved with the organization by declaring herself "a bitch." It helps to remember that some groups are expecting you to entertain them, but others only want you to focus on the issue at hand and to get right to the point, fast. Your opening words need to be compelling, luring your audience into continuing to listen to the rest of what you came to say.

As a journalist, I'd been trained to keep myself out of the story by remaining neutral in interviews and when describing events. What *I* felt about a situation didn't matter, and, in fact, was not supposed to show up in my writing. Further, it was all about capturing, as

What to Share, What Not to Share in the Opening

If you're talking about your expertise—let's say as a banker or wealth advisor—no one needs to know, or will care, that you were a football player in high school. Or a cheerleader. Or how many kids you have.

On the other hand, it might be relevant to tell them how you nearly lost your house to foreclosure. Or that you once racked up credit card debt and how you overcame that problem. Or how you helped someone in a similar position to grow the person's portfolio by 25 percent over a year.

Perspiration

accurately as possible, what was said, quoting or paraphrasing the experts and sources I interviewed.

As a speaker, I had to learn to undo that conditioning and trust that my own experiences had value when presenting to others, whether simply to brighten the moment with a true, humorous example or a more profound sharing. My metamorphosis as a speaker didn't happen especially fast. When you are trying to change habits, especially if you're past, say, twenty-five years of age, it's vital to give yourself time to adapt and acquire the new.

These days, I regularly describe incidents related to clients or my own speaking experiences—good and not-so-wonderful—when I believe it will help set the stage right away for learning and self-forgiveness.

Surviving My First Webinar

While I had been a guest on quite a few webinars and radio shows to talk about persuasive speaking and leadership communication, I didn't realize how different it would be when I was the co-host along with author and international performance coach Achim Nowak. We had decided to conduct a technology dress rehearsal the day before a scheduled noon webinar we had called *The Secrets to More Personal Impact*. The plan was that each of us was to speak for about ten minutes, followed by questions from the listeners.

To say I was awful during the first few minutes of the dress rehearsal would be an understatement. What made it worse was that I was supposed to cover being natural and confident as a speaker. But in fairness to myself, I had never before spoken to a computer monitor for ten minutes with absolutely nobody in the room and it felt awkward and uncomfortable. Even though I'd practiced intensely and prepared thoroughly, the audio performance with no audience was a first.

Achim teasingly said I sounded as though I had taken an illegal pharmaceutical. He tried to lighten my mood by wondering how many of my ex-boyfriends would be on the call. Jorge, our technical advisor, asked aloud where I had gone for the first three or four minutes.

But I hung in there, as you will no doubt do, as well. I found my voice and pace during the second half of the dress rehearsal. The next day, during the actual webinar, I was much more comfortable, felt myself emerging in this new medium, and we got great feedback. The slides, for some reason, did not work and I found myself having to tell the audience that we'd include them in the recording to be sent out afterward. And because the slides did not show, I also had to do my first-ever "upsell" at the end, encouraging the listeners to sign up for a one-day program that Achim and I were hosting a few weeks later.

Moral of the story? The first time you do anything new in the public eye—whether live or video or webinar—you may encounter not only technology snafus but some strong internal turbulence as well. As long as you're well prepared, and you practice extensively, it will all pass!

Not Meant to Be an Assistant

Another example of a memorable opening is the way the owner of a personal training company described how she began her business.

> *I was running a company that provided office assistance services, everything from filing to bookkeeping. I did it, and I was good at it, but I hated it more and more every day. Where I was happy was working out at the gym. Or hiking or walking outside. I loved fresh air and nature. I realized I wanted to be outdoors more, not stuck inside in an office. So I searched for personal trainer certification programs, found the best one I could, and after a few intensive months, graduated, started to get clients, and never looked back. I have never been happier.*

Her speech's purpose was to inspire women who were not satisfied with their bodies or what they were doing in life to seek out changes that could lead to new joys and satisfaction.

You, too, will develop that capacity to draw from your own personal and professional history, and to figure out what to incorporate into your openings.

The Prebody Summary—Setting the Stage for Success

"If you don't know where you are going, any road will get you there."
—Lewis Carroll

Following the opening in a well-crafted message is a part that seems deceptively simple when done properly, called the prebody summary, or for short, the prebody. It has two purposes. One is to serve as a tantalizing minicommercial, ushering in the rest of your message. The second is to act as a minicontent road map for your audience, advising us what you intend to cover.

From my experience, however, most people struggle with the prebody summary, often leaving it out of their speech entirely because it's often difficult to create, or if they do it, even the greatest fail to go the "extra mile." The result is a serviceable but boring overview of what's to come in their talk.

To write a sexy, intriguing prebody, you first need to have developed the two or three main points in your message and be fairly certain of the order in which you're presenting them. Consequently, for best results, it's one of the last things you devise, edit, and practice.

To give your audience good reasons to continue listening, after the opening, your prebody needs to incorporate either pain-causing or motivational words, or both, attached to your main points. Examples of pain words are *worried about*, *frustrated with*, and *concerned about*. Benefit phrases can be descriptors like *cost-saving*, *time-saving*, *brand-building*, and *delicious, low-calorie alternatives*.

Here's a prebody that a new dog food manufacturer might use in a talk to pet owners:

> *Today I'm going to show you how giving your dog healthier food instead of the type you typically find in the grocery store can save you money at the veterinarian, reduce the nighttime howling at the moon and other annoying behaviors, and also make your pet a happier, more energetic member of your family.*

Prebody: A Basic Summary of the Main Points Is Not Enough

Here's an example of what *not* to do in your prebody:

Today we're going to talk about changes in the legislation that affect your taxation.

First, we'll look at how taxes used to be assessed.

Then we'll examine the eighteen new provisions in the law in detail.

We'll wrap up with a comparison of the old versus new aspects of the law.

Don't know about you, but I got sleepy and edgy just thinking about having to listen to that talk!

The prebody above was clearly functional and logical, but it was also deadly. There were no problem words, no angst-inspiring or motivational phrases at all to compel us to listen further. Unless you're a die-hard tax information lover, chances are high you'd be tuning out immediately.

Uninspired

Notice that in the first sentence the dog food manufacturer talks about saving you money. In the second, he alludes to a pain point, "nighttime howling at the moon and other annoying behaviors." And in the last statement, he returns to a set of benefits for making the pet "a happier, more energetic member of your family."

Here's the often boring topic of taxation made a little more appealing with an intriguing prebody:

> *Today we're going to talk about changes in the legislation that will affect many things you hold near and dear to you in the days ahead. I'll help you know whether or not you will be able to take your vacation next year. Or decide if you can afford to renovate your home or have that plastic surgery you've been longing to do. You'll know you can go get that new car, update your computer system, or expand your office.*
>
> *I'll give you some easy to follow comparisons between what is now in effect versus what you were used to paying in the past, so you have a better idea of the impact on your family and your business going forward.*
>
> *And to help you avoid expensive fines and other headaches, I'll go over a few of the new provisions and their deadlines that you need to know about.*

A well-written prebody can sometimes serve as an opening by itself, especially if you've been asked to cut your message because another speaker or the meeting itself is running late. While you may be able to leave out the planned opening, if necessary, always keep intact the benefit and problem words you attached to your main points because these emotion-evoking words are what will attract and sustain your audience's interest.

The Body—Selecting Content That Rocks

In recognition of the shrinking attention span of most people, especially in the United States, I recommend no more than two or three main points of content in the main section, known as the body of your message. If you're speaking five minutes or less, consider just one main idea with subpoints. Between five and ten minutes, a maximum of two points will work the best.

If you feel strongly that you have more than three important points to present, and your time allotment is more than ten minutes, you can go up to four maximum main ideas. However, you'll need to move more quickly through your content and be prepared to cut out material when and if you find yourself losing the audience's attention. While it's sometimes necessary to address four key ideas, I believe you'll create a better impact when you make the effort to combine your thoughts into a total of three. Once you've identified your main points, embellish them with stories, stats, and stirring details instead of overloading us with too much to think about.

How do you decide what content could be the most relevant or impactful to present? Here's where the bread rises—or falls flat. An old trial test was the following:

If you shared the information with your mother or grandmother, would she yawn? Or, would she eagerly ask you for more details? Perhaps your topic is not suitable or relevant or even understandable by a close and honest relative?

What can you do to test out your content before you roll it into your message?

- Take it in pieces and present specific segments such as the opening or main points to a coworker, a board member, a friend in your field, or someone else you respect. Watch and listen to how they react and adjust or modify the material accordingly.

- Separately try out your anecdotes or stories *aloud* in different places to people you don't know well. Do they roll their eyes politely or are you gaining real attention?

- Relate your case history and its results. Line up the facts and research you've gathered, but only do it in three-four minute bites.

The Rule of Three in Content Development

Tied directly to your level of success in speaking is your mastery of The Rule of Three in crafting your message. The rule applies to the recommendation I've given you in this chapter to include a maximum of up to three main points in your presentation. It also governs the next level down, your subpoints, where you elaborate on your ideas and argument with stories, statistics, and examples.

Strive to offer your listeners *up to three* pieces of the most memorable, tantalizing, and worthwhile support data possible for each of your main points. More can seriously reduce the impact you want to make because your audience—no matter how receptive they seem at first—will only stay tuned for a limited time.

Definition

Why do I recommend these methods of testing your content well before you need to present it? It helps to remember that you are creating more of what ends up feeling and sounding like a theatrical production—a play—than a work that is meant to be read with the eyes. Most plays start out being performed in little towns and theaters, far away from the Broadway stages of New York, the ultimate destination for top artists and playwrights.

This preliminary creative phase is known as off-off-off-off Broadway production. The scripts are tweaked after these out-of-the-limelight trials so that when they get onto the important stages of the world, the words and their delivery seem natural and professional. Isn't that what you want, too?

The transition you're making is adapting the words that may *look* good on paper to the ones that *sound* good when you say them.

The hardest part of trimming down our content into the best of the best is often leaving out stories or data that we would really like to present. In a limited attention span environment—which encompasses nearly 100 percent of all speaking situations—genius speakers are those who can eject content as needed and retain only the top material for their time allotment.

Here are some guidelines to help you decide what to keep and what to cut:

- If you left the material out, would your message be any less meaningful or relevant?

- Will the story you plan to tell still work with fewer descriptors or every single step that happened? Try it, and feel free to cut as many elements as you can while retaining the most riveting parts.

- Can the assertion you're making be easily combined into another point and still provoke the interest you are seeking? If so, combine and cut. You'll enjoy the reward of a tighter, more rewarding message.

Remember, you can recycle that excellent material you chose not to present aloud into blog posts, articles, and other applications, all designed to promote your reputation, cause, or business.

When you have a limited time to speak—a presentation or a speech—how do you decide what's important to keep and what to leave out?

Here are some questions to ask yourself:

- Why would someone care about this story or fact?

- If I left out this description or example, would it be missed?

- What makes this statistic so important to include?

- Will this set of words get me an "aha" reaction?

- How did I feel about the idea/story when I first heard or experienced it? Can I convey that feeling?

When I'm faced with a last-minute request to cut my presentation down—regardless of the reason—the challenge is to slice out tried-and-true pieces of wisdom that usually evoke laughter or thoughtful reflection. My job is to be a professional and choose the best of the best to share while eliminating the rest, and make it seem as though nothing is missing.

You can more easily trim the fat and still retain the flavor of your remarks with a well-structured message: a strong opening, a well-crafted prebody, clearly stated main points and a solid close. The heavy lifting is sifting through your main points and the examples or supporting data you have for each one, and forcing yourself to eliminate the least powerful or illuminating.

Sometimes what I find necessary is to cut the three main points down to two main ideas. That means I also need to adjust the prebody and the summary close, to remove any reference to this idea as well. For example, if I'm doing a public speaking overview, I usually cover what I call the science, art, and law of averages in strategic speaking. If my time frame has gone from forty-five minutes or an hour to thirty minutes, I will cover only the science and the art, without ever mentioning the law of averages element.

You may be forced to reduce your presentation from two main points to just one. The same adjustments will apply, that is, eradicating any mention of the information you have eliminated in the other parts of your message. Your exact course depends on how much time you have been given in your changed scenario.

The Close—Your Purposeful Exit Strategy

As I've shared earlier, genius speakers know what outcome they want or need from a presentation *before* they start putting it together. In other words, what is your call for action? What do you want us, your listeners, to do once we've spent some time listening to you and your recommendations?

Sometimes, your close is fairly obvious.

The new head of a local museum was giving an inspiring history of Miami to a large audience, pointing out that it was founded by a woman and is the only major municipality in the country to have this claim. He packed his message with other fascinating tidbits, jumping from decade to decade, highlighting different ethnic groups and their role in the area's economic development.

Finally, he asked everyone to pull out a big orange-red folder on the table. Inside were membership enrollment cards and also sponsorship forms. He closed by inviting each of us to fill out the cards and become a member of the museum. The historical speech led us quite smoothly to the "ask" as they call this type of call for action in nonprofit circles.

Other times, your close will be more subtle.

I was part of a visiting delegation of business people from the United States to Mexico. In one of the sessions, a government representative presented a detailed analysis of industries by sector, percentages of increases in manufacturing, tourism, agribusiness, and other key components of his country's economy. His closing was simply a recap of the findings he had discussed with us.

The official never asked us to invest in Mexico, to open an office, or even to do business there. He simply said he'd be available to answer any questions. Yet it was clearly understood that his objective in providing the information to us was to foster interest and encourage further action.

A panelist at a technology group was educating us about 3-D printing and its future in manufacturing and for at-home use. He set up a demonstration with a 3-D printer that was producing a small plastic stand for a smartphone, a process he told us would take about forty-five minutes to complete. Meanwhile, the entrepreneur and a corporate counterpart with Hewlett-Packard traded stories about 3-D projects and innovations, comparing the evolution of these extraordinary printers to the advent of black and white and then color copiers in recent decades.

The Hewlett-Packard executive's ending was a simple recap of where the printers are today and what he anticipated we'd be seeing by year end. It was functional but didn't evoke much applause at the morning breakfast meeting of a local executive group.

What happened when the entrepreneur left the stage to return to the 3-D printer at the end of his comments on the panel? He reached into the printer, took out the finished copy of the tiny plastic smartphone stand, and raised it high with a big smile on his face. The audience broke into delighted applause, and he didn't say another word until the questions and answers started. His close had obviously been planned and hit the mark.

Whether you can be direct, or the situation requires a more indirect approach, you can elevate your chances of a successful outcome by devising a clear closing strategy at the outset of your preparation.

At the same time, I believe that when you genuinely provide value in your content, getting people to buy something from you at the close doesn't have to be painful or uncomfortable.

To Summarize...

- A well-crafted opening will engage your audience right away.

- Continue to keep your audience's interest with an intriguing prebody summary of what you'll be covering.

- Depending on your time allotment, develop from one to three main ideas in the body of your message.

- Define your goal and know how you're going to close before you start writing or delivering your message.

Chapter 11

Opening Techniques to Avoid Yawns or Worse

In This Chapter...

- Storytelling is not just for kids
- Suspense, startle, promise to shake things up
- To ask or not to ask
- The undigital way to open

No part of public speaking has more potential for deal-breaking than the opening. When you start on a boring or unprofessional note, chances are pretty slim that you'll be able to change that first impression later. In contrast, coming out of the gate with a truly attention-grabbing opening can immediately and unswervingly put you on the right path to audience engagement, regardless of whether your talk is formal or informal or if you're addressing one person or hundreds.

One of the most popular opening techniques is to tell a story. I believe that's because we all started in life as a child, and we've never outgrown our love for a good story. But it's not the only way. You can provoke curiosity, allude to rewards from listening to you, ask pointed questions and even use three-dimensional objects.

When you write your own speech or presentation, I encourage you to try out all of the techniques in this chapter to find which best suits your content and personal style. Choose a different opening for every new message to stay fresh.

The Speaker's Equivalent of "Once Upon a Time"

The story of Wilbur in *The Puppy Who Chased the Sun*, by Le Grand, was one of my favorites as a child.

Wilbur was a little dog who awoke one day especially hungry. He began to bark, and to his surprise, the sun started to rise from the horizon at the same moment. The dog surmised that he was responsible for this wondrous feat. Over the next few days, he lorded his new-found power over his doggie friends, each with a name that is permanently etched in my memory. I still hear my mother changing her tone of voice reading me the story, as Wilbur proclaimed to his pals, "Down Toothy Perkins! Down No-Tail Ryan! Down, Fido. I, Wilbur, make the sun come up."

As the story continued, Wilbur's friends grew annoyed with his antics and wouldn't play with him anymore. One day it rained, and though Wilbur barked and barked, the sun did not come out. He grew depressed. And the next day, tired from a rough night, the dog overslept. To his horror, when he got up, the sun was blazing through the windows. Wilbur realized that perhaps the sun rising was happening due to some other cause. He apologized to his friends and went on to be a happy puppy again.

The moral of the story? When we act like hot stuff without regard to the feelings of others, we will invariably lose.

The point of my telling you this story? A good story like the one about Wilbur from my childhood stays with you forever. It is one of the most powerful, yet deceptively simple, tactics a speaker can employ.

Why We Love Stories

Why do we never really outgrow our love for stories? And why are stories—especially as an opening technique—so powerful and effective?

I believe it's because most of us grew up with parents or grandparents reading to us and many of the tales began with "once upon a time." We knew to settle down and wait to be entertained. When you launch your message with a good story, we're conditioned to be eager to listen.

One of my required classes at the University of Florida was American history. I remember an especially outstanding professor who went far beyond the politics or battles in his lectures. He described and showed us the fashions and designers of the era in both clothing and home décor, played music you might have heard if you'd lived then, and read the names of book titles and authors who were popular. After each class, you felt as though you'd been transported to an America of yesterday.

Good teachers routinely tell stories to bring to life what could otherwise come across as boring, tedious material.

While most audiences really do want you, the speaker, to be outstanding and to learn something of value, patience and attention span are painfully low in nearly every age group these days. They are secretly hoping that, for a change, you'll be a really worthwhile and enjoyable speaker, instead of what they've come to expect.

What can you do to enable your audience to move beyond the ordinary, into the extraordinary, especially in the opening moments?

Shining at Cocktail Hour

Another reason for telling stories is our need to impress and delight others. Being able to offer an exchange of juicy tidbits

Why Stories Give You an Edge

According to scientific research, when you introduce just the facts and figures, only *one* part of your brain connects—the information processing section. But things really change when you tell a story! Instead of just one isolated region, several parts of our brain get in gear at the same time.

If the story you're telling touches on delicious food, for example, our sensory cortex kicks in, and we can smell or taste it as if it were real. A similar experience happens when you describe a type of motion, like competing in a marathon. Our motor cortex helps us create a sense of running or whatever you were depicting. The more elements and twists, the more our brain fully embraces your words and intentions. This type of brain activity certainly increases the odds of success for you as a speaker.

Pure Genius!

in a story format makes it easy to win people over in the conversation game, whether at a social event or in other situations.

When you can tell or retell a story as three dimensionally as possible—by vividly describing visual, emotional, and other sensory details—you are far more likely to get the results you expect from your public speaking than those who simply report the data.

It's like describing what you had for lunch in a matter of fact but uninspired way. "I had a sandwich and a drink."

Instead, you could make us hungry and envious with this kind of description:

> *On my sandwich was fresh-baked multigrain bread, hot out of the oven, along with a savory blend of roasted onions, peppers, eggplant, mushrooms, and spices. The mustard was a smooth and tasty Dijon. The turkey was tender and obviously not the smoked, processed kind. On the plate were oven-baked sweet potato fries, and you couldn't just eat one! The iced tea was a scrumptious blend of chai and other flavors, and you definitely wanted more than one glass.*

What you don't want to be is rich in facts but poor in stories. The first draft of a presentation to entrepreneurs and investors at a university by a young investment advisor was intellectually sound but dry, lacking emotion. He wanted to motivate the students and others in the audience to start new businesses and to encourage investors to take the leap to provide funding. I advised him to gather success stories that reflected the profitability of a few local small business owners as well as the return on investment that investors had received over time.

When he did the second draft with these real-life case histories included, the transformation was remarkable. You could sense his excitement about sharing these tangible results, as well as recognize how his credibility and connection with the audience would be much easier to score.

Make Them Wonder Where You're Headed

As you utter your first words as the speaker, envision an audience or a group in your office leaning in toward you. The people in the room are curious about the path of your message and anxious to hear more. The "arouse suspense" technique accomplishes that desirable goal. While you can share elements of a story to stir suspense, you can also employ other dramatic strategies to capture interest from the get-go.

Here are some examples. Try reading them aloud for best effect.

At the Market

The other day, I went to the farmer's market and I noticed some long beans that were an odd pinkish color. They were reasonably priced but I'd never seen them before. When I picked up one to smell it, there was no special odor. No one else nearby seemed drawn to these strange-looking beans except me. I managed to get the farmer's attention and asked him what these peculiar vegetables were called and how to prepare them. His answers were not at all what I expected!

Leaving the Hospital

My friend's stay at a local hospital for surgery seemed to go fine. Her procedure of nearly five hours to fix a broken bone in her neck, caused by a car accident earlier in the year, was uneventful. Her recovery took a bit longer than expected and she had to go on oxygen to ease her breathing for a while. Her trouble swallowing was not considered abnormal and by the weekend, she was able to handle liquids. After a few extra days, my friend was finally discharged to go home. And that's when the hospital's caregiving stopped being first class.

Music History

Long before rock and roll appeared on the scene, there was a type of music that also tended to divide older people from younger ones.

Diet Advice

Losing weight can be much easier than you think, but it does take a willingness to swallow a certain liquid with more frequency than most people usually do.

Notice that in these examples, the listener doesn't really know where the speaker is leading them. They are written to plant a hook, so to speak, and to then reel you in.

Remember, you can use these opening techniques to pump up your main points in the body of your message, too.

Here's a way I begin a part of a coaching session or workshop that is already underway: "After you discover what your own communication style is in our next discussion, you'll never look at your team or your clients quite the same way again."

Startle with a Newsworthy Fact

"Oh, my!"

Your audience members may not react with an audible "wow" or "oh, my" or even an "oy, vay" when you use a startling fact in your opening, but chances are high they'll *think* a similar sentiment—and pay attention! By introducing a moment of surprise, by presenting a salient piece of data, by sharing something eye-opening or even disturbing, you enable your listeners to move off their current thinking path and climb onto yours, pulled by the magnetic appeal of your words.

Here are some examples:

Breast Cancer

One out of eight women will develop breast cancer over the course of a lifetime.

Teen Pregnancy

Parenthood is the leading reason that teen girls drop out of school. More than half of teen mothers never graduate from high school.

From 1990 to 2008, the teen pregnancy rate decreased 42 percent from 117 to 68 pregnancies per thousand teen girls.

How Not to Keep the Suspense

To best put this method to work for you, the advice is similar to what I shared with the Tell Me a Story opening technique. Don't tip your hand. Avoid announcing that you are going to tell me something suspenseful! Instead, just dive in and set the stage for wonder or curiosity or a suspended state of mind.

IMPORTANT!

Charity from Sports Events

Billions of dollars have been donated to charities by sports promoters over the past twenty years.

Nature

Butterflies can't bite because they have no teeth.

Business

Business cards have been around since the Middle Ages and are believed to have originated in China.

Traffic Safety

Every sixteen minutes in the United States someone is killed in an automobile crash according to the National Highway Traffic Safety Administration.

Obesity

More than one-third of adults (35.7 percent) in the United States are obese and despite education efforts, the number is expected to continue to grow. Obesity-related conditions include heart disease, stroke, type 2 diabetes and certain types of cancer, some of the leading causes of preventable death. And the estimated annual medical cost of obesity in the United States is more than $147 billion.

Can You Use More than One Fact?

One shocking statistic, delivered with the right emotion, can turn an uncaring audience into a group of advocates or donors. Is that impact diluted when you pour on the facts? I believe the right set of statistics presented as a series can be just as effective as a lone statement. Both alternatives need to be practiced and delivered with as much emotion as possible.

Perspiration

When you employ a stunning piece of data to open your presentation, its purpose isn't simply to shock your audience into listening. The fact serves to move your listeners out of their comfort zone, to jar them out of their complacency, and to draw them into a world of information where they may never have stepped before, or perhaps never really wanted to go.

For a truly powerful presentation, your choice of opening fact needs to tie directly to the rest of your message.

Promise Them Something

> *You can lose weight, have more time in your day, and find more money in your bank account—and this morning, I'm going to show you how!*

When you begin your message with a big, bold promise, you're very likely to command attention right away. A related and equally effective variation is to kick off your message by talking about a problem or challenge the audience faces and then stating that you can provide a solid solution.

> *When your computer runs slow or keeps freezing, you not only lose time, you may also be experiencing a security breach. By the time we've finished our workshop, you'll know how to identify what is causing the problem with your computer and how you can prevent it from happening again.*

Keeping the Promise

If you announce that you're going to disclose "three ways to attract more hits and conversions in your social media marketing," it seems obvious, but be sure to present all that you have promised. Your audience will not appreciate you, and will think you are disorganized, if you only talk about two techniques instead of the three you mentioned at the outset.

Perspiration

The *promise* opening is one of the most economical to craft because you're essentially combining an opening technique with part of your prebody summary which we talked about in **Chapter 10**. You outline what the audience will gain from listening to you and at the same time, you disclose what information you plan to share to help achieve that promise, in the order you expect to present it. This technique is one of the most often used in business presentations because of this time-saving, two-for-one appeal.

At the annual goals conference for our local chamber of commerce—with more than one thousand in attendance—the new chairman kicked off the event and his leadership year with a spirited promise:

"Get ready, folks. It's going to be an awesome two days and an awesome year."

Other examples of the promise opening:

"In just two weeks, you'll have younger looking skin and fewer wrinkles, with just five minutes a day of treatment." —From an ad

"With just thirty minutes a day of listening to a set of CDs, you'll be speaking a new language—without studying a textbook or having to memorize a vocabulary list." —From an Internet video ad for a language program.

Ask for a Show of Hands

This tried-and-true opening technique looks simple but it really isn't. You are not putting in place a fact-finding system! When you ask the audience members to raise their hands in response to your question, your real goal is to stimulate interest in you and your message and to encourage a sense of their being a part of the show. With that objective in mind, your mission is to craft an enticing opening question that will encourage as many as possible to participate by lifting their hand up in the air, expressing their answer with that physical motion.

At the same time, just asking the relevant question and inviting folks to raise their hands is not enough. A key to making this technique successful is that you, also, need to raise your hand when you ask the audience members to perform this motion. They will mimic you, and help assure you get the desired results in the opening.

If you just ask the question without inviting a show of hands, what can happen?

Imagine a room full of grunts and mmm, mms. You could be getting either "yes" or "no" responses and may not be sure which you are eliciting. Only with a sea of lifted hands can you be certain that you're garnering a response on which you can build the next part of your message.

An international investment advisor from Central America launched his presentation with what he thought would be a solid question to a group of new business students at a Costa Rican university:

"How many of you have been to Costa Rica before?"

How Not to Ask

At a meeting recently, the president of a local public relations agency began her talk this way:

"How many of you, by a show of hands, have more publicity for your business than you want?"

Not one person raised a hand.

Without meaning to do so, the agency owner had suddenly created an invisible wall between herself and us, her audience.

What do you think would have happened if, Instead, if she had inquired: "How many of you would love to have more publicity for your business? Let me see a show of hands, please!" Quite a few attending would have admitted to wanting more publicity, and would have lifted their hand accordingly.

WATCH OUT!

To his dismay, none of the students raised a hand. Without meaning to do it, he suddenly created a wall between himself and the audience.

Quickly the advisor followed with another question to recapture interest. "By a show of hands, how many of you are here to get a really good corporate job or to start your own business?" This time, nearly every hand in the room flew up.

Here's one way of employing this technique that I always find works well, when I ask:

"By a show of hands, how many of you have ever had to sit through a really boring presentation or speech?"

Usually, nearly everyone in the room gets engaged, lifting their hands and laughing. I then follow it with a promise that using good public speaking practices, they never have to worry about being that boring speaker!

The Undigital Opening: Use an Object

Once upon a time, when there were no PowerPoint or video, speakers had to rely on other more traditional ways to capture an audience's interest to open a presentation or speech. In our now digitally-weary world, I believe you can stand out by creatively incorporating colorful and intriguing options such as drawings, maps, models, photographs, and objects. Actual things. Not projections on a screen!

Using theater parlance, these three-dimensional objects are known to speakers as props. The term "prop" is short for property, referring to the phones, hats, golf clubs, guns, and other equipment actors insert into the part they're playing on stage, in a television show, or in a movie to make it more realistic.

What prop or items can help you jump-start your talk?

Along with the rubber chicken I mentioned to you earlier that I've used for years in various parts of my presentations, is a prop box full of other "toys." Here is a quick inventory:

- A life-like plastic skull to illustrate the impact of too much dieting

- A clown-sized paper diaper to help convey the past-present-future approach to organizing ideas

  I say, "In the past, we all wore diapers. Today, most of us don't have to wear them. In the future, however… it depends." See more on this format in **Chapter 12**.

Openings Aren't Just for the Opening

Each of the six openings in this chapter can also be used to launch any of the main points in your talk's body (see **Chapter 10**) and even to rekindle interest in a subpoint.

So, if you create an opening and discover it doesn't really work as well as you intended in kicking off your comments, the work isn't necessarily lost. You may find that the statement would be perfect to lead into a main point or even as a story or subpoint within the body.

Pure Genius!

- Clown glasses with plastic eyeballs that pull out toward the audience together and separately, using metal extenders

  I display them to demonstrate how to make proper eye contact.

- Big orange monster-style hands

  They help me illustrate what to do and not do with gestures.

- A huge, oversized pin, a bag of chocolates, a city map, and assorted other objects, each brought to life in different presentations, depending on the topic and audience

Props can be simple or complex. A jar of peanut butter lifted into the air at the outset of a message can stir interest in and help motivate people to join a food drive to benefit hungry families.

What Props Can Do for a Speaker

A while back I worked with a mining lawyer who was asked to talk about the difference between United States contracts and Latin American contracts. He was on right after lunch, a miserable time at most conferences because the afternoon urge to nap runs rampant.

To capture his audience from the opening moments, the lawyer first held up a thick phone book, tucked into an oversized file folder. "This is the size of a typical contract in the United States," he announced, hoisting the folder into the air. Then, he lifted another folder, and pulled out four typed pages. "Here's a traditional Latin contract," he said, in contrast.

A bit later in the presentation, my client pulled out a toy phone. He pretended to be in a heated negotiation between himself and another international lawyer. In our debriefing when he returned to Miami, the lawyer told me that no one appeared to be napping during his presentation and that he was bombarded with questions afterward, a great sign.

Inspiration

How *Not* to Open Your Message

Unless you're trying to alienate your audience or set yourself up to lose on purpose, there are two ways I urge you to *avoid* opening a speech or presentation:

- *With an apology or excuse of some kind.* When you begin with the words, "I'm sorry," you can quickly lose credibility and status, especially if you go on and on about whatever you're apologizing about. If you're late, the computer doesn't work suddenly, you brought the wrong folder or flash drive, or otherwise you messed up, and you feel compelled to apologize, please say one brief apology and go on with your message. We don't really want to know what has gone wrong. We do want to hear what you came to say and use it to advance our own causes.

- *With a joke.* While I do advocate being as humorous as you can, I don't encourage jokes because you can inadvertently be politically incorrect without realizing it. Everyone is terribly prickly today, and you never know who you may accidentally insult. Further, jokes make the rounds and are easily found on the Internet. You don't know if a previous speaker to the group used the same one, leaving you in an unfunny place. Unless you're paying thousands of dollars for an original set of jokes, you don't want to risk opening with a joke that everyone's already seen or heard on the Internet.

Greetings and Your Throwaway Line

Regardless of where you are speaking or why, there are two other elements that I recommend you consider:

🖋 *Opening with a salutation or greeting.* When you walk into a room, you usually say "hello" or "good to see you," or some other greeting, yes? It's polite and friendly. In a formal speaking environment, the traditional greeting is: "Ladies and Gentlemen…" You can offer a more informal, "Welcome everyone!" Or, acknowledge the name of the organization in your salutation: "Good evening, members and guests of the National Association of Underwater Basket Weavers." This greeting goes *before* your actual opening.

🖋 *Adding an optional gracious throwaway line after the greeting.* The purpose is to give yourself a bit more time to gain control of your nerves by offering what appears to be a gracious and welcoming remark of some kind. Examples include:

◆ It's great to be here in the great state of Idaho.

◆ That blueberry cobbler dessert was the best I've ever eaten, and thanks!

◆ Your hospitality and welcome have been over the top!

◆ I'd heard about the incredible beauty of your neck of the woods but I'm truly in awe of how special it really is.

To Summarize…

🖋 Opening with the right story can help assure you're a hit.

🖋 Arousing suspense, creating a "wow"-evoking statement, asking for a show of hands, and promising something are other proven avenues for kicking off your talk.

🖋 Not everything needs to be digital to be cool.

🖋 Avoid jokes and apologies as part of your opening—and everywhere else in your remarks, too.

Chapter 12

The Fabulous Five Formats to Create a Genius Message

In This Chapter...

- Meet Monroe: Persuasion personified
- Formats for convincing, historical comparisons, and all occasions
- What usually does not work?

Some people are excellent cooks and rarely if ever consult a recipe. Others who don't follow recipes can produce dreadful eating experiences for themselves, their family, and friends.

When it comes to baking, as long as I follow the instructions on the package, I can make decent brownies. In contrast, my sister and sister-in-law are dynamite bakers, consistently creating exceptionally yummy desserts. While I'm not an outstanding cook, I believe I produce a few dishes well with recipes handed down to me from my mother and aunt—like stuffing for the turkey, roasted turkey, sweet potato pie with marshmallows, and beef stew. Sometimes I admit to improvising a bit, adding different vegetables or fruits or seasonings.

As a good recipe, the five formats in this chapter are designed to help you put together the content of your message. They are not designed to stifle your creativity, but to use as a base upon which to build with your flavorful additions, drawn from your experiences.

The right format allows you to convey your content in a thoughtful, coherent, and (forgive me!) a well-seasoned way.

Persuasion Personified: Meet Monroe

Alan H. Monroe, a communication professor at Purdue University and one of the industrial psychology giants of the last century, developed a sure-fire way to persuade others which he called his "motivated sequence." His timeless formula has five steps to enable you to build a case that convinces others to do what you're asking.

His technique is described as motivational because it appeals to the audience members' sense of not only being able to fix a problem you are bringing to their attention but also inspiring them to *want* to overcome it.

Here's how Monroe's motivated sequence goes:

- *Command attention.* Something's happening that affects you!

- *State the need.* Focus on the pain or the problem.

- *Satisfy the need.* Share your offer or solution.

- *Visualize the need.* Help the audience see themselves enjoying your solution or offer

- *Ask for action.* Say that you can help. How can *they* help, also?

I encourage you to write out one or two sentences for each of the steps of the sequence, saying them aloud as you complete each one. If the words sound awkward, false, or too strident, keep modifying until you get them right for yourself.

What kind of speaking situations would benefit from using Monroe's formula?

- Fundraising for a charity or cause

- Selling products like vacuum cleaners, wrinkle creams, exercise equipment, and anything that saves time or money

> Introducing a new policy or procedure where you need to get buy in to assure its adoption

> Getting people to vote for you or your candidate

AIDA—Tried and True for Persuasive Speaking

Another presentation structure with a goal of persuasion comes directly from the world of advertising and marketing; it's called the AIDA technique. Developed by the advertising industry's legendary Elias St. Elmo Lewis in the first half of the last century, the format is similar to Monroe but the pain motivation is woven into the message in a less obvious manner. Lewis devised the first three steps in 1898 as a sales strategy for the life insurance industry, based on research in *Scientific American*, and then later added the critical fourth step: action.

Attention. Why you need to listen—also can be promoting Awareness

Interest. Stimulates imagination, concern, doubt, or other reaction with the content

Desire. Invite listeners to picture themselves enjoying the issue you've raised in their own life, the product, service or program, so they'll want to own whatever it is for themselves.

Action. What you are expected or encouraged to do now. Based on his research, Lewis said the three initial steps are designed to lead to the final

---

Don't Overlook Emphasizing the Pain or Problem in Your Quest to Persuade

For some of us, emphasizing a negative feels uncomfortable. We've been taught to always focus on the positive or somehow make things seem less onerous than they really are. For others, especially those experienced in selling, pointing out the pain or problem is a totally natural, expected part of a presentation.

To be effective in persuasive speaking, you'll need to use problem or pain words that make folks squirm or bother them in some significant way, so they can be open to a solution—your solution. Popular pain words include: *frustrated with, nervous about, concerned with the lack of, unhappy about, worried that,* and similar expressions that stir doubt, fear, anxiety, and other reactions.

IMPORTANT!

AIDA Technique for Sales

Attention

If you're tired of looking and feeling older than you really are, you're not alone!

Interest

Now you can spend just minutes a day applying the same lotions that are keeping famous celebrities like Ellen and Cher so young and glamorous in appearance, without the need for expensive surgery and any loss of time at work.

Desire

Wouldn't it be wonderful to get compliments on how terrific you look, and to feel like yourself again when you look in the mirror? Isn't it your turn to attract the positive kind of attention you want?

Action

If you order today, you can enjoy a special two for one, and free thirty-day trial offer. Would you like to use Visa, MasterCard, or American Express?

Example

step, where the prospective buyer—or whoever you're trying to persuade—may raise these types of questions:

What kind of speaking situations would benefit from using the AIDA format?

The same persuasive environments as for Monroe: raising funds for a nonprofit, your school, team, a cause, or your business. You could be trying to convince a group or individual to invest in your venture. You are selling Girl Scout cookies or luxury vacations. Even getting out the vote lends itself to AIDA.

Traditionally, AIDA is one of the most commonly-used formats for sales presentations and advertisers—from cars, boats, and furniture to cosmetics and insurance. To see if this technique can help you advance your position when speaking to one person or groups, write out a sentence or two for each point, and recite it aloud immediately. I encourage you to cut and fix your message as much as you need to give you a smooth, natural-sounding pitch.

Organize in Four Steps: C-A-R-R and SOAP

From the world of resumes comes another model to guide how you organize your content. I was introduced to the format as the three-step C-A-R, but based on my experience with clients—particularly in the financial world—I added another R for Recommendations to reflect their considerable expertise and to more dynamically move their presentations forward.

C-A-R-R stands for:

Challenge(s): What's happening that I ought to care about?

Activities: What have you done or tried so far?

Results: Report on the revenues, changes, stats, and other outcomes

Recommendations: What you see as the next steps, and why

Using C-A-R-R for Reports

If you're asked to give an update report in your business, to city officials, or to your board of directors, the C-A-R-R model can help you look good and prepare relatively quickly. This approach also works well when you are presenting a proposal to a prospective client. It can also help you to gain support for a new project you'd like to see happen in your organization or community.

While each of the components of this format is important, the two "R's"— Results and Recommendations—are the parts most associated with what I call your audience's "greed buttons." Your goal is to stimulate envy and stir desire to do what you're asking; your summary of what you did so far and what you recommend is not the time for simply reciting the facts! Further, before you open your mouth, it's vital that you have a clear idea of what your recommendations are—for your boss, the prospective client, the board, for the audience—based on your own experience and evaluation of the industry, their market, or other related factors.

The SOAP Format

Similar to C-A-R-R, but straight from the world of educating doctors, comes the timeless format known as SOAP. You've seen it in TV shows like *Grey's Anatomy* and *House*, where a slew of doctors descends on a patient's room in the hospital, and the interns are expected to give a report on their findings to the critical assembly. Here's the formula, as shared by Dr. Rashid Taher, a retinal eye surgeon and founder of a website geared to educate health care students on key nonmedical issues relevant to their future success, *DrSmarts.com*.

Subjective findings. Describe what the patient has told you about health issues. ("Stomach hurts and constant vomiting.")

Using C-A-R-R for an Interview

C-A-R-R's original purpose—as a model for written resumes—can easily be adapted for your face-to-face interview. When the interviewer asks you about some of your key accomplishments, you can be ready to respond by following the steps of the formula, as one of my young executive clients did recently:

Challenges

When I started working at XYZ Company, we were only representing a few key areas of the market and my goals were to significantly expand both our presence and our revenues in our region with an eye to the national stage, too. We were nowhere to be seen in either the traditional media or social marketing.

Activities

I led the efforts to upgrade our presentation materials. We revisited and had redesigned our marketing packages. I helped create and select a core of our top executives to participate in a speaker's bureau, selecting qualified professionals who could appear on panels and keynote at conferences. We also identified who could take leadership roles in the chamber of commerce, Rotary, our industry association, and other places where our client base networks. We brought on interns to work with our marketing department to help us update our approach to dealing with the media and also revamp our online presence including the website.

Results

From our new marketing and outreach efforts, sales increased by 15 percent in six months, and we established relationships in seven cities where we'd never done business before. Our associates gave presentations in front of key audiences with a total of more than two thousand industry leaders present during that same year. Our new website is attracting more inquiries in one year than in the past four and we've attracted more than 7,500 followers on Twitter.

Recommendation

If you're looking to increase your results and expand your company's visibility and reputation, I believe I can help you.

Objective report. Relate what have you observed yourself or learned from others who have examined the patient. ("Patient has been seen grabbing the stomach area in pain and vomiting.")

Assessment. Share what tests have been performed so far and what are your conclusions based on what you know now. ("Stomach contents have been analyzed and it appears there is an infection.")

Plan. Summarize the care plan you recommend in terms of other tests that need to be performed, change in diet, therapy recommended, and anything else that needs to happen going forward. ("Patient is being advised not to continue eating three ice cream sundaes a day and to increase physical exercise once the vomiting stops.")

Whether you trot out CARR or SOAP for your message, stay focused on the outcome you're seeking from your presentation and double-check that the content you're covering is leading toward the response you want.

Historical Perspective: Past-Present-Future

A classic way to organize and convey information is the past-present-future format. This technique is also especially helpful for last-minute or impromptu speaking, because you can readily put your knowledge of the topic or issue into the three segments, in chronological order.

Past-Present-Future

Past. What happened, what are the origins, who did it, impact, and why does this still matter?

Present. What's going on now, what are the issues, who's involved?

Future. What do you see happening in the near and far future? How will the situation change? What will it look like going forward?

What's optimal for the Past-Present-Future format?

Technical and complex messages, such as conversations about tax issues and other financial matters, health care research, legislative changes, educational reforms, and advances in technology, are especially helped by well-crafted presentations in this format.

Past-Present-Future: Nelson Mandela's Incomparable Legacy

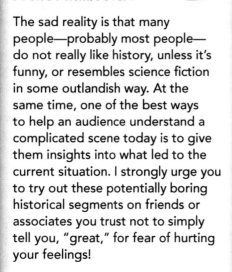

Special Challenges for Past-Present-Future Format Users

The sad reality is that many people—probably most people—do not really like history, unless it's funny, or resembles science fiction in some outlandish way. At the same time, one of the best ways to help an audience understand a complicated scene today is to give them insights into what led to the current situation. I strongly urge you to try out these potentially boring historical segments on friends or associates you trust not to simply tell you, "great," for fear of hurting your feelings!

Do your best to personalize the history. For example, many people do not know the origin of the icons "cut" and "paste" on their computer's word processor.

When I was a journalist, we had scissors and rubber cement on our desks because we literally cut and pasted the pages of our work together before turning it in to the city editor for review. I realize that sounds archaic now!

IMPORTANT!

Can you identify the elements of past-present-future in this tribute to Nelson Mandela?

With the death at age ninety-five of the world famous South African apartheid fighter and pioneering government leader, Nelson Mandela, in late 2013, came an outpouring of universal sorrow and admiration for his many accomplishments. He had been in prison for twenty-seven years for speaking out against the long, terrible history of oppression and violence against blacks in his country. When he was finally freed, Mandela set his sights on an unprecedented goal of uniting his country peacefully and overcoming its bitter racial divide. While in prison, he studied and became fluent in the language of the whites and even came to appreciate their most popular sport, rugby. Using the knowledge, patience and capacity for forgiveness he'd learned during his incarceration, Mandela succeeded in lifting his country to new heights and with its former white president, earned the Nobel Peace Prize.

Today, there appears to be no world leader—at least none of the stature of the former South African prime minister—who is taking the long view of forgiveness and forging collaboration that Mandela embraced. Instead, we are witnessing violence and pushbacks against democracy in many parts of the planet. Prejudice and racial divides continue to afflict nation after nation, limiting opportunities for economic growth, education for the young, and access to health care, and leading to many other debilitating social conditions.

Looking ahead, we can take some hope from the strides that are being made in digital education and the Internet, which are giving people throughout the world unprecedented access to information, political, social, and economic. What governments could once hide or deny is now much easier to lay bare. Perhaps some new leaders are formulating their own progressive views, studying, meditating, and planning, as Nelson Mandela did, awaiting for their moment to move mountains, to change the world, for the better.

In this tribute to Mandela I've taken you into his early years and life—the past. Then, we jumped ahead into analysis of political leaders of our time—the present. In the last segment, starting with the phrase "looking ahead," I lead you into speculating about what the future of our world might be.

Deliver What You Promise!

While the Triple T seems to be a straightforward way to organize your content, you can leave your audience wanting—and not in a good way—if you aren't careful about the details. If you tell me in the first step that you're going to give me four ways to save money on my next purchase of a computer or smartphone, and you only present three, I'm going to be upset when you're done. And most likely, I will raise my hand and ask you what the fourth one was, so be ready!

WATCH OUT!

Tried and True: The Triple T

When you strip away the four formats I've introduced in this chapter, an underlying structure emerges which is known as the Triple T. This structure is the core of all well-honed presentations and speeches. If any of the elements is missing, the message seems flat or poorly organized.

Here are the elements of Triple T:

🔦 Tell me what you're going to tell me. (The prebody serves this purpose. See **Chapter 10**.)

🔦 Tell me. (The body. See **Chapter 10**.) What are your one, two or three main points?

🔍 Tell me what you told me. (The summary, a review and highlights from your talk—the close. See **Chapter 13**.)

When Do You Use a Triple T Format?

Presentations you make that lean toward informative discussions, as opposed to persuasive messages, lend themselves best to the Triple T, although the format can be used for any purpose. Talks about the benefits of certain foods or health care practices, for example, work well with the Triple T. You may be speaking about trends that are impacting your industry or region or opportunities for investors. You could be giving an overview of topics such as social media, business plans, and even public speaking.

One of the ways I enjoy introducing this format is to promise to tell my audience members three ways they can lose weight without really trying. That's the "tell them what you're going to tell them" part.

Next, I share the three ways. I tell them:

> *First, always keep a lock on your refrigerator door. It won't prevent you from eating but it will slow you down just a bit.*
>
> *Second, drink lots and lots of water. You'll be running more frequently to the restroom, so you will have less time to eat!*
>
> *And finally, always eat with as many people as possible. Since it's impolite to talk with food in your mouth, you will consume less.*

To wrap up, I say:

> *To recap, I recommend installing a lock on your refrigerator. Keep a*

Using the Triple T to Answer a Question

You are at a meeting and suddenly you're asked:

Q. *What do you think about the mayor's decision?*

(No need to panic! In your mind, quickly identify two or maybe three relevant facts, figures, or anecdotes you could share to intelligently and effectively respond to the question at hand.)

A. *There are two ways I believe we could look at the mayor's decision.* (Tell them what you're going to tell them.)

First, we could examine what he did in light of recent disclosures about...And second, I would ask you to consider... (Tell them your answer.)

So to recap, I think the mayor's decision is first...And then...

Example

filled glass of water nearby at all times, and drink it to increase your bathroom visits and reduce your food consumption time. And party often, so you will talk more and eat less!

Not only does the Triple T help you structure a planned presentation, but it's especially suited for those unexpected moments when you find yourself having to answer a question or make a set of comments with no notice.

What Usually Does *Not* Work

From my experience, failing to choose one of the five formats can doom you to an uncomfortable, unprofessional experience. No structure usually means no thought has gone into the message, and you don't really care about the outcome or your audience.

You can try to overwhelm with facts but in most cases, despite their value and veracity, you'll lose your audience if the data is not organized into a coherent whole.

You have probably sat through a class, or a keynote address, where the speaker jumped from point to point, with no framework for you to attach the information. You may have found some entertaining or engrossing moments, but, by and large, a rambling message is just that, rambling. It's actually hard on both the audience and the speaker, because neither knows where they are going to wind up.

As I mentioned earlier, cramming too much information into your message,

Know Where You're Going

Two men committed to clear communication in the last century offered similar views of the importance of knowing where you are going in your public speaking:

A talk is a voyage. It must be charted. The speaker who starts nowhere, usually gets there.

—Dale Carnegie, Author and Motivational Speaker

A speech without a specific purpose is like a journey without a destination.

—Ralph C. Smeadley, Founder of Toastmasters International

Quote

no matter which format you choose, can overwhelm and turn off even the most eager audience. More than three main points for a presentation over ten minutes can stir your listeners to peek discreetly or not so secretively at their smartphones, or simply tune you out.

Other tactics that don't usually work include:

🔦 Stating too many facts or references without a personal story or case history to bring them to life

🔦 Too many case histories or success stories without enough data to back up what you're saying

🔦 Jumping from point to point without clear transitions that encourage the audience to keep on listening

While I do not love rules that others create—only my own, I readily admit—I strongly encourage you to give yourself time to create a structure that liberates you. With the right format for your content, you can deliver your message with poise, confidence, and style.

To Summarize...

🔦 Your odds of being persuasive can increase significantly when using Monroe's motivated sequence to organize your content.

🔦 There are four other tried-and-true formats to give you the edge in both planned and impromptu speaking situations. The key is to find one that works for your particular message.

🔦 Too much information and a disorganized message spell doom for most speakers.

Chapter 13

It's a Wrap: Closing with the Right Words

In This Chapter...

- In the home stretch, recaptivate and convince your audience
- Spell out your call for action clearly
- To quote or not to quote, that is the question
- After the last word, what's next?

You may have heard a speaker, anxious to wrap up, utter these unfulfilling words: "Well, that's all I have to say. Are there any questions?"

While expedient, I don't recommend this approach to ending your message, whether you're delivering a keynote speech or a report to your team. It is a poor substitute for one of the most critical parts of your presentation, the close.

The closing of your presentation is no place to wimp out. In this chapter you'll get tactics to assure that you don't.

Instead of just trailing off, with no definitive closure, I encourage you to end as strongly as you started, sending clear signals indicating what you intend the outcome of your conversation to be. In addition to your choice of words, there are also accompanying movements of your body that you'll want to incorporate into your close. If you're considering ending with a quotation, I've shared some of my favorites and also a few guidelines for using them effectively.

Once the applause is over, you can connect with your audience in other ways.

Summarize to Recaptivate and Convince Your Audience

After you've wowed the audience with your impressive stories, data, and plans to successfully gain the agreement you're seeking, it's vital to provide an equally powerful summary of the highlights of your content. Your closing summary is going to be structured similarly to the prebody summary you presented right after your opening, and before the body of your speech (See **Chapter 10**), but here's the difference:

In the prebody summary, you gave the audience a taste of what was to come, with key benefit or pain words attached to stimulate interest. Now, in the closing summary, you not only briefly go over the main points you covered in your comments, but you also remind the audience of a startling fact or particular story associated with each point. By summarizing and highlighting the significant and memorable parts of your message, you reinforce your expert status and more readily pave the way for agreement.

You may be thinking, "But they've already heard what I had to say. Won't a summary be overkill? Won't they be annoyed that I am going over the same stuff again?"

It's a fair set of questions, and if you simply recite the facts you shared, again, with no real changes, I believe your audience could have the right to be aggravated with you. That's why I strongly recommend that you carefully sift through what you covered and emphasize the special or even spectacular moment in a brief but powerful recap.

For best results, I encourage you to give your summary of main points in the actual order you presented them. It seems obvious, but sometimes we find ourselves wanting to retell an especially well-received anecdote or a fact that drew enthusiastic applause at the outset of the summary, even if that was

Franklin's Words of Wisdom

I especially like this quotation from one of America's founders and pioneering inventors:

Remember not only to say the right thing in the right place, but far more difficult still, to leave unsaid the wrong thing at the tempting moment.

—Benjamin Franklin

When it comes to summarizing, the skill comes in sorting through all of your wisdom and identifying what is worth restating and reminding your audience that you said it in the first place.

Quote

not what we talked about first. So, if your main points were delivered as one, two, and three, your closing summary needs to correspond to that order.

Spell Out Your Call for Action Clearly

"But I told her everything and nothing happened," the young man said, as he related his failed efforts to convince his girlfriend to marry him.

"I told her I loved her. How happy she made me, and how I loved spending time with her. I told her how I envisioned us spending the rest of our lives together and how wonderful that would be," he said, sadly. "But she didn't say anything!"

The young man's missing words, of course, were what people in sales and in fundraising call "the ask." If you do not ask for what you are seeking, nothing will happen.

But how do you ask? How can you create what is known as a "call for action" closing?

First, write out exactly what you want to happen at the end of your message. What kind of outcome or actions are you anticipating?

- An agreement to go ahead?

- A decision choosing one plan over another?

- People to show up at the polls and vote?

- Funds to be donated to your cause?

- The team to adopt your plan?

- New volunteers to step forward?

- Investors to come aboard?

Consider and Speak to Their Motivators

Next, identify which primary attitudes or values you believe are driving the decision-makers you're addressing. Color your call for action with language and outcomes that match their motivators.

Are they bottom-line focused? If so, be sure your numbers are attractive and convincing. Spell out the expected return on investment in time, money, resources, and whatever else applies. Adding graphs, flowcharts, and other visual representations of your data will also help you state your case more effectively with this motivation.

Would you describe the decision-makers and others in your audience as helping-oriented? Do they care about how your request impacts the individuals on the team? Reiterate how your idea will translate into better working conditions, more opportunities for advancement, how relationships will improve, or other similar personal benefits.

Using Social Media to Add to Your Call for Action

With a nod to the role of social media, you can hand out a flyer or put the information on your first and last slide, inviting your audience to:

◆ Tweet about your presentation—by stating your hashtag (@AnneMiami is mine).

◆ Share a recommendation on LinkedIn—giving your personal or company name as appropriate.

◆ Post a comment or post a photograph on your personal or company Facebook page.

◆ Write a brief story, for their organization's newsletter or blog, about your presentation.

When your audience participates in any of these postspeaking activities, it helps build your reputation as a speaker and as a business or community leader. These actions can contribute to your achieving the results you set out to accomplish with your remarks, whether for your company or for your cause.

Perspiration

If possible, cite examples of how similar efforts in the past have evolved into the kind of improvements you're envisioning as an outcome.

Do they highly value advancing their own position or power? Show how they'll be viewed as brilliant, effective leaders. Describe what kind of strategic alliances can be formed to their benefit by endorsing what you're recommending. Be as specific as possible regarding the type of competitive edge you are giving them with your proposal or product. Mention the names of powerful people or organizations that have come onboard with your idea or service as part of your persuasive strategy.

Do they spend much of their time pursuing knowledge? Illustrate how your product, service, or idea will give them an opportunity to learn new things immediately and on an ongoing basis. Showcase the exclusive source of the information you are providing, if applicable, along with its depth, facets, and any unique aspects you can reveal.

Are they interested in beautiful things or other sensory delights like the arts, décor, fashion, the outdoors, fine wines, or foods? Portray your proposal as a ticket to access the finer things they appreciate. I advise that you make your presentation as visual, colorful, tactile, and even tasty as you can to stir their senses and spur the reaction you want to your message.

Would you say they throw themselves into certain causes with gusto? Align your call for action with parallels to the rewards they receive by working for the causes they support. Dig a little deeper to identify whether the causes they support center on children or the environment, a disease or hunger, an institution, or world peace. It's far easier to target your call for action with the universe narrowed to their particular interests.

Finally, practice your close aloud in a confident tone of voice, eliminating any words or phrases that sound stilted or simply don't work. Remember, what works on paper does not always sound natural or conversational when you say it aloud.

Calls for Action That Changed History

American presidents and other important leaders have issued critical calls for action both at the end and during their messages, and some have propelled the nation and individuals into pursuits that otherwise would have never happened. It's okay to put a call for action in the middle of your presentation as long as you build your case throughout your remarks and again state it in your closing statement.

"Ask not what your country can do for you, ask what you can do for your country."

That challenge was issued by President John F. Kennedy in his inaugural address. His words led to a renewed volunteerism and civic-mindedness among Americans of all ages, but particularly the youth.

On May 25, 1961, Mr. Kennedy stood before Congress and proclaimed, "This nation should commit itself to achieving the goal, before the decade is out, of landing a man on the moon and returning him safely to the earth."

In 1969, the Apollo project saw American astronauts step onto the moon.

One of the most inspirational messages of the last century was the oft-quoted "I Have a Dream" speech of civil rights activist and leader Dr. Martin Luther King, Jr. He is credited with sparking the movement that led to the desegregation of America, notwithstanding much heartache, bloodshed, and resistance. He delivered his historic remarks on August 23, 1963, in the March on Washington, D.C. for jobs and freedom.

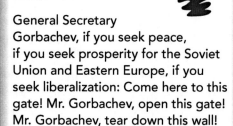

What Four Words Did

General Secretary Gorbachev, if you seek peace, if you seek prosperity for the Soviet Union and Eastern Europe, if you seek liberalization: Come here to this gate! Mr. Gorbachev, open this gate! Mr. Gorbachev, tear down this wall!

The last four words of this demand issued by President Ronald Reagan to the head of the Soviet Union were considered by many to be the most important of his presidency. The quotation was actually midway through a speech he delivered on June 12, 1987, at the Brandenburg Gate in Germany, and he was talking about the notorious Berlin Wall, which had been erected in 1961, and which divided the West from the Eastern European bloc in the Cold War.

Two years later, in November 1989, East Germany opened the wall, allowing people to travel freely into West Berlin, reuniting families separated for decades. It was finally torn down late in 1990, marking the end of the Cold War era.

Inspiration

You can easily find the speech in its entirety by searching on Google, "I Have a Dream" and Martin Luther King.

In digging around for notable calls for action by women speakers, I decided to jump forward into our more recent history. Here are two that I especially liked:

> *If several years ago you stopped challenging yourself, you're going to be bored. If you work for some guy who you used to sit next to, and really, he should be working for you, you're going to feel undervalued, and you won't come back. So, my heartfelt message to all of you is, and start thinking about this now. Do not lean back; lean in. Put your foot on that gas pedal and keep it there until the day you have to make a decision, and then make a decision. That's the only way, when that day comes, you'll even have a decision to make…*
>
> *So go home tonight and ask yourselves, 'What would I do if I weren't afraid?' And then go do it.*

Lean In Circles

To further help women reach their full potential as leaders, Sandberg launched a nonprofit with a website: *leanincircles.org*.

According to the website, "Lean In Circles are small groups of women who meet regularly to learn and grow together. Circles are as unique as the individuals who start them, but they all share a common bond: the power of peer support. Women are asking for more and stepping outside their comfort zones, and men and women are talking openly about gender issues for the first time."

Inspiration

Facebook chief operating officer Sheryl Sandberg gave this much-reported speech at the commencement of Barnard College on June 10, 2011. Her popularized admonition to aspiring women to not "lean back; lean in" resulted in changed attitudes and the formation of Lean In Circles across the country.

> *Frankly, what keeps me in the business, seriously, is not always the love of my work… sometimes I really don't love it. What keeps me in the business is hope, and that's the hope that women of color are also a part of the narrative, that our stories are just as potent, because we also have*

When Not to Use a Quotation

When your closing needs to be a strong call for action, I do not recommend quotations at the end of your message. This advice applies to most persuasive speaking situations such as sales or investor presentations, proposals to your board of directors or team, or other similar times. Further, it's not a good idea to open a speech or presentation with a quotation because you are shifting the "expert" position from you to the author of the quote, even if it's only temporarily. By the end of your outstanding talk, if you interject a quotation in your closing, there's no longer a question as to whether or not you're the expert.

In this book, I broke my own rule by using quotations to open some of the chapters. I believe a quotation on paper, read silently, does not compete with your expertise as it would if spoken aloud at the beginning of your message.

Perspiration

the power of transformation. We also have the power to be quirky, and sexy, and different, funny, heartfelt, and all of those things…

I believe and I really hope that we have the imagination, that we have the courage to bring those stories to life, because I want to do for other young women of color what Cicely Tyson did to me in that apartment with the slats showing underneath the plaster, and the bad plumbing, and no phone, and hardly any food, and rats… she allowed me to have the visual of what it means to dream… she threw me a rope. That's what we do as actors… we throw other people the rope.

Actress Viola Davis, accepting the *Elle Magazine's* Women in Hollywood award for her role in the movie, *The Help*, recognized the ongoing challenges of women and especially black women in the cinema in her extemporaneous remarks. Asked what made her different from the others at the ceremony, she reportedly said, "I'm black."

What a Quotation Contributes

When you want to create a moment of reflection or transport your audience for just an instant into another realm, the right quotation can be a wonderful way to end your message. It comes after your summary and can reinforce your message in a powerful, distinctive manner.

Ending with a memorable quotation can be a successful technique for inspirational messages and can add a lift to talks that are mostly informational.

To create the optimal impact, it's best to memorize the quotation so you can look everyone in the eye as you share it. Practice the pitch and pace. Usually, a slow, firm delivery works to capture the tone and intention of the person who originally said what you are quoting.

When you use a quotation during a speech, cite the person who said it before you begin reciting their words. If the source is unknown, announce that to your audience.

Here are some of my favorites:

In the words of the philosopher Voltaire, "Common sense is really not so common."

As the Duchess of Windsor was quoted as saying, "You can never be too rich or too thin."

Popular U.S. author Mark Twain apologized to a friend by commenting, "I'm sorry I don't have time to write you a short letter."

Helen Keller, the famous blind author and teacher said, "Alone we can do nothing. Together, we can do everything."

One of my postcollege roommates, Hope, always noted when the trash needed to go out or it was time to perform some other unpleasant task, "It's a hard, cruel world but somebody's got to do it!"

For all speakers, everywhere: "When in doubt, leave it out!"

The one I quote most often is what my mother, Natalie B. Lyons, always pointed out when talking to overachievers who wanted to be everywhere, do everything: "No matter how hard you may try, you can't put your tush (also known as derriere, butt, and bottom) in two places at the same time."

Another one from my mother: "You're just greedy for life! You don't want to say 'no' to anything."

A few more pointers on using quotations:

🖋 Consider cultural backgrounds when you select a quotation. What is familiar to Americans may not fly in the United Kingdom, even though the common language is English. The reverse is also true. If there are an abundance of foreign attendees, your quotation and its context may be completely lost.

🔊 Try to keep the quotation as short as possible so you don't dilute its impact by requiring your audience to listen too long.

🔊 Give yourself a chance to experiment with your pitch, pace, and punch. Where does the phrase need pausing, and where does it need a louder or softer voice?

Signal When You Are Done

In proper dining, United States style, when you've finished eating, you're expected to put your used silverware on your plate, with knife and fork pointing in the same direction, laid out parallel to each other. That signals to the waiter that you're done and your plate can be removed. Other cultures have different customs.

As a speaker, if you've been effective and the audience is enthusiastically or even just politely listening, it's still expecting signals from you when you have ended your message.

Once you've said your summary, and either your call for action or quotation in closing, here's what to do:

1. Pause for a few seconds.

2. Say a sincere, simple "thank you" to your audience. Some organizations and speaking consultants do not advocate for a speaker to thank the audience, suggesting that it is the audience that ought to thank the speaker. It's your call, but I prefer to err on the side of graciousness which means uttering thank you.

3. Take a few steps back, away from the lectern, microphone, or your final speaking position.

4. Nod your head, looking down momentarily.

5. Await the thunderous applause you so deserve!

6. Smile back at the audience.

In a formal speaking situation, it's up to the person who introduced you to invite any questions from the audience *after* the applause. That's because the agenda responsibility and time control are in their hands.

If it's a more internal meeting, where there isn't likely to be any applause after you speak, I still recommend steps one and two above, to let your words and ideas sink into the room. You may want to then follow up with a request for questions or comments.

Your Postclose Activities

It's easy to give in to a tendency to keep talking because you're finally warmed up and cooking on all burners. The challenge is to end your presentation or speech on a suitably high note and then take the next steps that lead to the results you are there to accomplish.

To maximize the return on your speaking, you can employ a number of different strategies. One approach is to start dropping hints about two-thirds of the way through that there's something really worthwhile coming ahead, and they'll want to stay around to hear it. The hint resembles when an organization provides door prizes, shows you different, tempting ones throughout the event, and then states, "you must be present to win."

If your goal is to secure enrollment in a course or program you're offering, or sell tickets to an event at a discounted price, you may state that the offer you're giving at the end of the program will only be valid until midnight or another close date.

What else can you do after your closing and thank-you?

Depending on your objectives, there are different strategies you can employ once the applause has finished and your question-and-answer period is over. With the okay of those who invited you, consider selecting "winners" from business cards collected earlier or on the spot for the following:

- Free entry to an event you and your organization are sponsoring

- A one-hour complimentary consultation for a service you offer

- A sample product in your line

- An invitation to a webinar or other online experience

- A free subscription to your valuable newsletter

- A plaque with a famous or humorous quotation, with your company logo and website at the bottom

- A bottle of wine, champagne, balsamic vinegar, bouquet of flowers, certificate, or some other notable gift

With the business cards previously gathered or provided at the drawing, you have a set of contacts who are now familiar with you and what you do, making it easier to follow up—whether your goal is for your business, your cause, or for any other purpose.

To Summarize...

- Putting a good summary together for the end of your message can reengage your audience and help you reach your goal.

- Spend time deciding on your call for action to assure a strong finale.

- The right quotation can reinforce the end of a motivational message.

- You can include a variety of tactics near the end, and afterward, to further connect with your audience for business, career, or community purposes.

jpegwiz @ 123RF.com

Turning Yourself into a Speaking Genius: The Art of Public Speaking

Why is it that some speakers seem to mesmerize their audience and others only stimulate the desire to nap? Why do you look forward to hearing about a certain topic but find yourself sneaking frequent peeks at your smartphone or dying to disappear to the restroom because the speaker is droning on unbearably? Why does a speech that reads well on paper sound so different when we try to say it aloud?

In this part of *Public Speaking for the GENIUS*, we'll explore how you connect your words to the hearts, minds, and wallets of those in your audience.

Chapter 14

Curtain Up: Face to Face with the Attention Span Factor

In This Chapter...

- Overcoming the global attention deficit disorder
- How long will people really listen to you?
- Tactics to reignite interest
- Not just for cocktail parties

You've worked really hard to gather enticing content that brings real value to your audience and that will convince them to act according to your plan. You are now ready to go face to face with the world! You roll up your sleeves and jump into your message, only to realize—to your horror—that you've lost their attention.

Instead of listening, you see people texting, looking at their tablet, phone, or computer screen, whispering to each other, or otherwise engrossed in something that is not you or your remarks. It's every speaker's worst nightmare and sadly, a scenario that happens all too often in today's world of ever decreasing attention span.

In this chapter, I'll take you into the realm of fighting back against this frustrating audience tendency. You will gain an understanding of what you are up against, with practical pointers to help you engage and reengage even the most reluctant groups. I'll show you simple ways to keep your content fresh and more fun, including how to bring relevant experiences drawn from your everyday pursuits into your presentations.

The Global Attention Challenge: What Mark Twain Said Then versus Now

"No sinner is saved after twenty minutes of a sermon." The iconic American writer, Mark Twain, made that observation more than 150 years ago. In contrast, smart clergy today are adopting a seven-minute format for sermons to satisfy their congregants' preferences.

When I first started consulting with executives and community leaders on their presentations, experts were saying the maximum length of our attention span correlated to the seven-eight minutes between commercials on television. Learning research at the time was showing that both adult and child learners needed to be stimulated at least every three to four minutes to maintain interest in the material at hand.

With the advent of digital devices and their instantaneous capacity to answer nearly any question or desire, the latest

Reasons Why Your Audience Isn't Listening

◆ The average worker checks emails thirty to forty times every hour, and that often doesn't stop during your talk.

◆ People are spending seven hundred billion minutes on Facebook every month—and it's increasing. These folks are also looking at Facebook when you're making a presentation.

◆ Many are receiving their news Twitter-style in 140 characters or less. You're most likely talking far more than 140 characters of text!

◆ While movies may still be ninety minutes or more, the time people will watch a video is shrinking constantly. Think one to two minutes tops.

IMPORTANT!

findings suggest attention span has dropped to a new low, an average of only five to eight *seconds*. In contrast, a goldfish has a nine-second attention span.

The attention span situation is even more treacherous for speakers than ever before because of a device on the sofa of most homes. The television remote control, aka "the clicker," empowers the user with instant gratification, the ability to change a program anytime boredom strikes.

Good teachers, speakers, trainers, and managers work hard to come up with material and interactive moments to maintain attention, despite mounting odds against their best intentions.

You and I, when we're in presentation mode, are fighting the clicker mentality, the tendency to tune out anything after a few seconds of attention because its value or entertainment level is not readily apparent or appealing.

In other countries not yet ruined by the clicker syndrome, audiences have a longer attention span. A certain amount of formality and protocol remains commonplace and expected, and it's generally practiced.

For example, in Brazil, when government officials and even corporate leaders speak, it's customary to identify everyone of importance in the room, which can take up to a half hour or longer, depending on the size of the gathering. That's before a single word of the speech is uttered! I believe you'd agree with me that custom would not play well in the United States.

When I consult with foreign executives who want to do speeches and presentations to English-speaking markets, part of the work we do together is helping them learn how to deliver their messages in a more concise and relaxed manner. Many are accustomed to commanding a certain level of attention and respect simply because of the position they hold in their company, country, or community. Celebrity or not, without a well-targeted message and a practiced delivery that seems natural, they are likely to fall flat and not connect with demanding international audiences.

Psychology Today's Online Test

You can take a free five-minute online quiz to determine your own attention span, thanks to Psychology Today. (*http://psychologytoday.com/tests*)

In the test, the authorities point out that a "really boring lecture/meeting can definitely make anyone's attention span run thin." However, some people

What about an Accent?

While nonnative English speakers with heavy accents are often especially concerned about being understood, I've heard the same trepidation from Americans with deep southern accents or some other strong dialect.

It's true that in some cases an accent can hinder communication, especially if the speaker talks too fast, doesn't pause enough, and fails to pronounce words properly. My experience, however, is that the accent is often not the challenge the speaker thinks it is. More often, I've found that the speakers' level of preparation and their willingness to streamline the message—or not—can make or break the performance. Bottom line, you can be just as boring and ineffective doing a presentation in Spanish (which I do speak fluently) or any other language, as in English!

Observation

find having to focus on any routine, ordinary task as torture.

I thought my own attention span was pretty high, but not according to the test result. My score was a forty-seven out of one hundred. Here's what it said:

According to your score, you seem to have a rather short attention span. You tend to have a great deal of difficulty maintaining your focus on a task and following it through until completion. People who have short attention spans tend to jump from project to project and are often known to be quite disorganized. This frequently results in missed deadlines, tardiness, and bills being paid late.

An inability to pay attention for an extended period of time could be a result of fatigue, a medication side-effect, or you may simply have a personal issue weighing heavily on your mind. However, it would be a good idea to visit a psychologist in order to assess whether Attention Deficit Disorder may be an issue.

Yikes! These results made me wonder how many other people are out there—in our audiences—with a mild or even major version of attention deficit disorder, aware or oblivious to their inability to pay close attention to our messages. While I recognize that we cannot control the attention span of others, I believe we can overcome the odds against us as speakers. We can maintain the most attention by crafting our message in as interactive a way as possible, and by making sure our mission matches the interests of those in the room.

How Long Will They Really Listen?

There are four major factors that can interfere with your ability, as a speaker, to keep an audience listening:

🔍 *The speed of our brain.* The average person speaks between 150 and 160 words a minute, but we can process information almost twice as fast. Most experts, including me, recommend your pace for a persuasive presentation be 140 to 160 words a minute or even less. What that means is that while we're listening to you, we can be thinking about something you said and simultaneously going off mentally in any number of directions, while still seeming to be paying attention.

🔍 *An urge to reply to the speaker.* Wanting to talk back to the speaker can overwhelm our capability to listen. We get caught up in what we want to say and start mentally rehearsing our thoughts and words, thinking of better ways to make our point, all of which interrupts our listening to

The Elephants in the Room versus You and Your Message

Not so long ago, children and adults were regarded as lazy and disrespectful if they displayed a short attention span, were always late, disorganized, and tended to jump around a lot, both physically and mentally. Psychologists began studying this behavior and labeled it Attention Deficit Hyperactivity Disorder (ADHD).

Studies have shown that more than one in ten children in America suffer from ADHD, and that nearly five percent of all adults do not outgrow the symptoms, which usually start at about age seven. Males tend to be afflicted with these tendencies more than twice as often as females.

What that means to you as a speaker and a leader is two-fold:

◆ You may have some form of this disorder yourself, making the job of creating a viable speech or presentation even tougher.

◆ You can overcome limited attention spans by developing highly interactive and fast-paced presentations, with strong visual components.

Perspiration

you. When we are paying attention, we are not listening to content. Instead, we are awaiting a space where we can insert our reply.

🔖 *Poor content and bothersome delivery style.* When boring, difficult, or irrelevant material is discussed, we listeners tune out. Other contributors to losing an audience are talking too long, being insulting (even accidentally), speaking in a flat tone, an absence of supporting body language, and no avenue for the audience to reply or react. So keeping up our personal *mojo*—our own magical talent and energy source—no matter how we really may be feeling is vital.

🔖 *Self-absorption.* When you're the speaker, you control the conversation and typically have your own agenda of what you are trying to accomplish. It's easy to overlook or simply not focus on what others are doing because we're caught up in our own goals, in the stories we're sharing, the position we're defending, and the recommendations we're making.

Part of the responsibility of the speaker, I believe, is to read the audience members' body language, too. If they are drooping in their seats, if their eyes are shutting, and it's not with the ecstasy of listening to you, perhaps you've been too caught up in your own conversation, at their expense.

You could say it's a miracle when a speaker does experience a grateful, engaged audience! I suggest that the wondrous exchange of energy between the speaker and listeners is possible because of the combination of thoughtfully crafted content and honed delivery skills coming together for mutual benefit.

Four Proven Tactics to Recapture Attention

Skilled speakers have developed what appear as intuitive responses to the drifting attention span that can happen when you are face to face with a small group or a big audience. While some of these turnaround efforts may truly be intuitive, most are learned behaviors, usually from painful experiences.

I've identified some proven tactics you can begin to practice right away so you'll look and sound in control, too.

🔖 Pose questions and elicit answers

🔖 Make use of opening techniques throughout your message, not just for the opening!

🖋 Match content to images that provoke responses

🖋 Include good "cocktail conversation" items to maintain interest

Ask an Open-Ended Question

At regular intervals in your speech, throw out a question not answerable by a simple "yes" or "no"—and seek out responses from your audience. This tactic is often in play among experienced speakers. You not only stimulate interest by converting what could be viewed as a lecture into a group discussion, but you also create the element of surprise and a sense of anticipation, which most people truly enjoy. No one knows in advance what will be said by the nonexpert members of the group. And will you, as the speaker, agree, disagree, praise, or criticize the response?

The value of posing questions to your audience is immense in terms of promoting audience involvement and appreciation.

Potential Downside of Asking Questions

Given that most people like to keep talking once they get

Open-Ended Questions You Can Pose

Depending on who's in your audience, you have a variety of possibilities of questions to trot out and reenergize your speaking situation. Here are some:

"Have you ever had a similar experience? Tell us about it."

"Why do you think this kind of practice could work or might not?"

"If you were writing the legislation, what would you want to see included?"

"What was the best place you ever traveled and why?"

"When is the best time to exercise for you, and what to you do to stay in shape?"

"What would you say was the biggest challenge you had starting your business?"

"As a parent, what has been the most rewarding aspect of raising your children?"

"What gets in your way when you're trying to lose weight?"

"What was your biggest 'aha moment' in the last few weeks?"

Example

cranked up, you risk losing control of the speaking situation when you ask a question and encourage audience members to answer it. Several other awful things can also happen:

🖐 The person can say something truly inappropriate, off-color, racially biased, or worse.

🖐 Your facts, position, or credentials can be challenged in a less-than-friendly way, even to the point of someone trying to trash your message and you.

🖐 You thank the person for responding and try to move on, but the individual refuses to stop talking or to return the microphone to you.

To prevent some of these occurrences, especially in a large crowd setting, always insist on two microphones. One is for you, and one can be available to the audience, whether portable or in a fixed location. That way, you can override the unwelcome participation, if needed.

Try to set some ground rules right after you pose the question. Request that the responses be as brief as possible to give time for others to participate as well. Be sure and acknowledge each respondent before taking the next answer, even if it's an extremely brief thank-you.

Despite the potential for loss of control, I find this question-asking technique works beautifully most of the time and it can really help your presentation to be well received.

Opening Techniques—Not Just for the Start!

One of the best ways to boost listening levels throughout your presentation is to treat your main points and subpoints as if each were the original opening of your message. In **Chapter 11**, you were introduced to the six most popular ways to open a speech or presentation. One of the rewards of brainstorming openings is that your written rejects—the ones you didn't use for the start of the speech—could be just perfect to open up different parts of the body.

Here they are again:

🖐 The speaker's equivalent of "Once Upon a Time"

🖐 Get them to wonder where you're going

🖐 Startle with a newsworthy fact

- Promise to give them something

- Ask for a show of hands

- Use an object or exhibit

A story or personal anecdote you considered using to open the presentation, but that just didn't have the right punch, could be just the best way to launch a main point or subpoint.

You sensed that asking the audience for a show of hands to answer a particular question would not be well received in the opening of your speech. But, later in the message, that question and getting the audience to raise their hands in response could be just the right strategy to revitalize the crowd and reengage them with your message.

"And now that we've been talking about the role of chocolate in our lives for a little while, by a show of hands, who believes that chocolate can provide health benefits as well as satisfy our sweet tooth?"

Similarly, you have a clever prop or a remarkable graph that you know will get the group to react, but it only pertained to one of the points you planned to present so it was wrong for the

Applying Openings to Pump Up Your Message

Say you're introducing a main point about changing a longtime procedure in your organization. A typical, unimaginative approach might be: "The next aspect of the transition we need to go over is how this change will impact the support staff."

Instead, you might want to try out the "promise to give them something" opening and "the startle with a fact" technique, to see how you can energize the beginning of this important point.

(Promise.) "By the time we've finished showing you what this transition will mean to our support staff operations, you're going to see how much faster and more secure both routine and special project data storage will be, with no increase in anyone's workload."

(Fact.) "The largest, fastest-growing counties in our state have already adopted the new case management that we're about to discuss, and they report a 75 percent satisfaction rate once it's installed and working up to potential."

Example

opening of your presentation. That commanding visual element, placed in the right slot, is another ideal way to reinvigorate those attending.

Match Content to Provocative Visuals

While many folks rely heavily on programs like PowerPoint and videos, just having images is not enough. We've all suffered through a boring PowerPoint presentation with dull slides and too many words. Or endured an amateur video with awful lighting, sound, and questionable content. Even professional videos that are dressed with spiffy images but say nothing can be frustrating, as you wonder why they spent money and time developing something so useless.

Remember that not every set of ideas needs a visual, and that you can sometimes more effectively use words in a good story or a well-crafted description to help paint a picture in your audience's mind.

Think about the tons of images viewed daily on electronic devices in social media and websites, the treatment of photographs and graphics in popular publications, and all the special effects we expect in movies and TV shows. Ordinary no longer suffices, not if you really want to come across as an up-to-date pro.

I'm not encouraging you to use a visual for shock value only. When I worked with a surgeon who insisted on putting in a PowerPoint slide of a girl in a skimpy bikini half-way through his talk "to wake everyone up," I pointed out that his approach was more than a little sexist in that half of his audience was female. Further, he was belittling his own research and remarks by interjecting an irrelevant slide. Better, I recommended, that we identify some uplifting success stories or other content that would more suitably maintain a high-interest level.

What Goes into Making Great Visuals?

With the world's shrinking attention span, you can increase the odds of getting folks to listen and act when you use visuals the right way. Here are some recommendations that I've found helpful:

🖉 *Less is more.* An old guideline which I believe remains somewhat valid is to include no more than six words on a line on your visual. Fewer words, carefully chosen, will position you even stronger. Why? You don't want people to be reading the slide instead of listening to you.

🔍 *Limit the number of lines of text.* Ideally, display two or three, maximum. The same rationale as the previous recommendation applies. Remember, the slides exist to complement your spoken words, not replace you. Too much text and as the speaker, you may find yourself reading it aloud instead of maintaining your conversational tone with the audience. No one appreciates a speaker who reads their presentation from the screen instead of delivering it in a straightforward, engaging manner.

🔍 *Use a large type that is simple to read for headlines and subpoints.* An absolute minimum of twenty-four points and ideally larger, thirty points or more, works best. Avoid fancy typefaces that don't project well. I find traditional fonts like Arial, Helvetica, and Tahoma best-suited for text. You can be more adventurous with headlines but be sure and do a trial way before your presentation to assure readability.

🔍 *Keep headline colors and type fonts consistent.* Try to resist the creative urge to make every slide look different by changing the color or type fonts. Too much variety and your audience doesn't know where to look first and their attention will be diverted from your key messages.

🔍 *More images, less text.* Do pack a positive punch by selecting powerful, relevant images that help you make your points. You can choose photographs, pertinent illustrations, and even videos. It's okay to have just one or two key words on a slide accompanied by an attention-grabbing image.

🔍 *Don't settle for mediocre.* Just as you have worked hard to hone your message itself, give yourself time to locate and insert the right images to make your points pop.

🔍 *Don't be afraid to ask others.* Reach out to people who have presentations, websites, or publications you admire and ask where they've found their visuals.

🔍 Be on the alert for photos and videos of relevant images you can create or download yourself, also.

Visuals Can Take You Down Memory Lane a Good Way

When I was asked to speak at a local university leadership class, I decided to talk a little about what had influenced my becoming a writer. I went online to locate photos and included the historic huge chair in the park of my

Finding Better than Average Images

When I recently redid my PowerPoint slides and website, my graphic designer and web developer shared a site for stock photographs she'd found especially creative, and encouraged me to check it out. "*123rf.com* has the best bang for your buck," she told me. Compared to other stock photo sites I'd frequented in the past, the new source was fantastic.

At the same time, just as you gather more than one source of information for your presentation to create a balanced, dynamic message, the recommendation applies to locating visuals as well.

Perspiration

hometown—the Chair City of the United States—Gardner, Massachusetts. The city was a well-known furniture manufacturing center and my parents owned a small colonial-style factory behind our home that produced one of the rockers that President John F. Kennedy used to ease his bad back.

The other visual I showed was the home page of the *Gardner News*, the local daily that had given me my start. I was a scribe of my Brownies troop, beginning at seven years old. In those days, the paper printed a few lines monthly from every Scout troop in the area. Unlike now, there was no shortage of news space.

I loved seeing my words in print, a feeling I confess never having lost!

Add Good "Cocktail Conversation" Tidbits

You don't need to have imbibed anything to engage in worthwhile cocktail conversation. The idea is to gather and be ready to add content to your messages that is enticing, stimulating, and could be repeated at a cocktail party to impress others.

I'm not recommending that you gossip or bring down anyone or a particular group with your version of these conversational wonders. I am encouraging you to give yourself time to find gems you can sprinkle into your message that will light up the house.

Part of the reason that I'm out going to meetings and networking is to meet potential clients. But the other motivation, equally important, is to keep abreast of what the so-called "thought leaders" are saying in our community. My goal is to come away from every meeting with at least one example, story, or insight that I can share in my next presentation.

Sometimes these gems come unbidden. When I left my husband in his hospital room the night after his surgery, he had no roommate. But the next morning when I came to check on him, there was a young man in the next bed with three young women and an older woman hovering nearby, and the constant ringing of their cell phones. Soon, two doctors showed up and started discussing his condition.

"You're not going to be happy about how your hand is after the bullet is removed," the doctor said. "But it could have been much worse." He went on to tell the patient that he would be in surgery for at least two hours, but it could be four hours. Ed and I were listening, trying not to be obvious, but it was a bit shocking to be so close to a victim of crime. We didn't think he was the perpetrator because there were no police officers present.

And the diagnosis got worse.

"Now, about your leg. The first x-ray didn't show that the bullet hit the bone but we're going to do another to be sure," the doctor continued, adding that the result would influence the patient's walking capability.

The doctor then asked, "What kind of work are we going to get you ready to go back and do? And who do you live with?" The young man answered that he worked in a warehouse and that he lived in his mother's home. The doctors told him that he probably would not be able to go back to do the kind of lifting his job required and that it was good he would be home to have someone take care of him as he recovered.

Cocktail Conversation to Avoid in Private or Group Settings

Good manners were once taught at a tender age and their importance reinforced as you got older. Some parents have continued this practice and other people have been left to discover the value of manners on their own. In that spirit, I offer some generally off-limits topics and questions to avoid:

◆ The income of those in the audience

◆ Personal tragedies (unless they are relevant to your topic)

◆ How much you paid for anything

◆ Off-color or discriminatory statements

◆ Political or religious positions (unless relevant to your topic)

◆ Details of personal relationships or sexual orientation

◆ Health or diet information (unless relevant to your topic)

Example

We were at Jackson Memorial Hospital, the biggest public medical facility in South Florida, which has a working arrangement with the University of Miami and its wonderful surgeon who operated on Ed. Jackson is known for its many excellent departments but also for its exceptional trauma unit, where gunshot victims and motorcycle accident patients usually wind up.

A few minutes after the doctor left, a short, stocky guy in a long black blazer strode into the room, carrying a black leather briefcase. In a voice much lower than the doctors, obviously for privacy sake, he discussed the legal options of the patient. We could not hear much of what he said.

In telling some friends of this episode, the reply was "only in Miami."

Needless to say, I got some good mileage out of this experience! Be alert to what is happening to you and be open to incorporating these experiences into your remarks, when appropriate.

Bottom line, some of us are more sensitive than others to the feelings and attitudes of those we encounter as speakers and in our day-to-day lives. "Think before you speak" remains timeless advice.

To Summarize...

- If you're concerned about losing your audience's attention, right on! Increasingly, speakers everywhere are facing intense competition from digital devices, multitasking, and overstressed work and home situations.

- You really only have seconds these days to capture and keep people tuned into your message.

- It's possible to restore interest in your talk even if people have drifted away when you apply specific techniques.

- Staying on top of the news and other current events makes you a more relevant, timely speaker, increasing the odds of your maintaining attention.

Chapter 15

Communicating Like a Genius: More to It Than You Think

In This Chapter...

- Different communication styles: yours, theirs, and ours
- Why are some folks apparently 'naturals' when speaking?
- Dealing with the direct and interacting with the influencer
- Connecting with the steady and coexisting with the check-lister

Many people have confided to me that what they truly want is to come across as a talented, poised professional when public speaking. I have seen the quietest, most Nervous Nellies communicate like a genius, when they craft a solid message and devote enough time and energy to practice. At the same time, Jovial Joes can bomb despite their natural charm and effusive personality, if their words are off-target or their ideas simply fail to connect.

It's true that some people come across as natural with no hint of nervousness. But stage presence alone does not assure success. I have found that speakers become remarkable and exceptionally productive when they acquire knowledge about their own communication style along with the characteristics of those in in their audiences, workplace, or nonprofit organization. In this chapter, you'll be exploring how to apply these valuable insights to your formal speaking situations so you can increase the odds of achieving your goals. You'll also see how you can become more successful in your critical day-to-day presentations and conversations as well.

Different Communication Styles: Yours, Theirs, and Ours

Looking at the world of leaders and aspiring speakers, some of us tend to be introverts: understated, low-key, and risk-adverse. Others are extroverts: bold, vocal, and fearless. And some of us see ourselves as in between, changing depending upon the circumstances at hand.

Another distinction is how we relate to the world. Among us are task-focused individuals keen on getting the job done, often by themselves. And there are those who are more people-oriented, accomplishing work through others.

To be an effective communicator, it doesn't matter whether you are an introvert or an extrovert, whether you're task or people focused. What matters is for you to recognize and accept your own communication style, and not let it interfere with your ability to connect to audiences or individuals who are not like you.

Looking back, I have realized that I was an introvert growing up. I played the clarinet, was a Girl Scout, liked to write, and didn't do much to attract attention to myself.

For reasons I don't recall, my freshman year of high school, I ran for and was elected president of my temple's junior youth group. It was a great experience and I got to go to a special summer camp in North Carolina, representing our group. When I lost the bid for the senior group presidency the following year to a boy named Kenneth, I was devastated.

At the same time, I decided to give up the clarinet in favor of writing for my high school newspaper, the *Nova Vue*. I was able to advance up the ranks to become editor. Early on I knew I was comfortable interviewing others and asking classmates questions, then turning those conversations into articles. The behind-the-scenes role of reporter and editor was fine with me. I didn't feel any need to perform or be center stage, unlike the cheerleaders, thespians, or the student broadcasters who did the daily closed-circuit television news reports.

Introverts Are Not Limited; Extroverts Have No Guaranteed Success

Popular books now abound that shout out to the introvert that it's okay to be who you are. I'm not advocating that it is necessary to dance on a bar counter to draw attention to yourself. However, classic, stereotypical, introverted behavior that is withdrawn, understated, and designed to make a person nearly invisible, usually does not bode well in public speaking. Instead of focusing on the message, we are distracted by the apparent discomfort of the messenger.

At the same time, just because extroverts may exude personality, they may deliver only puff and illusion. They may be entertaining and appear confident but have no real substance to impart.

IMPORTANT!

In college, I continued as a student journalist, covering the rapidly changing campus life as the Vietnam war raged, curfews for women students disappeared, celebrities visited, and phones started to be installed in every dorm room.

Fast forward to my postcollege stints as a newspaper reporter. I found myself in situations far outside of my comfort zone. The singles bar scene was gaining popularity in Miami and my editor wanted me to go and write a story about what was happening. It was doing that series where I believe my more extroverted tendencies began to emerge. While the real Anne would never go to a bar and start talking to strange men or even unknown women, with my assignment as a journalist, I was liberated from my own fear. And in fact, I was being paid to ask people questions and write up their answers.

In subsequent years, doing investigative pieces and features, I was undaunted when approaching elected officials, business owners, and community leaders in the pursuit of a story. It was a professional fearlessness that I was able to take into my assignments when I began to be a freelance writer as well. Though I wasn't a full-fledged extrovert by any means, I certainly was less timid and more willing to put myself into the limelight when necessary than I had been as a younger person.

Insecurity Can Return Unbidden

A few years later, after I'd established a public speaking consulting business, I was asked to lead a networking event for a business group at a cocktail reception. I'd been doing a version monthly for a small chamber of commerce and didn't think it could be that different for this group, even though it would have between one hundred and 150 in attendance. But when I walked into the room, it turned out to be all suits. I was only one of a mere a handful of women in the room and I was definitely, surprisingly, intimidated.

I led group members through about three networking exercises and then could not regain control. They were busily engaged in conversation and exchanging business cards and refused to respond to my request at the microphone to stop so we could do another exercise. I was mortified. My host, however, appeared unfazed. He asked the group to thank me with applause, which it did. I left quietly, feeling my tail between my legs.

The next day I got a call saying how terrific they thought the event was, and maybe I could do it again next year!

The moral of the story? Looking back, I realize now that I was in a room with a disproportionate number of extra-strong extroverted personalities. There were many lawyers and entrepreneurs in the room, accustomed to being in charge. They wanted to be and acted in control of the networking and the event.

You may find yourself in a transition just now. You may have one foot in the past, the kind of speaker you once were, and another lifted into the present, striving to become a more memorable and impactful communicator. You may already be a confident and remarkable presenter, and yet you are demanding more of yourself, wanting more consistently to obtain the outcome you desire.

Why Some Are "Naturals" and Others Have to Work Harder

As I started to do public speaking, first as a freelance writer and then as a consultant, I noticed some key differences between myself and some of the elected officials and business leaders with whom I began to work.

Whenever I had a speaking engagement, it took extensive practice for me to appear natural and relaxed. (I still practice thoroughly for new programs and review and refine constantly for existing ones.)

In contrast, a few of my clients were good to go after reviewing the message we'd developed together and after just a few rehearsals. These folks were most often the more experienced public officials who had given dozens if not hundreds of speeches over the years. My role was to help them devise fresh ways of talking about the themes and issues that were important in their communities. Once they were in front of a crowd, they knew how to work the room, establish rapport, and "naturally" engage their audience. Some sales leaders also seemed exceptionally at ease in public situations, particularly doing motivational speaking.

The vast majority of my clients, however, were not "naturals" like the politicians or the sales leaders. It took hard work to not only craft their messages, but commitment to devote enough time to rehearsals so they would appear polished, poised, and professional.

What kind of speaking engagements were they doing?

Over the years, the range of topics has included:

- presenting to their own organization at annual meetings or for other significant occasions

- speaking as industry experts at conferences

- pitching to prospective investors

- rolling out new initiatives in-house

- leading team-building sessions during mergers and acquisitions

- delivering state of the government addresses

- announcing strategic plans as a new chamber or organization president

- introducing advocacy positions for a political, business, environmental, or educational issue

- promoting fundraising messages

My take away for you to remember is that 95 percent of good public speaking is due to preparation and practice. The other 5 percent may be attributed to exceptionally good luck, pure moxie, and factors over which most of us have no control!

A Lasting Gift for Speakers from Wonder Woman's Creator

Working with clients accused of crimes, in the early 1900s a Harvard-educated lawyer discovered a relationship between blood pressure and lying. He built a device to measure changes in a person's blood pressure while the subject was being questioned, inventing the first lie detector in 1915. He formally published his early polygraph findings in 1917. This discovery was to be just the first of many extraordinary gifts that William Moulton Marsten would develop over his lifetime.

Marsten was fascinated by the behavior of ordinary people rather than abnormal psychology, which was unusual for his time. Continuing to build on his work with accused criminals, he studied the role of a person's sense of power and its impact on behavior and emotions. He also explored consciousness, colors, primary emotions, and body symptoms which led to his landmark book published in 1928, *The Emotions of Normal People.*

If you've ever had your communication style analyzed with a popular assessment like the DISC report, Myers-Briggs, or any of dozens of other assessments, they are based on the findings of this remarkable man. His work categorized people into one of four main types by their relationship to power and energy—dominance, influence, submission, and compliance (DISC). Over the years, industry leaders modified the names to make them more universally acceptable. In the next section, I'll be introducing you to the modern-day version of what Moulton Marsten identified in the last century, and how you can use these insights to be more effective in your public speaking and team communication.

While Mr. Marsten didn't actually design a test from his model—others did later—he did apply his research to help Universal Studios in 1930 to transition from silent pictures to movies with audio.

Perhaps as valuable a legacy as the personality types—especially for women—was his creation of the comic book heroine Wonder Woman, who first appeared in 1941 at the back of an All Star Comics book. Using the pen name Charles Moulton, the lawyer-turned-psychologist took inspiration from many diverse sources. These included his studies of Greek and

What Is Your Style and Who's on Your Team?

For more than fifteen years, I've used the assessments of Target Training International (*ttisuccessinsights.com*), based in Scottsdale, Arizona, and have found them easy to administer and interpret. The reports are available not only in English but in many other languages. You can also find many other companies that also offer similar assessments and check them out for yourself.

Perspiration

Roman classics along with his own personality style findings. But I believe his close involvement with the earliest movements for women's rights, voting, career equity, and birth control was the driving force in this unprecedented and historic cartoon venture.

To achieve her missions, the comic character Wonder Woman was portrayed with Greek and Roman goddess archetypes, a lasso for truth and imbued in a stereotype-breaking move with power and will. She relied on the four personality characteristics—dominance, influence, submission, and compliance. Moulton and Max Gaines of DC Comics, considered the grandfather of American comic books, weren't sure how a feminine hero would be accepted by the public. Despite their misgivings, Wonder Woman soon attained her own prominence and comic book. Moulton wrote her stories until he died in 1947. In 2006, he was inducted into the Will Eisner Award Hall of Fame.

Some employers use surveys based on the four communication styles to screen candidates and also to develop team strategies that Mr. Marsten identified nearly one hundred years ago. In the next segments, you'll be introduced to what makes each tick. Try to identify who you are and who may be on your team, or perhaps, who your clients or prospects are, as you read through their descriptions. Think about who will be in your audience or attending an upcoming meeting.

Why Charles Moulton Created Wonder Woman

In Moulton's own words:

Not even girls want to be girls so long as our feminine archetype lacks force, strength, and power. Not wanting to be girls, they don't want to be tender, submissive, peace-loving as good women are. Women's strong qualities have become despised because of their weakness. The obvious remedy is to create a feminine character with all the strength of Superman plus all the allure of a good and beautiful woman.

It's too bad for us 'literary' enthusiasts, but it's the truth nevertheless—pictures tell any story more effectively than words. Realize what you really want. It stops you from chasing butterflies and puts you to work digging gold.

Quote

Dealing with a Direct Personality

Many would agree—including me—that the most difficult kinds of communicators are the direct types. They are classified as extroverts, dominant, outgoing, and forceful in their speaking. Picture a lion, king of the jungle. They are big-picture focused, love to solve problems, are exceptionally goal-oriented, task-driven, and will roar out exactly what they want and rarely shy away from a direct confrontation. They tend to make fast decisions and don't tolerate slower-thinking individuals too well. Maybe you're a direct, like I am, or you know one.

When you craft a message and you have directs in the room, your message needs to be visionary yet practical, clear, and concise. They care about saving time and want to know specifically what's involved. They are not usually particularly sensitive to how their roar may affect others.

Presiding Over a Direct-Heavy Group

We had quite a few directs on our board of directors of the Miami Chapter of the National Association of Women Business Owners (NAWBO), when I served as president. I described our group in somewhat politically incorrect terms as, "All chiefs, no Indians."

While the directs unquestionably helped us move forward into exciting avenues, it wasn't without ruffling a few feathers along the way. We were able to hire an administrator, acquire new corporate partners, form alliances with other groups, and expand our involvement nationally, internationally, and with other chapters in the state. Other members with different communication styles wanted more time to think about the proposals, expressed concern about our finances, and insisted on putting more systems in place to accommodate our growth and plans.

My job as president, as other leaders find themselves doing, was to try to balance the opinions, goals, and personalities of our talented and strong-willed team. Since I am a direct myself, I had to learn how to share the news about possible projects in a nonthreatening way, and to secure

How to Persuade a Direct

Since directs often see themselves, like the lion, as the king in their world, it's not a good idea to tell them what to do.

Instead, lay out the big picture and the specific options and probabilities for action. Give choices to them along with the ultimate decision-making capability. Even if they ask your opinion or recommendation, try not to make your solution absolute. For better results, reiterate the pros and cons or options from which they can choose.

Perspiration

agreement among the board members before forging ahead. I confess that some of my recommendations were better received than others, despite my best efforts to appeal to the different styles on my board.

Involving an Influencer Personality

You know you're around influencer-type communicators when they get excited and expressive about an issue and try to motivate everyone in the vicinity to climb onboard. Envision a magnificent peacock with its colorful feathers fully extended. Influencers, like the directs, are big-picture and result-oriented extroverts. The differences are their passion for enjoying themselves, for enthusiastically promoting what they find fascinating or important, and their capacity to be charming and people focused.

Influencers can be easily bored, especially if you try and give them too much detail. They like to be in the spotlight and seem to carry an inner energy that draws people to them.

When you communicate with influencers, your message needs to fly high and be as entertaining as possible. They care about being able to enjoy life even more, so demonstrate how your plan or product can help them do that. Impressive name-dropping can reinforce your efforts when you refer to other people and organizations who have previously embraced your idea, product, or service.

How to Persuade an Influencer

Influencers generally think highly of themselves and value the opinions of others who they see as experts or leaders.

Rather than pile on too many facts or research findings that they may find dull, search for testimonials from recognized experts. Identify and offer incentives that will propel them to action, such as pleasurable outings, time off to experience new things, a chance to hobnob with celebrities, or ways their reputation or personal life can be enhanced.

Perspiration

Connecting to a Steady Personality

As the name suggests, the steady is a person who prefers life without too much drama, and favors a consistent, predictable course of action in most things. Marsten, the psychologist who first published his research on these personality types called this style submissive, giving in to the dictates of others as a core element in their behavior. Over the years, the name was modified because the description only yielded a small portion of their true characteristics.

In animal terms, I usually describe the steady as an elephant. As the majestic elephant, the steady has a remarkable sense of balance and loyalty.

The steadies are classified as introverts, quieter and less in your face than extroverts. They tend to resist change and delight in celebrating and carrying on traditions. They function best as part of a well-managed team, a family-like group that is supportive and sensitive to the feelings of its members.

In communicating with the steady, it helps to understand that relationships are one of the most important parts of their world. When you talk about change, they naturally get upset or feel threatened because change always impacts relationships—whether with coworkers, vendors, systems, the community, or any other regularly occurring pattern. They want to know exactly why you are proposing something new or different, so be prepared to explain it in detail.

How to Persuade a Steady

It's key to provide as much reassurance and if possible, guarantees, when you try to persuade a steady. They generally do not like change and most likely, you're trying to get them to buy into some kind of change! In addition to personal reassurance, include a discussion that shows your recognition of their concern for the relationships in their circle, and what you have planned that will help reduce any negative impact.

Perspiration

Convincing a Check-Lister Personality

Whenever I visit my accountant, Marvin, and I want to give him an update on a new project, he always says, "Anne, give it to me… one, two, three, four." Since I'm a direct, my natural style is the opposite: to first provide an overview, then scale down to the details.

But the check-listers, like Marvin, are the heavy-duty details folks. You want that in a good accountant! They are introverts, usually soft-spoken, who want all the facts, figures, and rationale behind them. They thrive on rules and procedures and insist that these practices be followed precisely. In the animal world, picture the wise owl that appears to see everything and everyone.

How to Persuade a Check-Lister

Naturally skeptical and distrustful of the new, to help overcome the check-lister's reluctance to go forward, you need to prepare a thorough and orderly analysis of the data behind your plan or about your product. They never want to be wrong and insist on proof that what you're asking for approval will, in fact, work. Find and arrange your evidence carefully, and you're on your way to a home run.

Perspiration

Check-listers moan when decisions are made too fast, without enough of what they regard as necessary, careful deliberation. They need to be right most of the time, to save face, and they only respond well if they're told exactly how something will work, step-by-step. So when you're communicating with the check-listers, be sure you're presenting an approach that has a high likelihood of being successful or you may never hear the end of it! Also, give them a robust explanation of the method you're recommending, in as much detail as you can manage.

How to Adapt Your Style for the Challenge at Hand

As I mentioned earlier in the chapter, I'm a direct when it comes to communication styles. You'll find me happiest when I'm getting to solve a problem, create a new solution, and I'm head-to-head with other like-minded innovative folks. I'm terrible with following most rules—except, perhaps, for good writing—and I admit that I'm not thrilled if anyone tries to tell me what to do.

Needless to say, this style of communicating has not always endeared me to those in my world. And to become a successful speaker and communication consultant meant moving past my natural tendencies—getting out of my own way.

How Can Directs Adapt Their Behavior?

As a direct, I've had to learn to adapt, to put on a mask, so to speak, to tone down my directness at times, and to try to be more patient. It has meant becoming more accepting of how others think and act, and to be less confrontational. What I like to say is that we directs need to become mavens at biting our own tongue with some frequency, overriding our inclination to respond immediately to any given statement.

Does adapting your behavior to meet the situation at hand always work?

No, alas. But from my experience and the research I've done on this aspect of communication, it helps to know that adapting our behavior is an acquired skill, just like improving a golf game or mastering a new software program. Set your mind to it, become familiar with the way things work, dive in, practice and you can do anything!

How Can Influencers Adapt Their Behavior?

Okay, so you're not a direct. You're a fun-loving, outgoing influencer. Mostly, the world loves you!

But the "I" part of you can take over and make you appear so self-centered and egotistical that you turn everyone off. Your lack of interest in the details and talkative nature can further hamper your role as a leader and communicator.

Begin to stuff an imaginary cloth in your mouth—so you can listen more instead of talk constantly. I'm exaggerating only a little bit. Try to remember that the big picture is grand, but it will work well only if the underlying foundation is solid.

Harness your inherently wonderful energy to get behind the plans of others, not just your own. They'll welcome your support and be more likely to jump in and back you in the future, too. Force yourself to get into the weeds now and then, to more carefully examine the details than you might really want to do.

You'll be surprised at what you learn and how it can help you advance your position.

How Can Steadies Adapt Their Behavior?

In the spirit of equal treatment, let's visit with you, the steady. While you're unquestionably the glue that can hold together a team or family, and your sensitivity to others is no doubt a blessing in most places, you can also be a stick-in-the-mud! The steady prefers the tried and true and sometimes that isn't the best course of action any longer. The steady also wants everyone to embrace a plan and take a role in making it happen, a wonderful ideal, when it's feasible.

Try not to look at every new plan as a threat to your existing relationships, whether they be with people or procedures. Instead, allow yourself to imagine how your team or community would benefit from the recommendation at hand. It's fine to ask why a change may be necessary, your customary and thoughtful response, but put the answers you hear into a new context that allows you to make a judgment without being totally tied to the past. Tradition matters, but it's not the only thing that does!

How Can Check-Listers Adapt Their Behavior?

And last, but not least, let's consider the role of you check-listers. You are the quality-control chiefs of the planet, the ultimate inspectors in fields such as finance, the law, logistics, and editing, carefully striving to be sure that every "t" is crossed and every "i" is properly dotted. While such precision is critical in many situations, it can absolutely throw a monkey wrench into the path of a train traveling faster than you like or perhaps in a direction you don't think you want it to go. In your quest to follow the rules, you may overlook a situation that requires special consideration and a different treatment.

Let go of the red pen in your hand for a moment, or your digital equivalent. Try not to be so judgmental of every action before you. Give yourself the right to step back and look at the question at hand from a bit of a distance, instead of being right on top of the matter. Use your gift of being systematic to analyze what could work well, not only what might fail.

To Summarize...

- To be an outstanding speaker, it doesn't matter whether you are an extrovert or an introvert; you need to adapt your style to connect with your audience effectively.

- Behind the façade of confidence is a set of skills honed by practice and a determination to be an excellent communicator.

- Paint the big picture as clearly and concisely as you can, and give options when you're trying to persuade a direct personality. Lay on the charm, be entertaining, not detailed, and provide incentives with the influencer type.

- Reassure and gain agreement with the steady that what you are seeking won't adversely affect existing relationships. Give as much research validation and background as possible to prove your position to the check-lister.

Chapter 16

Gaining Control of Those Body Parts

In This Chapter...

- Avoid unwanted sounds and words when you're speaking
- Add impact with posture, gestures, and eye contact
- Forget the fig leaf position
- Make the microphone your new bff (best friend forever)

"Can't live with them; can't live without them." This popular expression is often trotted out to describe how men feel about women, and vice versa, and other relationships as well.

In the world of speaking, we sometimes feel this ambivalence about our various body parts, from head to toes. Just as we can have and appreciate those good hair days, the bad ones are a plague that can disrupt our entire confidence and performance. While most men don't complain about bad hair days, other worrisome physical complaints can intrude including a shaving nick or a pimple in a highly visible place on the face.

In this chapter, we acknowledge that our mouth and our other body parts sometime fail to cooperate or respond the way we'd like when public speaking. To counteract these unwelcome tendencies, we look at strategies to help you get and keep things under control. These tactics include regulating the words and sounds you utter so they are intended, not unintended. Helping your hands and the microphone become your allies instead of enemies is also addressed.

Conquering Errs, Uhs, Kind Ofs, and You Knows

Verbal fillers are the sounds we make between sentences and midsentence when the right words are not coming out as needed. Our subconscious mind does not like empty spaces and it encourages us to produce inelegant sounds that temporarily replace words. These familiar and unprofessional sounds often include:

"Err, uh, and um."

You've heard a speaker stumble while everyone inwardly groans:

"*Um*… I want to thank *err* my team, my mother *uh*, and *um*… my cat… for helping me *um* win the marathon today."

Word versions of these fillers also appear in our conversations and speeches. Probably the most widely heard is: "You know."

"It's a green way of handling office waste, *you know*, and the approach has been recognized by the Environmental Protection Agency, *you know*, Audubon, and the chamber's natural resources committee, *you know*, when they have their annual meeting."

My internal response when I encounter someone saying "you know" too many times is the urge to respond rather curtly, "Yes! I do know. So why are you telling me this?"

A similar but equally annoying variation that you hear more and more often is the phrase "kind of."

She was "*kind of*" a graphic artist and web designer who "*kind of*" knew how to put together a website that "*kind of*" gave you a clear presentation of what the company "*kind of*" offered. You wonder, was she or wasn't she a professional

Imagine a Bucket of Nails

Early in my business career I joined the Miracle Mile Toastmasters International Club to give me a weekly audience to practice my presentations, and I wholeheartedly recommend you check out your local club, also. One of the responsibilities that we took turns doing at every meeting was being the "Err-Uh" counter.

Whenever a speaker uttered an "err" or an "uh" while delivering the message or even in the more informal table topics, a nail was noisily tossed into a bucket, making a distinctive and somewhat embarrassing sound. Worse, the job of the err-ah counter was to keep track of your violations of the rule not to say "err" or "uh." At the end of the meeting, a "prize" went to the winner—or loser—of the err-ah contest. The technique definitely helped me and I saw it make a big difference in many other members, too. Other clubs have different practices but seek the same result.

Inspiration

webmaster? Did she or didn't she do good work? You might not find this kind of referral too helpful.

Other verbal fillers are opening phrases such as "So…," and sentence-enders such as "and stuff like that."

Most of these unbidden sounds and unconsciously used phrases will disappear with sufficient rehearsals and a conscious effort to get rid of them.

One of the simplest techniques for banishing verbal fillers is to close your mouth at the end of every sentence. Try saying "err," "uh," or "um" with your mouth shut. You can't!

It also helps to imagine if you kept it open that a fly or mosquito could force its way inside.

When you emit these verbal fillers, you unwittingly signal to your audience your nervousness or lack of preparation.

Ideal Speaker Posture

The knee bone connected to the thigh bone, the thigh bone connected to the hip bone, the hip bone connected to the back bone, the back bone connected to the shoulder bone, the shoulder bone connected to the neck bone, the neck bone connected to the head bone, them bones got up and they walked around.

From the song, Dem Bones or Dry Bones, an African-American spiritual.

A lectern, with a proper stance, can make you appear in total control, relaxed, and an expert.

Podium versus Lectern—A Rose by Any Other Name

When speakers stand on a raised surface—like a stage or a platform—the technical name for it is a *podium*. The term comes from the Greek word *pothi*, which means foot. It's the same source as the word "podiatrist" or foot doctor.

Where speakers can *put their notes*—on a slanted, raised stand often with a microphone attached—is a *lectern*. The word lectern is derived from the Latin word *lectus*, meaning "to read," the same as the word "lecture."

Many people refer to the podium when they mean the lectern. It's only a problem when you, as the speaker, try to make plans for your presentation. Be sure to clarify that you need a place for your notes—a *lectern*—or you may simply wind up with an empty stage.

In this book I will use the terms correctly. When you call the lectern and the podium by the right names, too, you'll sound more professional and come across as a true genius speaker.

> **Definition**

When you need to stand before an audience, the bones in your body suddenly become important. Let's start at the bottom and work your way up. We'll assume for now that you're standing at a lectern.

- Plant your feet about shoulder length apart, about one foot from the lectern. If your feet are too close together, you'll wind up rocking forward and backward. If they are too far apart, your behind will start swaying.

- Gently pull your shoulders back into an erect but not stuffy posture. Breathe.

- Adjust the microphone so that it is pointing at your vocal chords in the middle of your throat, not close to your mouth.

- Place both hands on the lectern, palms down, without gripping or touching any of the sides. Both hands need to be free to move about without any restriction.

- Lift your head up and look out at your audience, making sure you can comfortably sweep the room with your eyes.

To me, the most miserably designed lecterns are the clear plastic ones. They may be modern and sleek in appearance, but everything is exposed. Your notes, your glass of water, your watch to keep track of time, and everything below your waist, are visible, too.

Keep that *Dry Bones* song in mind when you speak at one of these clear lecterns.

Your good posture along with control over your hands, movements, and everything else is especially critical!

Your Eye Contact Says It All (Or a Big Chunk, Anyway)

The process of looking around the room of people you are addressing is known as eye contact. The best eye contact occurs when you actually connect by looking directly at a person or a set of individuals, as you would do in an ordinary conversation.

If you're a bit timid about direct eye contact as a novice speaker, you can temporarily fake it by looking a foot or two over the heads of the individuals seated in front of you, roaming your eyes from left to right to encompass everyone. You'll give the illusion of eye contact.

As you gain confidence, you'll be able to drop your eyes down and actually see the audience engage with you. Avoid looking at someone who is yawning, on their cell phone, or otherwise not engaged in your remarks because their apparent disinterest can bring you down psychologically. You will find true eye contact an important and often gratifying experience that leads to applause, agreement, and good questions at the end of your presentation.

I find that making a clock-wise motion with my eyes, around the room, helps me be sure that I've appeared to look at everyone. It's sometimes easier for left-handed people to make a counter clock-wise motion.

No Lectern? No Problem!

What you see, more and more, are speakers, leaders, and entertainers appearing in front of groups without lecterns. If you've ever watched the popular TED talks on the Internet, you'll notice that a microphone is never visible. In all of these cases, the presenters are wearing wireless microphones, attached

The founder of Toastmasters International, an organization devoted to developing public speaking and leadership skills, Dr. Ralph C. Smeadley, wrote this:

The speaker who stands and talks at ease is the one who can be heard without weariness. If his posture and gestures are so graceful and unobtrusive, that no one notices them, he may be counted as truly successful.

Quote

to their clothes, for greater ease in roaming around the stage or in the meeting room itself, and to better engage their audiences.

My friend, author, speaker, and performance coach Achim Nowak, CEO of Influens, Inc., works with the highest level executives in Europe, Asia, and the United States. He does not permit his clients to use lecterns at all and never uses one himself.

A few caveats for the no-lectern presentation are in order.

- 🔍 You really need to know your presentation cold, because there's no place to put any notes.

- 🔍 If you're using PowerPoint or any other image program, and you need to advance the visuals, try out the remote ahead of time to avoid any embarrassment. After all, without a lectern, you're the only thing the audience has in its range of vision.

- 🔍 Your posture and gestures become even more significant because your entire body is now exposed to the audience, not just from the waist up. Avoid sticking your hands in your pockets or placing them behind you. Do use them to help illustrate your points and reach out to the audience.

- 🔍 You may have been able to get away with jeans on the bottom and a jacket on top

To Lectern or Not to Lectern

Some professional speakers, corporate leaders, and many technology execs I know refuse to use lecterns, citing the distance erected artificially between them and their audiences. Instead, they insist on wireless microphones and remotes so that they can freely walk around the stage or boardroom.

I say it depends on your role and what's customary in your community and your industry. While I believe in breaking outdated rules when appropriate, a lectern with a microphone is still commonplace in many public settings such as city hall, sanctuaries of religious buildings, and school auditoriums.

If you are relying on paper notes or a tablet with software as a teleprompter, a lectern remains a convenient and unobtrusive way to hide your support accessories.

Perspiration

with the lectern. Be certain that kind of casual attire will fly in front of the group you're addressing.

🖑 Walk the talk but don't overwalk. By that, I mean do move around the stage, but avoid pacing back and forth, which can be distracting.

Speaking When Seated

President Franklin Delano Roosevelt once advised his son about public speaking: "Be sincere. Be brief. Be seated."

While I agree that the advice is good and timeless, if you find yourself having to do public speaking while seated, you risk coming across as less powerful, less dynamic, and less impressive than if you were standing up. Why? When you sit down, your energy level can go down, too, leaving you to appear as a watered down version of your true self.

What are some of the seated speaking situations in which you may find yourself?

🖑 In a classic panel discussion setup, with regular straight-backed chairs located behind a table and microphones placed before each speaker, or shared.

🖑 A living room style layout where you are expected to speak while sitting in a comfy, deep chair or sofa.

🖑 The board room or a conference room with plush, high-backed chairs that roll.

🖑 A one-on-one or small group conversation in an office, around a desk.

One big and tempting distraction is the chair itself. You may find yourself on a chair that's too hard or narrow, and you just can't seem to get comfortable. On the other hand, if it's way too comfortable, you can sink in and abandon all pretense of professionalism, looking ultra-relaxed but not an energetic contributor or expert. Alas, your voice strength will also suffer because you're not physically able to project from this sunken sitting position either.

But you can turn your seated speaking into the same kind of success story as the standing variation of you. Here are some tactics to help you:

Foundation for Your Feet and Bottom

When you're standing up, both feet need to be firmly on the floor and shoulder length distance apart, as I mentioned earlier. The same holds true for when you're seated. But there's more! Located under the flesh of the bottom (butt, derriere, tush, etc.) that you sit on are bones known as the sit-bones, or sitz-bones. Allow yourself to experiment in your chair until you can feel the sit-bones gaining traction, so to speak.

To acquire the kind of posture that leads to a powerful presence when sitting, you want to let your sit-bones rest flat on the bottom-forward part of the chair. When you do, you'll find yourself naturally sitting up erectly, literally unable to slouch in the chair. You won't look stiff, just in control. A good thing, yes?

The Right Breathing

You can have access to the same necessary breathing when you are seated as when you're standing, if you don't inadvertently shut off the air supply because of poor posture. Falling back onto your tailbone—instead of staying on your sit-bones—interrupts your in-breath air flow. Keeping your body relaxed and aligned allows you to breathe deeply, even when you are seated.

Voice-Quality Control

To cultivate the full, rich sound vibrations you want for your voice in speaking, known as the resonance, your body needs to be grounded, relaxed, and open. The right position, standing or sitting, helps to assure that your breathing is deep and strong. Sit too far back in your seat, however, and you can interfere with those vibrations. One instructor I had used the analogy of a bell laying on its side. It can't easily transmit sound properly. But when you stand the bell up—as you do for yourself when you're on your sit-bones—the sound can freely transmit. So, too, will the vibrations from your body. Your speaking voice will have the type of effect you intended.

A caveat is that nobody wants to appear overeager when everyone else looks laid-back and relaxed in their chairs, legs crossed, casual. At the same time, I believe you owe it to yourself and your audience to take control of your chair the same way you would a stage or lectern. Don't worry about what everyone else is doing when it's your turn, whether you're in a panel discussion or talking with your board of directors. Own the chair! Sit up straight, on your sit-bones, bring yourself up to full height, remember to breathe and use your entire body to speak. Your reward? You'll come across as a strong, confident, well-spoken expert.

Making Gestures for Impact

Bobblehead dolls of the *America's Home Video* host Tom Bergenson have been the gift prizes awarded to some of the show's winning contestants. These winners were able to correctly match certain funny sounds with a particular video.

In some of the Progressive Insurance Company's commercials, a bobblehead doll of Flo, the popular dark-haired character, appears on a car dashboard.

What makes a bobblehead funny and appealing in an odd way? I think it's because only the head bobs, propelled by a spring-like extension.

A bobblehead is not a good model for speakers. So as not to be mistaken for a mere bobblehead, you want your entire body to participate in your presentation—most especially, your hands.

Gestures are those motions you make with your hands, on purpose:

- to reinforce points

- to appear to reach out to your audience

- to create the impression of a certain movement, like climbing, throwing, rowing, or getting dressed, among others

- to count in the air

- to hug yourself

- to extend shrugged shoulders

A good speaker intersperses words with gestures in strategic places in the message—and practices them in front of a mirror or on video to be sure they work.

What's Not a Good Gesture?

- *Pointing your finger.* I don't recommend ever pointing your finger at anyone, in an audience or up close. Your mother was, of course, right on that admonition. When you point, you put everyone on edge. Instead, wave an entire hand in the direction of the area or person you're trying to bring into your sphere of attention.

🖋 *Wagging the middle finger, even in jest.* You never know if someone is videotaping or photographing your presentation and you could be caught totally out of context. Express your displeasure some other more neutral way.

🖋 *Not checking out local norms.* In some cultures, the use of hands or fingers in a particular way can cause great offense. Get guidance before you ruin the day.

The Infamous Fig Leaf Position

Ever since we were little boys and little girls, we've been standing in a position that seems comfortable and natural. Our fingers are nestled together. Our hands are holding each other, leaning gently against our thighs, covering our privates.

It's called, aptly, the fig leaf position and the stance is not recommended for speakers over five or six years of age.

Instead, take those clasped hands and move them up to waist height. Immediately, you'll look more in control, less vulnerable and child-like. For some people, this clasped hand motion gives early speech confidence and acts as a home position, to return to periodically. As with any gesture, you don't want to overuse it or lock yourself into a particular motion. Such activity can become annoying or distracting for the audience.

Make the Microphone Your Friend

If you're a singer like my favorites, Gloria Estefan, Barbra Streisand, and Jodi Rozental, interaction with the microphone can appear to be sensual. For the magic of their music to work, the singers need to be up close and personal with this amplifying technology, mouths appearing to almost kiss the microphone.

Since I love music but cannot carry a tune, that kind of intimacy is not a part of my world. However, I do believe that speakers need to develop a comfortable relationship with the microphone to present themselves and their messages in the optimal light.

Microphones come in different sizes and shapes. By arriving at least an hour early for your speaking engagement, you'll have time to meet and try out yours.

Lavalier or wireless microphones have different ways of being attached. From my experience, attaching a wireless microphone is simple and seamless when you wear a jacket and pants or a skirt with a waistband.

On the other hand, I have found that they are not always designed well for women's clothes. Instead of being hands-free, on several occasions I've had to hold the amplifier unit of a wireless microphone because I could not anchor it on the dress I'd chosen to wear to the conference.

The control unit had a clasp that easily attached to a belt or pants; since I was wearing neither, and there was no alternative available, I was out of luck.

If you find yourself in a similarly awkward position, my advice is to put on your best face and act as if everything is just fine. They won't pay attention to the fact that you're holding onto a microphone instead of having it attached to you unless you point it out.

Whether you're using a wireless or a fixed microphone, I strongly recommend that you make your new best friends the audiovisual technicians where you're speaking. It's their job to make sure everything is working well so you can focus on your message and not the technology. I try to learn their names during the prespeaking test of the equipment, so if something goes wrong, I know who to ask for help.

Lectern microphones and floor microphones can be moved up or down

---

The Two Most Common Microphones

You're going to find yourself using two kinds of microphones in most of your public speaking situations:

◆ The lavalier (*lava-leer*) microphone attaches to your clothing, typically a lapel. The wire connecting the microphone to the small amplifying unit is usually hidden inside your jacket. The unit itself is attached to your pants or belt. These mikes are also called self-attached or wireless because they don't rely on wires to connect directly to the audiovisual system.

◆ The traditional microphone is generally larger than the lavalier. When speaking, you either hold it in your hand or use it in a fixed location on a lectern or a stand. The handheld versions can have a wire attached or be wireless.

A microphone can become your best friend or your worst enemy. As a friend, it helps you project your words in a crisp, clear way. When malfunctioning or not working, it disconnects you from your audience.

Definition

to adjust to your height. Ideally, the microphone does not cover your face or mouth, and is optimally located below your chin, picking up the sound from the vocal chords.

I encourage you to have a decent meal before your speaking engagement so you won't try to "eat" the microphone! By that, I mean, do not stand too close to the microphone so that your mouth is right on it. You'll risk sounding too loud, fuzzy, and even cause unpleasant sound effects you really don't want.

Regardless of which kind of microphone, here are a few additional pointers:

🖋 Make sure it's on before you start talking! Test the microphone by asking if everyone can hear you before you actually begin your message. Don't wait to find out something isn't working! Even though the mike may be working at the start, it may not *continue* to work! That happened to me at a national conference where I was speaking. After five minutes of frustrating off-and-on sound, the technician realized the microphone was defective and went to get me another, more functional, unit.

🖋 Vary your vocal variety and loudness, but avoid yelling. It's not only likely to offend people in your audience, you may also stimulate unwanted feedback from the acoustical equipment.

🖋 If you move to a certain position and begin to hear screeching or some other unpleasant sound, note the location and move back to where you were previously. Avoid moving in that direction again!

I spoke at a conference in Orlando and discovered that moving in front of a floor speaker resulted in a horrific screech. When I interacted with the audience, I had to keep myself on the right-hand side of the room and not move around the entire audience as I would have preferred.

🖋 Aim your voice so it reaches the top surface of the microphone whenever possible. You'll get the best voice quality that way.

If you do enough speaking, you might want to invest in your own portable microphone system. The technologies keep evolving, so check out what's best in the online audiovisual stores and with the a/v technicians you encounter in top-drawer hotels. They're usually on top of these developments.

To Summarize...

🖋 You can prevent annoying verbal fillers from creeping into your talk by becoming aware of how they disrupt your good intentions.

🖋 How you stand or sit, and the ways you incorporate your hands into your presentation, contribute to making the impression you want.

🖋 Taking control of your hands and other body parts gives you peace of mind and helps you connect in a professional manner with your audience.

🖋 Once you get comfortable with microphones, they can make your speaking life more rewarding and enjoyable.

Chapter 17

Practice like a Genius without Getting Bored or Frustrated

In This Chapter...

- The shower is not just for singing (and other tips)
- Take the message apart, in pieces, and change the order
- Don't be afraid to cut or modify—but not too much!
- Schedule at least one "off-Broadway" rehearsal

Every so often I meet a businessperson or a candidate for office who seems stunned to learn that being a good speaker requires a ton of practice. The executive invariably confides, "I don't need to practice. I know what I'm talking about." And the candidate shares, "I just speak from the heart and it's usually enough."

Just as outstanding dancers, musicians, athletes, and actors practice for hours and even years to perfect their performance, I have found that speakers and leaders who are serious about making a difference with their words do the same. In this chapter, you'll find techniques to help you rehearse without driving yourself or others crazy in the process. You'll discover that one bonus of being a speaker—as opposed to a performer who is part of an ensemble—is that you are free to change the words, order, and pace of your message as you perfect it. Once you've thoroughly prepared, finding a local audience for the equivalent of a dress rehearsal before your big day, helps assure you'll be the hit you want to be.

In the Shower and Other Places—Just Do It!

"Practice does not make perfect, perfect practice makes perfect."—Vince Lombardi, American football coach

"You can't hire someone to practice for you."—H. Jackson Brown Jr., author of *Life's Little Instruction Book*, and many others

Although I cannot carry a tune, when I sing in the shower I seem to sound much better to myself than outside. I recommend the shower for early-stage practice of a speech or presentation because it's just you, the falling water, and the nonjudgmental walls of your bathroom.

Another good place to practice, especially at the beginning, is when you're driving in the car. Anyone passing you on the road will think you're engaged in a cell phone conversation. With windows up and no passengers, you have a similar safe, noncritical environment as your shower.

Some people I know have snuck into empty churches or synagogues on weekdays, vacant conference rooms or auditoriums, and other similar spots to rehearse. You really don't have to sneak into those places. If you call and ask about being allowed to practice in nonpeak times, most locales are glad to give you the space with no hassle.

I did this with a client who was giving his first-ever speech to an audience of more than one thousand people in his home country of Colombia. He had attended the University of Miami so I called a contact there and got permission to use an empty auditorium, during the week, to rehearse. It was a big space and I stood near the back so he could imagine having to speak to the back of the room, as well as to the front.

A week later, my client's speech was televised and live-streamed on the Internet. He wound up getting a standing ovation, so I can tell you that serious practice does pay off big time!

The cameras in your computer, your tablet, and smartphone can become instant allies, too. Turn the camera on yourself (or ask a friend) and practice!

Video remains a powerful prespeaking way to see what's working and what isn't, giving you time to fix content and adjust your physical presence as well.

🖋 Don't overlook that full-length mirror or even a smaller one, either. You may feel a bit awkward looking at yourself but it's another proven method for detecting ungainly stances or behaviors you might want to eliminate.

🖋 Have a dog? On your morning walk, pretend you're talking to your dog as you recite parts of your message aloud. Who's going to know—or care—what you're really saying?

🖋 Do you have a walking, exercise, or jogging buddy? Try out bits and pieces of your presentation as you go through your routines together.

Often the hardest part of practicing is making ourselves take those first steps to do it. Once you make a commitment to rehearsing and experience the stress-relieving benefits it brings, however, you'll find yourself more consistently setting aside rehearsal time.

Take the Message Apart, in Pieces

Whether your remarks are just a few minutes or an hour, trying to practice the entire message at one time can doom you to failure. Instead, I recommend learning to deliver it in chunks, in a similar way to how you developed the content.

Let's revisit the basic four elements of a speech (from **Chapter 10**):

🖋 Opening   🖋 Body

🖋 Prebody   🖋 Close

Whether you choose to practice using an electronic device like your smartphone, a tablet, your computer, or on paper, there are a few steps I recommend to put yourself on the most optimal practice track.

🖋 Take your written speech or presentation apart and put the elements above into separate documents or at least on separate pages.

🖋 Depending on the number of main points in the body, you may have one, two, or three components to list and practice along with their associated subpoints.

🔋 If you have not already done so, rewrite your content for each segment into a series of bullet points to make your practicing easier and more efficient.

🔋 Write out the opening, transition lines from one segment to the next, any specific research points or complex data, and your call for action. These more detailed cheat sheets are temporary crutches that can help you as you gain traction in mastering your material.

A benefit of breaking your message into pieces to rehearse is that it's much easier to detect any awkwardness, boring segments, or areas that need more data or a story to keep them engaging.

Plus, I find learning a few lines at a time much more feasible for a speaker than trying to master the whole talk at once. When you know your message in pieces, out of order, any unexpected interruption will not throw you off as much, because you're not so dependent on the linear flow of your content.

Practice to Make Your Opening Gracious and Sizzling

For a quick review of the six opening techniques, see **Chapter 11.** To get off on the right foot, practicing the three key elements of your opening can assure you of a strong start.

1. *Thank-you to your introducer—or introducing yourself.* If you're being introduced, try to find out in advance the name of the person assigned to you and ask how to pronounce the person's name and any title that might be appropriate, such as Doctor, Dean, General, and so forth. If it's customary to acknowledge the name of the organization you're addressing, reconfirm that you have it correctly, and practice so you don't stumble.

   If no one is introducing you, practice telling the group your name, your position, and something else briefly about you that is relevant to your presentation and purpose for being the speaker. It's more difficult than it seems to talk about ourselves in a purposeful manner! Failing to practice this section can cause you to go on too long or to forget to include information that will help the audience understand your background and expertise, and help them willingly pay more attention to you and your message.

2. *Optional gracious throwaway line.* If you choose to use a gracious throwaway line, remember its purpose is to help you, the speaker, gain

control of your nerves and also, give the audience a little more time to settle down into a listening mode before your amazing opening.

Your line can be as simple as, "It's so great to be with you all today in the great city of x." Other variations include: "Wasn't that dinner/lunch/recital/performance absolutely terrific?" You could be a cheerleader for the local team: "How 'bout those ABC's?"

Practice saying your line aloud. Ask yourself: "Is it too long? Do I think it's engaging? Do I appear to be in the moment? Does it seem forced?" Remember, it is optional; you don't have to incorporate these words unless they work for you.

Whatever you decide, treat the line with same importance as any other part of your message, especially because it's one of the first things your audience will hear you say. You want it to hit a home run, right?

3. *Your opening words.* Having crafted one of the six recommended openings (see **Chapter 11**), your practice needs to focus on the pace, volume, enthusiasm, pauses, and other elements of a professional delivery. You don't want to race through it nor drag the words along too slowly. It's better to project a louder voice than a softer one, especially at the start, to reinforce the tone of authority versus a submissive tonality. Strategic, planned pauses contribute to grabbing and controlling attention.

Keep Changing the Order of How You Rehearse

I usually recommend that you rehearse the close or ending first, practicing your energizing summary, followed by your call for action or quotation. Why? If the spoken version is falling flat, or too hard for you to say, modifying the concluding text early on can prevent more serious problems later.

After that, anything goes, as long as you tackle one specific piece at a time. Try main point two and then the opening. Practice the prebody and follow it up with point three.

Depending on how long your message is, you may have anecdotes or facts associated with your subpoints. It's okay to mix up the order of these subpoints as well while you are practicing, especially in the early phase of your rehearsal. Why? Your goal is to identify what's working and what could be better, as soon as possible.

To keep things fresh and avoid becoming bored with your own material, do change up the order of the segments every time you practice. That doesn't mean you change the content itself, just the positioning for the rehearsal.

Clues That Your Words Might Not Be Working

As you practice, listen to your voice and be aware of your own energy level. Are there certain points where you feel on top of everything, and others where you seem to sag?

When you're practicing out of order, as I've recommended, you can more easily identify those phrases that seemed fine on paper but are not coming out of your mouth as you expected them to do!

Sometimes the word choice itself is the culprit and in other instances your pacing can be throwing you off.

For example, "indubitably" is a delicious word and it means without a doubt, but many folks can't pronounce it properly without sounding a bit stuffy. Saying "without a doubt," instead, will keep your message more conversational.

Speaking too fast, which many of us do when we're nervous, can force us to trip over words that we would normally find easy to articulate. If you slow yourself down and still find a particular set of words not coming out of your mouth properly, it's a clue that you probably need a bit of editing.

In other instances, some sections of your speech may literally suck the air out of you. You can feel your energy vanish. Quickly identify those draining portions and rewrite them in language that you can say with your full personality behind it. If you're stuck finding the right words, reach out to a friend or colleague for help. Don't continue to practice what you know is not working!

Don't Be Afraid to Cut or Modify—But Not Too Much!

Recording yourself as you practice can reveal where you've nailed the presentation and where you still need to work at it. You may want to adjust the text, simplify the language, or completely change the content, if repeated rehearsals still produce a less than stellar performance in a particular part.

You can also obtain an accurate reflection of how long your message really is by writing down how long each recorded piece takes, and tallying up the results. Most smartphones have a timer. If you need to trim, you will readily see where you can cut a few minutes or more, to make your talk fit the allotted time you have been given.

Be sure and practice using your visuals because you need to know how much time they will take up when they are incorporated into your presentation.

When you do the final run-throughs, make sure you have remained in the time frame that is expected of you. No one appreciates a speaker who runs longer than expected, as it usually throws an entire agenda off track. You don't want to be the cause of that!

What to Keep? What to Cut?

Here's what Alejandro Espinal, CEO of AF International (*afiexpress.com*) whose company provides competitive business development around the world, told me he does when faced with having to tighten his planned presentation:

I always include examples that connect the audience with the topic I am presenting and those stay in, as a priority. They need to be real and enjoyable stories and examples that relate to the audience and get its attention.

What I wind up leaving out are the technical information and charts that people have to process in order to understand the content of the presentation. They can be given this data as a handout or it can be sent to them after the meeting.

Perspiration

What is too much self-editing and what can you do about it? You'll know you've crossed over the line into self-doubt and self-punishing when you begin to think nothing is good, that nothing is working. You may be right, alas.

One way to find out is to ask a close, honest friend or colleague to listen to your best shot, without indicating the parts you have doubted. Presenting the message in its entirety to someone who has not heard you tackle the pieces may be a wonderfully redeeming experience. You may realize that, after all, your speech is sound and nearly ready to present.

On the other hand, you may be told which parts are not working, and get the help you need to fix them.

One of my favorite speakers is Rabbi Edwin Goldberg of Temple Sholom of Chicago who for seventeen years served Temple Judea in Miami. He's also the author of numerous books including his most recent: *Saying No and Letting Go: Jewish Wisdom on Making Room for What Matters Most.*

Here's how Rabbi Goldberg looks at the challenge of winnowing down content for a speech:

> *Taking a cue from my latest book, I like to remember when I speak to include only what is most essential. If you cannot say in one sentence what you are saying, then there is something wrong. I call this big idea a 'pearl' and it is a key component of judging in advance whether or not the sermon will work.*
>
> *The art of speaking is really about saying something pretty common in a new way. So I don't pretend to come up with a new idea. Instead I find a relevant idea and then make it interesting.*

Allison Maslan is CEO of Allison Maslan International, a global business mentoring company. Her company teaches business owners how to successfully structure their business so they can multiply their revenue, attract customers, and create more free time in their lives.

Here's what Allison said about the challenge of choosing the right content for your time frame:

> *Speaking is one of my favorite ways to teach and inspire entrepreneurs on how to strategically grow their businesses. I love connecting with the audience members and making sure they leave with an elevated perspective as a business owner, and result-oriented practices they can put into action right away. That said, if I am presenting a keynote or a workshop, I always consider which content is going to give the attendee the highest impact in the shortest amount of time. I ask myself: 'What is the best value I can offer the audience in a clear, concise, and exciting manner, and make sure that I stay in the required time constraints?'*
>
> *If I am given a limited amount of time, then I literally go through my entire talk and pull out the crucial components that they must have to understand my success process.*
>
> *For instance, if I am teaching the Secrets of Millionaire Business Owners, I start with eight characteristics that I explain deeply, using stories to illustrate my points, and then I narrow them down to four or five. I am still happy with the shorter presentation because even one new shift can be transformational for their lives.*

Michelle Villalobos is a personal branding and small business strategist, speaker, and founder of Mivista Consulting, Inc. She stages popular branding events for entrepreneurs and speakers.

> *I've learned that in a short period of time (say, anything under fifteen minutes), I can deliver just one outstanding 'A-ha!' moment. So everything I say and do around that one takeaway is meant to create emotion and engagement to ensure the audience really gets it, remembers it, and applies it. My favorite ways of doing that are 1) repetition, 2) story, and 3) drama.*
>
> *Last week I was asked to do an impromptu five-minute presentation to an audience of teenage aspiring entrepreneurs. So I started with a brainstorm of everything I thought this audience in particular needed to know—from identifying their strengths and surrounding themselves with winners, to finding their purpose and investing in personal development—plus about nineteen more items. Then I went back and grouped together items and combined them into themes, like 'mindset,' 'people,' 'vision,' 'investing in personal development,' 'personal branding,' etc. With that pared-down list, I circled the ones that I really thought would resonate, ruthlessly crossed out the rest, and looked for ONE theme that could tie them together—which turned out to be personal branding (one of my favorite topics). So, stressing the importance of them focusing on THEIR brand rather than their business brands became the crux of the presentation.*

Do Not versus Do Tips When Practicing

Do not allow yourself to use any distracting, nervous habits like playing with a ring or necklace, continually tucking hair behind your ear, clicking a pen open and closed, or any similar mannerisms.

Do remove any jewelry you might be tempted to play with, take away any pens, and tie your hair out of reach.

Do not put your hands in your pockets or keep them crossed while you're standing. You limit your ability to use gestures this way and can also send the wrong signals to your audience.

Do stand tall, about a foot back from the lectern and deliberately incorporate gestures at key places in your talk as you practice.

Do not hold onto your notes while you practice. You won't be able to use your hands to make gestures.

Do simulate the lectern where you'll be presenting by finding something where you can position your speaking outline, such as a high counter, phone books piled onto a table, or a music stand. If there won't be a lectern, you won't be able to use written notes; instead, your visuals will be your guide.

Do not practice by looking behind you at the projected visuals, because you won't want to do this during your actual presentation. It's distracting and makes you look uncertain about what's coming next.

Do set up your practice so you can see the images on a monitor in front of you to use as a prompt while you're speaking.

Do not say "I'm sorry" aloud or apologize while you are practicing (or during your talk). Nobody except you knows what you were supposed to say!

Do simply correct whatever mistake you made and keep going!

Do not practice in a totally quiet vacuum because real public speaking life is never that way.

Do turn on the TV for background noise, let the phone ring, permit the dog to roam as normal, and otherwise allow for some normal, minor distractions, so you can practice staying focused regardless of what else may be happening.

Do not put on any old thing in your final practice.

Do wear whatever outfit you planned for your actual presentation at least once to be sure the shoes and clothing are comfortable and fit well.

Schedule Your "Off-Broadway" Rehearsal

There's an old show business adage that says something like this:

"Bad dress rehearsal, great show."

It suggests that despite a poor performance at what is called the dress rehearsal—the final, fully staged practice before a theatrical production's debut—the actual show can be terrific anyway. Most show business professionals will tell you that a bad dress rehearsal is a nightmare, albeit a better time for things to go wrong than at the opening night.

I highly endorse the idea of having a dress rehearsal for speakers, and I call this kind of practice your "off-Broadway" performance. You address an audience that is not your ultimate target, but one that still expects a certain level of professionalism from you.

Where Can You Give Your Off-Off-Off Broadway Trial?

You often find startups seeking investors, and even those more established companies trying to secure investments, doing mock pitches at universities, conferences, incubators, and in other protected settings to get feedback that can help them improve their ultimate presentation. These off-Broadway performances can be in person, online, or by video.

Perspiration

Making Yourself a Local Speaking Star

Regardless of where your off-Broadway pursuits take you, here's what you need to secure the engagement.

◆ Identify who books the programs and how far in advance they're scheduled. Ask how long their typical talks are, the format, day of the week, and time.

◆ Come up with a catchy title for your talk and some bullet points of description that can be used to help promote your message and you. Prepare a one-sheet description with a photo that you can email that can be used in their publicity.

◆ Let them know about your audiovisual requirements, if any, i.e., a screen, projector, microphone, lectern, room layout. Offer to provide a door prize or two.

◆ Write up a summary of your remarks that can be put into their newsletter afterward for additional exposure.

◆ Be outstanding so they'll recommend you to their friends, too. Ask for testimonials you can post to your social media or website, if you're a coach, consultant, or sales rep.

I encourage you, whenever possible, to go to the room where you will give your presentation to get a first-hand sense of the setup. Try to prearrange a full out practice in front of a friend or friends without stopping, performing the same way you'll need to do on speech day.

If you're in a community fortunate to have at least one or multiple Rotary Clubs and other similar service organizations, you're lucky for many reasons. Not only do these groups work diligently to make their communities healthier, better educated, and safer, they give you as a speaker the chance to become part of the Rotary circuit. Seek out the local program chairperson and offer a noncommercial version of your message.

Early in my business, the South Miami Rotary Club where my husband belonged invited me to speak. I confess to being a bit more nervous than normal because, after all, these were his friends! My topic was public speaking and while the group was friendly and attentive, there was no hesitation from the members to jump in, ask questions, and make comments along the way. While the sense of family and friendship in the club, not found normally in other speaking situations, made the engagement especially fun, it was also quite challenging to stay on track with all the questions and kidding around. I did answer every question and finished with a truly warm round of applause.

Surviving the experience added to my own confidence and it also resulted in speaking to other clubs in our region, eventually leading to consulting assignments with a few of their members.

You can bring your expertise to local classrooms, at the college level, and in high school, depending on your topic and background. I've been a guest speaker in marketing and journalism classes, at after-school programs for disadvantaged girls, and for many nonprofits. Whether you do this type of speaking for your own practice purposes, as a way of giving back, or to expand your relationships in the community for your career or business, everybody wins.

Remember, neither Rotary nor any of the other community organizations wants to be pitched for your product or service, but they will welcome your speech on industry trends, tips to avoid problems in business, health, raising kids, and dozens of other topics. Most of these clubs meet weekly or monthly, and they have a healthy appetite for speakers on all kinds of topics throughout the year. Plan to talk for twelve-fifteen minutes to give yourself time for questions and answers. These off-Broadway, or off-off-off-off-Broadway talks, as I sometimes call them, give you a chance to try your wings.

The range of good work that Rotary and other service organizations undertake is especially important in a world where volunteerism is dwindling. They also provide a hands-on leadership training environment, with programs for officers, board members, and anyone else who wants to expand their leadership capabilities. (For more information on Rotary go to *rotary.org*.)

No Rotary Club where you are? No problem. Your off-Broadway practices can be local schools, churches, synagogues, before a classroom, at a public library, a community center, parent-teachers association, or any other place where people gather together to learn, have fun, or support a cause.

To Summarize...

✎ Practice aloud anywhere you can, as often as possible, to give yourself the best chance of being a hit.

✎ To avoid getting bored and to improve your spoken message, rehearse in pieces, out of order.

✎ Good writing is rewriting, just don't get stuck in revisions.

✎ Find an "off-Broadway" location to try out your speech or presentation before the big day.

mipan @ 123RF.com

Disaster Preparedness: Planning for the Unexpected

Nobody anticipates a power outage, a button popping off, birds pooping from the sky, or a verbal attack in the midst of public speaking, but these unexpected happenings, and more, can interrupt your best-laid plans. As a leader, you can also find yourself being asked to do what is called ceremonial speaking, helping to showcase others, making introductions or presenting awards, and being asked to toast the bride and groom, a colleague, or visiting dignitary. You can even become the recipient of recognition as well.

In this final part of *Public Speaking for the GENIUS*, I'll help you think about and be prepared for the kinds of scenarios that produce both nightmares and dreams.

Chapter 18

What Separates Geniuses from Losers on Stage?

In This Chapter...

- Mental readiness strategies to reduce speaking trauma
- Prespeaking rituals to help stave off disasters
- Creating your own speaker's emergency kit

On stage, the truly self-centered are the ones who cause everyone to lose. They make those of us in the room to feel uncomfortable, tense, and awkward when things go south. Losers give in to their emotions and fail to plan for both the expected and unexpected that occur in public speaking. In contrast, the geniuses not only practice intensely to earn their applause, they insist on learning how to overcome—and even prevent—any obstacles that could interfere with their success.

The unexpected in speaking can be caused by many factors: a personal upset, something happening or not happening in the environment, a verbal challenge from audience members, and when technology doesn't work the way you planned.

In this chapter, I'll guide you through some of the steps you can take to prepare psychologically and physically *before* you speak so you can always do your best, no matter what you encounter during your presentation. Just as winning athletes and top performing artists have preperformance routines, you'll want to develop your own, too. You'll be glad you did!

Mental Readiness for Out-of-Your-Control Events

I don't think anyone would ever describe me as serene. Not calm, cool, and collected, either, most of the time. I can be upbeat and funny, but also highly disorganized in certain areas of my life and constantly find myself struggling to be on time. My mother was frequently annoyed with me before school. I recall her saying, exasperated: "The school bus comes the same time every day! Why are you always late?" While I do love order, I find it a challenge to put things back where they belong on a consistent basis, recognizing the effort as necessary and admirable, if tedious.

However, when it's my responsibility to serve as a leader, running a meeting for an organization to which I belong, or presenting a workshop or speech, I know that my behavior is critical. I have an obligation to be ultra-ready, ignore what I may be feeling at the moment, and focus on the interest and well-being of my audience. I believe that anyone who accepts the mantle of leadership or who finds themselves committed to speaking in public shares the same obligation.

In all the years we worked together, I never saw my husband and partner, Eddie, go into an important presentation flustered. He always carried himself forward with what he called a "positive mental attitude." After serving in Vietnam and living six years in Puerto Rico, he landed in Miami working for what was then called Combined Insurance Company of America (now AON). Founded in Chicago by W. Clement Stone, author of *Success through a Positive Mental Attitude* and other books of that ilk, Stone's system was designed primarily to motivate sales people to produce, no matter what.

The salespersons' lives were not easy. Every day, all day, they walked into business after business, making presentations, trying to persuade strangers to buy insurance from them. Part of the philosophy and training the agents received was to say aloud: "I feel healthy, I feel happy, I feel terrific!" They were instructed to repeat this phrase fifty times, at four intervals throughout the day. The expectation was this repetition of a positive thought would help salespeople overcome the inevitable rejection of their profession, giving them the inner fortitude to keep on selling.

Now I admit, when I was first married to Eddie and heard him doing this daily in the shower, I thought it was silly and a little weird. As a former journalist, I was cynical and unaccepting. As time passed, however, I realized how ingrained this attitude was in Ed, and how helpful it is to be inclined toward the positive, rather than mired in the negative.

Some people invoke their faith in moments of stress. Others find solace in other ways, ranging from a small glass of an alcoholic beverage to a dish of ice cream to listening to music or a relaxation recording. It's vital to know your limits and how you'll react with alcohol or any other drug you may take for nerves, or you could wind up embarrassing yourself, your organization, and the group that invited you to speak.

I do believe it's critical to your success as a speaker to identify an antistress technique that works for you. Having this ally allows you to present your most positive side on demand, regardless of whatever may be going on around you.

Prespeaking Rituals to Help Counteract Nerves and the Unplanned

"We are what we repeatedly do. Excellence is then not an act but a habit."
— Aristotle

To prepare myself for speaking engagements—especially when I'm doing a new presentation for the first time—I engage in a few practices that have helped me over the years.

- In the shower, I put on a lavender-scented body lotion, which seems to calm my nerves. I also dab my wrists with a lavender essential oil afterward, and peppermint oil, which together help take the edge off. There's also a combination of oils that comes in a bottle with a roll top, called Past Tense, which I buy from doTERRA (*doterra.com*). According to research, certain fragrances and oils, strategically applied to our bodies or inhaled, influence our nervous system in positive ways.

- Food is a source of strength and calmness. It's not a good idea to avoid eating before a presentation—even if you don't feel hungry— because your tummy could grumble aloud and embarrass you at the microphone. To have the right energy for my early workshops and speeches, I need a healthy, substantial breakfast with some kind of protein. I've learned not to rely on whatever might be served because just fruit and little rolls aren't enough for me. If you're a coffee addict, try to limit your caffeine because it can make you even more anxious.

🔦 Treating yourself to a delicious massage, a long run or walk, listening to your favorite music, and watching a funny movie are other rituals you can adopt to help you relax before the big performance.

🔦 Mind/body advocates recommend deep breathing exercises, yoga postures, meditation, self-acupressure, and even pressing your index fingers to your thumbs for up to a minute at a time.

🔦 Clients have told me they always wear a certain suit, scarf, or necklace for key engagements, believing they look sharp and ready, and helping them feel that way.

Keep searching until you find and create your own prespeaking rituals.

From Fun to Intense Preparation

Ana Gazarian is an attorney and CEO of Employee Mobility Solutions, which represents companies with employees who need to work in foreign countries, helping them with immigration, housing, education, and other matters. With offices in Argentina, Brazil, Chile, Peru, Spain, Trinidad and Tobago, and in the United States, she frequently speaks on these issues in the United States, Europe, and South America.

I had the privilege of being her first public speaking coach years ago. Her prespeaking rituals range from personal and fun to more serious investigation.

Her tactics?

Some Rituals Are Literally Inside Out

Borrowing from a New Year's Eve tradition in Ecuador, where you put on new yellow underwear representing the color of gold to usher in twelve months of prosperity, I have accumulated a drawer full of yellow and silver-colored panties. The tradition was introduced to our family by a dear friend, Rosa Peralta, when our daughter was a toddler.

For really important speeches or presentations, I don these "prosperity panties," as I call them, to give me confidence literally from the inside out.

Inspiration

"Before the presentation, I enjoy a bit of chocolate or drink a Coke. This gives me energy and helps me relax," she said. She also listens to music. At the event, "I try to maintain my sense of humor, laughing and relaxing with the people because it's always fun to learn something new and get to meet new people."

Before she speaks, Ana also adjusts her presentation style, content, and visuals according to the location, based on her experience with different cultures and expectations:

> *In Brazil, to keep the audience interested, I need to speak louder and have a stronger intonation than in I do in other places. You need to move your hands and body freely to make your points, too.*

In the United States, it depends on the state.

> *If you are in Miami, and the audience is Hispanic, you can freely use your hands to express yourself. However, you need to pay close attention to use the correct translation of words for the American and Spanish speakers. You can't assume that there is a uniform understanding in a Hispanic audience, because there will be many cultures present. While Cubans predominate, there are also Venezuelans, Colombians, Brazilians, Argentines, and Spaniards. Be careful with expressions in the language, even if it's entirely done in Spanish, because the idioms are different.*

Ana says about speaking in Texas:

> *It's a more relaxed and accepting audience in terms of how you express yourself and your body movements than in New York, where how language is used and even what you wear matters. Observe the stereotypes about clothing—dress, jacket, and tie—and be up to date on financial and legal matters related to your topic.*

Moving to South America and Europe, she finds more formality:

> *In Argentina, the business community is even more formal and favors darker color, so it's best to follow suit. When you're presenting in Spain, it's best to keep your language as formal as possible and minimize your movement on stage. Generally, unlike the United States where interaction and movement between the speaker and audience are expected and often create a good impact, you don't want to move around too much in Spain.*

Another prepresentation variable is adjusting for who will be in the audience. Ana noted that "you have a totally different focus, speech, and set of visuals to present if the audience is business as opposed to academic."

Take Cues from Firefighters' Training

When a public speaking situation moves out of your control, it's like a fire. Once underway, fire takes on its own life. The training and skill of firefighters stand between total destruction, walls collapsing, windows blowing out, possible death, and chaos. They prepare extensively throughout their career, both mentally and physically, to throw themselves into harm's way.

While I may seem to be exaggerating a little, when you're in the midst of a speaking disaster, you can feel as though everything is on fire. Tempers can flare. Your argument, like a building's walls, can collapse under scrutiny. What once seemed predictable and orderly is now hazardous and swallowing up all in its path.

You can mentally gear yourself up for maintaining your cool in these trying situations by taking cues from the firefighters. Their professional education encompasses both tactical training and psychological conditioning, especially for those awful cases when adults and children die despite heroic efforts.

As a leader, you may not find yourself in the same life-threatening position as a firefighter, but the threat to your role, your organization, or your community can be deadly serious—if you do not maintain or regain control of your emotions in public speaking.

Firefighters are trained with live fire drills to help them learn to solve problems quickly, and think critically and clearly, especially under extreme stress. The following steps are adapted from National Fire Protection Association.

First, students are required to dress in high-tech, multilayered specialty clothing that can withstand temperatures up to 1,200 degrees Fahrenheit. In addition, each student wears specialized equipment, tacking on an extra thirty pounds or more.

Every item of firefighting clothing is planned and has a purpose. When you tackle your wardrobe planning the same way, there's less likelihood of a wardrobe malfunction getting in your way. You want clothes that move with you and breathe, shoes that are elegant yet comfortable, jewelry that doesn't clunk against the lectern, and nothing extraneous to distract attention from what you are saying.

Next, the aspiring firefighters enter what's called a burn building, with a prescribed series of steps, where some carry a hose and some don't, keeping a specified distance from each other.

You want to be aware of where your audience will be sitting in relationship to you, where the microphone will be, the projector, screen, and lectern, if any, before you step on stage.

Then the action really starts. Once the instructor gives the go-ahead, the students open the nozzle and start attacking the flames. They take turns, positioning the nozzle away from their bodies to avoid steam burns on exposed skin. Once the fire is put out, everyone leaves except a final crew that makes sure the fire does not reignite.

As a speaker, you have almost as many moving parts as the firefighters! No wonder you may feel under fire at times, right? With live, on stage practice, however, you will learn to watch the audience behavior while maintaining control over your emotions, your hands, body, and the actual delivery of your words and ideas.

Creating Your Own Speaker's Emergency Kit

Just before I began my speech before one of the local chambers a few years ago, I ran into the ladies' room for a last-minute check in the mirror and other necessary activity. The chamber was only about fifteen minutes from my office, so I didn't think there would be much to worry about. Normally, this once-over procedure can help you avoid potential embarrassment from hair standing on end, something green stuck in your teeth, or an unbuttoned shirt, preventing other similar distractions for your audience.

After I washed my hands, I looked down and discovered that the sink had emptied into my crotch area. It was that kind of older sink that splashes wherever it feels like splashing. Rather than get upset with massive wetness now obvious in an inappropriate and highly visible area, I flew out to my car where I had left my extra suit—which I always carry for just such emergencies—and quickly changed into it. The response when I reemerged a few minutes later in a purple outfit: "Weren't you just wearing a blue suit?" I answered, "Yes, but I was tired of it." And the show went on, nobody being the wiser.

I have been carrying an extra suit as part of what I called my speaker's emergency kit since the beginning of my business as a speaking consultant, but other contents over the years have changed somewhat. Here's what is with me at all times, in my briefcase or carry-on, and I strongly encourage you to create your own variation:

❑ Migraine medication. I get them and you never know when they'll strike.

❑ Extra compact, blush, and lipstick. (Gentlemen, you might want a razor and shaving cream, if you need to freshen up for an evening talk or television interview.)

❑ Kleenex packet

❑ Mints

❑ Toothbrush and toothpaste

❑ Dental floss

❑ Raisins or a cereal bar (in case I've missed a meal or am hungry)

❑ Over-the-counter stomach medication

❑ Allergy medicine

❑ Colored markers. If the digital fails, you can usually find a flip chart to enhance your remarks

❑ Copy of my introduction, in large type, even if I have previously sent it

Other essentials:

❑ A printed copy of my PowerPoint slides, six to a page in handout format.

Pop Goes the What?

Wearing a royal blue suit with big, navy buttons, I was doing a last-minute bathroom visit before starting a half-day session for a cruise line. Satisfied with my hair, my nose not shiny, and my lipstick not smeared, I proceeded to button my jacket. And that's when the middle button fell off in my hand.

If you've ever seen what's behind a button on a blue suit, it's not pretty. There was no time to sew it back on. Even though I had a tiny sewing kit in my speaker's emergency kit, the truth was it probably would have looked awful even had I tried.

In an instant, I went back to the meeting room, grabbed my purple standby suit, flew into the ladies' room, and changed.

A few of the participants asked me what happened. I mumbled something about changing my mind, a woman's prerogative, and the rest of day went off without a hitch.

Uninspired

- An *extra* copy of my introduction, in large type to make it easy to read

- An extra suit or dress that goes with my shoes. Even locally. (I used to also carry extra panty hose. Now, I do that only if it's cold.)

- In my new-and-improved speaker's emergency kit, there's now a digital version. Its contents are:

- Two flash drives with my presentation, in case one doesn't work, even if I've sent the presentation via email already

- Power cords for iPhone, iPad, and laptop computer

- Information on the link to my Cloud application if I need to access my presentation there

You may be thinking to yourself, "I've never had anything really awful happen to me so far." Well, you are lucky! While plan may be a four-letter word and an annoyance to some when it comes to public speaking, I have found that taking the time to equip yourself to withstand hurricane conditions on stage really pays off.

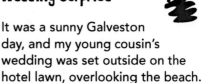

The Unwelcome Wedding Surprise

It was a sunny Galveston day, and my young cousin's wedding was set outside on the hotel lawn, overlooking the beach.

As the couple exchanged vows, a flock of seagulls in a perfect v-shaped formation flew overhead. It seemed a good omen. In seconds, however, I heard—and smelled—a series of "plop, plop, plop." Next to me, covered in poop, was an unsmiling cousin. A few seats over another cousin was similarly adorned. I noticed that the mother of the groom suddenly had a brown spot on the front of her dress. A few of us uncontrollably started to laugh, trying to hide our grins.

Fortunately, no one in the wedding party realized what had happened. The ceremony concluded with the traditional breaking of the glass and shouts of "mazel tov," congratulations.

Moral of the story: You cannot always control what is happening around you. Poop happens. You can only control your own response.

Uninspired

To Summarize...

🖎 What separates speaking geniuses from losers is the capacity to remain focused on delivering your message to the audience, instead of worrying about yourself.

🖎 When you establish prespeaking rituals, you increase the odds of maintaining control even under the most trying circumstances.

🖎 By putting together your own speaker's emergency kit, you will be as self-sufficient as possible, adding to your psychological well-being and your professional presence as well.

Chapter 19

Dealing with Hostile Questions and Technology

In This Chapter...

- The Ins and Outs of Answering Tough Questions and Disruptions
- Dealing with the Word Gremlins
- You're Still the Boss with Technology

Once you've finished crafting your message, your next assignment is to wonder aloud to your team, or quietly to yourself: "What kind of things could happen that I need to be ready to handle?" These "what if?" situations can range from being asked questions that are neither friendly nor positive, posed by your audience or the media, to the malfunctioning of your presenting technology, and more.

The process of getting these potentially disruptive or damaging questions out in the open can help you a) admit that they could be asked, and b) mentally begin to ready your answers. The same prepresentation consideration of the potential for equipment failure, poor Internet connections, and other technology nightmares will give you time to focus on a realistic backup plan.

In this chapter, I give you practical ways to approach answering hostile or otherwise challenging questions from any group or the media. You'll also find ideas to help you overcome those inevitable technical glitches that usually show up at the most inopportune times. They may not be avoidable, but you'll know what to do!

Heckler's Delight: Anticipate Hostile Questions or Interruptions

No matter how much you have rehearsed your message and prepared for all contingencies, there will be someone who wants to steal the spotlight from you. It could be one person or several, an audience member or a media representative. Their mission is not the same as yours for being at your presentation, is it? You're there to share your ideas and expertise. Critics want their side of the issue heard. A potential or existing client may try to poke holes in what you're proposing. The media's interest is to get a good story to print or air.

Creating an Oral Headline

Amid the noise of the question-answer session or a broadcast media interview, to be sure your key messages are heard right away, begin with your conclusion and then follow up with further explanation. That way you are "headlining" the issue, also known as "flagging" the point. To amplify what you're trying to say, you can add phrases to frame your remarks.

"The most critical (or important) fact/issue/idea is…"

"What we want to stress/make clear is…"

By the way, the idea of an oral headline also applies to your self-introduction or elevator speech. Can you telegraph in a few powerful, clear words what is important for people to know about you?

Answer Fast and State Your Real Point

You can transform every question—even the dumb or awkward ones—into an opportunity for you to make your point by giving a short answer and then plunging ahead to talk about what is important to you.

"… (your brief answer to their question) and that reinforces our goal to…"

Try the Football Defense: Blocking

A reporter or someone in the audience directs a question to you that you absolutely do not want to answer, perhaps because your organization's policy is not to discuss certain matters like the one on the table. You can state that clearly, "It's not our policy to discuss this," and then go on to say what you do want to focus on.

I don't recommend that you avoid answering a question without explaining why you can't answer it because you appear suspicious or uninformed, neither desirable impressions to make. Only the White House gets away by saying "no comment."

Take Your Speaking Genius Further: Bridging

You could be asked a question that doesn't allow you to make the points you want or that you really don't want to answer at all. One of the techniques you can try is called bridging, finding the connection to your issue and then turning the question toward it.

"I think what you really are asking, what you really want to know is…"

"Yes, and that speaks to a bigger point…"

Pick the top three or four most miserable questions you think you could be asked first, and devise your answers, on paper and then saying your responses aloud. If you don't have anyone with whom to practice, record the question, then play it back and respond. Simulate being asked and answering as much as you can.

What happens if you get stuck trying to answer a question and the words don't come out well or at all? Better to have this happen during your practice than at a critical moment, yes? Just keep trying to develop a solid, coherent answer, and you'll soon find the right way to respond will emerge. If you hit a dead end, do seek help from a colleague or friend who may be able to help you unlock the blockage you've inadvertently created within your brain.

Brain Freeze Can Happen at Any Time, to Anyone

It's not only the hostile question that can trip you up. I was recently asked a question I did not expect during a last-minute interview by Mexican journalists.

What started as an informal lunch invitation I'd extended to a Mexican entrepreneur had grown into a formal media event. The media came to cover the signing of a memorandum of understanding between the Miami chapter of NAWBO, of which I was president at the time, and AMMJE Yucatan, the Mexican women's entrepreneurs association.

The first question went well. "Did I see this agreement increasing trade between the Yucatan and Florida?" I answered that I thought it would eventually, as the relationships among women business owners throughout Florida and the Yucatan developed.

It was the second question that caught me by surprise. "Tell us about who's in your organization."

For some inexplicable reason, my brain went suddenly dead. I couldn't think of anything clever or particularly interesting, and could only rattle off a description of some of the categories: lawyers, accountants, software developers, and financial planners. Later, when my brain unfroze, I kicked myself. I could have told them how we had a member who used to be in the Central Intelligence Agency and now does high-level personal security. And about another member who has invented a device that translates information into any language for medical information and menus. About the member who has three bakeries. And on and on.

The point is that getting tongue-tied can happen to anyone, especially when we have never given any previous thought to a question.

One of the ways to minimize appearing tongue-tied or insecure is to avoid language that sounds defensive. That includes the words, "I'm sorry but" unless you truly are sorry and are admitting to doing something wrong or bad. Instead, point out the data you have supporting your position. Be ready with whatever evidence, testimonials of significance, and anecdotes you can share to diffuse the hostile questions and recapture the confidence and interest of your audience, whether it's the board of directors or an industry group.

If you're speaking and you keep getting interrupted by an audience member and it's not a question but a statement, allow it only once. You can interrupt and ask, "Do you have a question for me?" Most likely, there won't be one. But if there is, you have several choices. One is to answer it immediately, as quickly as possible, and then continue your remarks. The second is to thank the person for the question and tell the audience member you'll be covering the answer shortly and just keep going. The third is to acknowledge the question, stating it's outside your realm of expertise, and that you'll try and locate someone who can answer it the next day.

Most people who interrupt a speaker are simply trying to seize the spotlight for themselves, instead of waiting for the regular question-and-answer period.

Fighting the Gremlins: When Things Don't Work

When a disaster strikes during public speaking, whether a miniversion or a major catastrophe, I usually blame it on one of two groups of gremlins.

The first I call the "word gremlins." Their home base is in our brain, our natural technology system. If you hear yourself saying something you never intended to say, if words pop out of your mouth totally unbidden—and usually undesired—you are experiencing an attack of the word gremlins. Think back to my example in **Chapter 7** where I found myself saying our hero, James Bond, was in a different *bed* every eight minutes—instead of in a different adventure. You will find yourself stunned and muttering: "Did I just say that?"

A related phenomenon is when the words suddenly vanish from your brain entirely and you have no idea where you are in your speech. This dreaded type of word gremlin is known as a *memory lapse*.

It's not unusual, despite a ton of practice, for you to realize that you are out of

You've Lost Your Train of Thought

What do I recommend? Here a few different techniques to try.

◆ Ask a question of your audience and smile, "Now what was I just talking about?" Of course, it's easier if you have slides and you can take a quick peek at your previous and upcoming one to give yourself a prompt. When you are speaking with no visual backup, if you appear calm and unflustered, most likely an audience member will help you get back on track.

◆ Make the pause look planned. Start a quick recap of the theme of your message to give your brain a chance to fall back in gear. Sometimes that little jump-start will get you going again. If not, act in control by saying, "This point I'm about to make is so important that I want to be sure I get it absolutely right for you." Waltz over to your notes, pretending to double-check your statement.

Inspiration

gas mentally, in the midst of a speech, experiencing a total blank screen in your head. This unnerving occurrence happens to veteran as well as novice speakers.

It is the second group, the "technology gremlins," who have taken a particularly strong foothold in our speaking world of late. The technology gremlins attack at the worst time, without provocation, and can drive you completely nuts. They can cause great harm to your reputation, too, if you are not prepared to get past their presence.

One of my clients was doing his off-Broadway practice at a local Rotary Club in anticipation of a speech before five hundred industry leaders the following week. We had tested the PowerPoint several times and everything was working fine. Upon arrival at the restaurant, and putting the flash drive into a computer provided by a member, nothing showed up on the big screen. Having prepared for such a scenario, Tom was able to use the printout of the slides to guide him along. He appeared confident and focused on his topic, and no one seemed to miss the visuals. After his remarks, he was peppered with good questions, helping him anticipate what might be asked from an audience with more knowledge of his topic.

At a venture capital conference where startups were pitching investors, I saw the opposite result when one of the presenter's deck of slides failed to operate. Instead of going forward to seize the moment and the opportunity being in front of potential funders, the entrepreneur kept trying to make his slides work, using up his allotted time and losing his chance to be heard. Everyone was uncomfortable, too, watching this technology drama play out. If he had been really well-versed in his presentation, the lack of visuals would not have mattered.

The following technology gremlins have attacked me, personally:

🔍 I had the technician double-check the microphone, the video setup, and computer during the break in the conference before my presentation. When it was my turn, the audio with the PowerPoint did not work. I just kept going in front of three hundred plus prospective investors, acting as though nothing was wrong, because no one could really tell anything was missing— except me.

🔍 For some reason, every outlet was dead in the hotel meeting room where I was scheduled to speak. No other space was available. Fortunately, because

I was on site an hour early, there was time for the audiovisual people to find enough extension cords to bring electricity into the room.

At the last moment, the clicker to advance the slides decided to stop functioning. The battery was changed and still nothing happened. It would have been awkward for me to be going back and forth to where the computer was situated, so I had to ask an audience member to help out. No fun but no choice.

Even though a screen had been requested in advance, when I arrived at the meeting room, I was told no screens were available. The walls were ornately decorated with virtually no white space. After some experimenting, I found that only the doors were light enough for the images to show up. And that's where we projected the slide show, albeit far smaller than usual.

To Summarize...

Identify questions that could throw you for a loop and prepare answers in advance. Know you can't be ready for everything!

Your natural technology, the brain, can take you on journeys you weren't expecting, too. But the "word gremlins" can't win when you maintain control of your thinking and actions.

Technology can be a friend or foe at times. Remember, you're always the boss of your own speaking and leadership presentation. Be ready to go on without your technical support.

Chapter 20

Become a Genius Speaker... and Get Ready for Success!

In This Chapter...

- There's no such thing as too ready
- As the expert, the spotlight belongs to you
- You didn't do it overnight, no matter what they say
- The world needs your voice—and your future awaits!

In my all-time favorite movie classic, *The Wizard of Oz* with Judy Garland, one song continues to tug at my heart: *Over the Rainbow*. Dorothy, the heroine who wakes up in a strange land, sings her longing for things to be better and to return home, a mission she wants to accomplish by wishing upon a star.

By now, you've figured out that great speakers aren't created by mere wishing. Neither is it an accident of birth. They are made through hard work, dedication, and a special spirit that is unwilling to bore others or show up unprepared to do their best.

In this final chapter, you'll meet some characters in the speaking world who might make you seek help from the Wizard of Oz yourself, following the yellow brick road as Dorothy did. No need! I've given you strategies to deal with them along with additional tactics to show the world what an expert you really are.

Why You Really Can't Be Too Ready

Even when a firefighter has been in the department for years and years, emergency drills are still mandatory. Olympic athletes practice for years to compete for minutes in front of the world. Award-winning actors rehearse tirelessly to perfect their part in a play or movie.

What separates the adequate from the extraordinary in public speaking is a commitment to practice, to rehearse the carefully crafted words so that nothing gets in the way of your top notch delivery.

When you truly know your material, the unexpected interruption, whether welcome or not, will not throw you off your game.

Some clients have complained that they are afraid of becoming wooden if they rehearse too much. To that concern, I remind them that I recommend practicing out of order, in pieces, as frequently as possible, to help keep you from getting bored or sounding like you've memorized the content and are saying it by rote. Delivering a message in its entirety, in order, only needs to happen a few times in rehearsal when you have nailed the individual pieces.

There's another reason you can't be too ready. Despite your best efforts to anticipate who's going to be in your audience, you don't really have any control over who will show up. Here are four of the most dreaded audience types who could plague you, and some strategies for winning them over:

The Bully Type

Remember the person motivated by power we talked about in **Chapter 13**? Sadly, you're going to encounter groups of this type often in the extreme intensity in your audiences and during an interview as well. In a sales or internal presentation, they're going to try and put down what you're offering because they believe their connections are stronger and more influential than what you're bringing to the table.

When you're a speaker at a conference or before a local group, the bully type is likely to publicly challenge your statements or even your expertise. In an interview, this type tends to get carried away with the wielded power and may also have forgotten what being new feels like.

Your challenge is not to wimp out, to not back down under the pressure, and instead, to show how your expertise, your ideas, your products, or your services can add value to their organization and efforts. You can try to turn these people around by acknowledging their leadership in the industry or in their particular organization or club. You can express your desire to learn more about their own role and vision for the future, as well as the company's plans.

The Poker Face—Shows No Emotion

Sitting right in front of you, with a mission of throwing off your confidence if you're not ready for them, are those individuals who will not give you any emotional or physical clues to let you know how your talk, your sales presentation, or your interview is going. I can tell you this type can be truly disconcerting if you, yourself, are an especially expressive personality type.

Instead of worrying about giving the audience or the interviewer what you think they want to hear at this tense moment, continue with what you've planned carefully to share. You won't be able to read their nonexistent reactions anyway. Impress them with your knowledge in your area of expertise. You can pose thoughtful questions to get them to respond mentally, if not in an obvious way to your presentation.

If it's an interview, point out how you've taken initiative in your position and try to get them to open up by asking questions that encourage them to talk about their experiences on the job and what they see as future opportunities.

The Investigator

These type of nosy and sometimes almost paranoid audience members, prospective clients, and interviewers will have thoroughly checked you out before your appearance, online and in your industry or professional circles. They will insist on your verifying every statement you make.

Listen carefully to what questions you're being asked for insights into what their real motivations or concerns may be. The questions can also give you clues to how their own company operates and how you can supply what they need. Don't hide behind but do take advantage of whatever technology is available to help you overcome their overly-curious nature.

If you really don't have an answer to a particular question they raise, do assure them that you'll get the information they are requesting and send it immediately following your presentation or interview.

The Chicken without a Head

You're in a meeting where the schedule was messed up or those attending didn't have a clue they were supposed to be present. As my Aunt Maxine would have said, "Oy vay!" Or, "oh, my."

Individually and collectively, the folks in the room are acting like a chicken running around without its head. Whether you arrived to make a speech, give a pitch, or be interviewed, you may suddenly have to take control of what's happening to salvage your time and reach your goal.

Try not to give in to the disorganization spinning around you. Avoid making your audience or interviewer aware that you're disappointed by their lack of readiness for your visit. Instead, seize the moment to lead with your best material and bragging rights, as soon as you can, because chaos could erupt at any moment. You may decide you don't want to do business or work with a company that operates this way. Listen to your intuition.

From a Fire Alarm to Flying High

Ana C. Martinez, a former client and a longtime development executive for local nonprofits, is legally blind and a community activist for disability issues. She told me:

> The worst public speaking experience I ever had was when a fire alarm went off in the middle of my speech.
>
> The sudden reality was that everyone needed to get out of the room, fast, and they flew out the door. I took some comfort knowing that they weren't leaving because of my message.
>
> But a few minutes later, the organizers announced that it had been a false alarm and people started drifting back to their seats. They encouraged me to 'just go on,' but how do you do that? You take a deep breath and start again. You trust that you know what you're talking about and go forward.

No matter what you plan as a speaker, life will take its own turns.

Forever Out-Maneuvering the Time Grinch

You've been told you have an hour to go over your findings and recommendations but, arriving on the scene, you learn it's now only thirty minutes.

Or, every board member was supposed to get ten minutes but the meeting is running late and five minutes is all you've got now to be convincing.

Or, you're the guest speaker and instead of twenty minutes, the host has asked you to limit your remarks to twelve minutes.

The Time Grinch usually shows up at the worst possible time. What can complicate the scenario is not only revamping the content of what you were ready to present, but what to do with the visuals as well.

Remember, You're the Expert—and the Leader at This Moment

Regardless of who is in your audience, no one is inviting you to speak just because you're someone's child or you're too beautiful for words. You are in front of a group because there's a perception—right or wrong—that you are an expert, you are a leader. We think that you know what you are talking about, and that you have something of value to share.

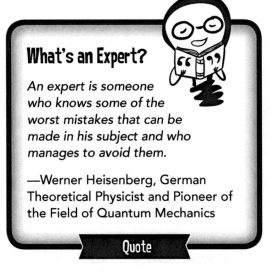

What's an Expert?

An expert is someone who knows some of the worst mistakes that can be made in his subject and who manages to avoid them.

—Werner Heisenberg, German Theoretical Physicist and Pioneer of the Field of Quantum Mechanics

Quote

As an expert, your obligation to the audience is to be as helpful, informative, and inspiring as possible. It is also to not be boring, to honor the time you've been given, and to be on your toes, ready to deliver more than is expected.

How would someone know if you're really an expert? Why does it matter?

Your Bio Had Better Be the Real Deal

It's critical to put together an impeccable bio as part of your speaker introduction and any package you may present to be considered as a speaker. Today, it's

The Inventor's Grandniece versus the Time Grinch

As a sought-after keynote speaker on innovation and inventing who is also the great grandniece of pioneering American inventor Thomas Edison, Sarah Miller Caldicott has become quite adept at having to adjust to her planned presentation when time expectations change. She is CEO of Power Patterns of Innovation and author of *Midnight Lunch, Innovate Like Edison*, and *Inventing the Future*. She produces a newsletter called *Edison's Notebook* and blogs for *Forbes*. She told me:

> *While having a brief presentation window is not the ideal, I've learned short speaking intervals are a reality for every platform professional.*
>
> *When I know ahead of time that I'm facing a short time slot, I will choose just three core points to make with my audience. I organize all my stories, all my insights around these three key points. In such instances, I use only ten presentation slides rather than the roughly thirty-five I would normally use in a full one-hour keynote.*
>
> *The ten slides rotate between a single word or theme on the slide and a photo or compelling image linked to one of my three key points. There is no verbiage and the slide deck has a completely different visual feel than my longer keynotes.*
>
> *When I don't know ahead of time that my speaking slot will be shortened, I work with the technical rep on site to pull out as many as twenty slides from my prepared speech. I keep slides that I've specifically prepared for the client combined with slides that I use in every single keynote I give. I will then deliver the keynote using just the roughly fifteen slides remaining.*
>
> *In these situations, I once again select three key points to make for the audience, always remembering to emphasize the specific theme of the event as my guideline.*
>
> *Shortened speaking slots are an acid test for every professional. But rather than fear them, embrace them and recognize you'll learn something new from each one.*

relatively simple to verify online whether or not you actually graduated from a particular university or if you are truly certified in an industry. Once it's discovered that your background check does not match up, anything and everything you say may be suspect. Your credibility as a speaker, as a leader, or as a candidate for a position will vanish.

State the Facts with Conviction and More

If you cite facts in your talk, identify the source or, if from multiple places, mention at least one of them. Unless it's your own research—and then be sure to announce that—citing whose discovery or findings you are sharing will reinforce your position as the expert in your field.

Talk about and Answer the Questions People Want to Know— and More

Sometimes you're sought out to speak on one subject and it turns out they want you to modify your remarks with a different focus. Your ability to shift gears to share your know-how from another perspective reinforces the idea that you are, indeed the expert.

The More You Speak, the Better You Can Become

Can you become an overnight sensation in public speaking? Maybe, if your talk goes

I Can Do That!

A women's entrepreneur conference I'd approached about doing a public speaking workshop for leaders, instead, asked me to put together a talk on how to use motivation, for chapter leaders. As the conference approached, the organizers contacted me about changing the focus again, to make the session appealing to any kind of aspiring leader, not just those already serving on a board.

Since my expertise is communication, I was able to switch gears and craft the workshop they wanted. If they had asked for guidance on chapter financial matters, however, I would have had to decline the opportunity. Although I've been a member for more than twenty-five years, I never handled the books, and would have been entirely the wrong person to comment.

Example

viral. Years of preparation can pay off in wild and wonderful ways. A truly outstanding performance can skyrocket your career and reputation.

If you examine the success of speakers who make it—in business, politics, the arts, and academia—you'll find that they started as I mentioned to you earlier in the book, "off-off-off-off Broadway," talking to audiences of all sizes, seizing opportunities to acquire and perfect their presentation skills. They spoke in classrooms, at Rotary Clubs, in their church or synagogue basements, at orientations, to women's groups, at coffee klatches, and village council meetings. Some went on to top-tier leadership positions and to become professional speakers. Others have claimed a place of respect in their companies and in their communities.

Just as you did not wake up one day with all the expertise and leadership presence you now have, so it is with acquiring and perfecting your public speaking skills. It's a never-ending polishing act, and every day you can continue to get better and better.

Here are a few more things to ask yourself to insure your status as a respected authority *and* a great speaker:

- *Am I respectful of what they're afraid of or concerned about?* If you have young parents in the room, for example, they may be fearful of missing out on doing something critical for their child's development. If you reassure them in a cavalier manner that they probably won't make any serious mistakes, you could alienate everyone.

- *Did I bring my knowledge level to where they are?* Assuming they know as much as you do on your topic can doom you to a huge disconnect.

- *Do I make myself likable and believable?* Are you connecting person-to-person? Keeping yourself emotionally distant from the audience dims the light that you could be spreading.

- *Have I stopped too short?* If you haven't inspired the audience members to go forward and do something for themselves, their company, or their community—if you haven't specifically called for an action of some kind—what was the point of your being there?

- *Does what I have to say really matter?* With the intense, ongoing information overload everywhere, what is the value—the lasting worth—of what you are presenting? If you can't state it now, go back and work a little more on your message. It will come to you.

The World Needs to Hear Your Voice

Before going to press with this book, a friend who had founded and led a highly respected local nonprofit organization for many years decided to run for office. It was her first foray into the world of politics and while I was thrilled for our community, I was concerned about her well-being, jumping with both feet into the often negative realm of politics.

I quoted to her my mother's favorite saying for such decisions: "Are you sure you don't want to lie down and let the feeling pass?"

She assured me that she was clear on her purpose. She wanted to continue to serve the community, but in this new way, as an elected official, in government.

I worked with her team to help craft her announcement message, jumping in after reviewing some drafts that had been provided by another expert she'd hired.

What was missing, at first, was my friend's voice. Though well-written, the speech did not ring true. To gain the support she needed to be elected, to convince those who did not know her, who did not know that they could have a better government with her contribution, her voice needed to be heard loudly and clearly through the message.

We modified her words and approach to help her let her own voice surface. She continued her campaign, refining the message and adapting her delivery for

Over the Rainbow— Not Just for Dorothy

The lyrics from the classic *Wizard of Oz* song I mentioned earlier often come to mind when I'm up against a particularly tough challenge. (Google: Over the Rainbow.)

Other inspiring music for me includes many of the Beatles' songs: "Yesterday," "Here Comes the Sun" and John Lennon's "Imagine All the People." I also love "Don't Stop Believing" by Journey, "Ain't No Mountain High Enough" by Marvin Gaye and Tammi Terrell, and "Don't Worry, Be Happy," by Bobby McFerrin.

I encourage you to identify a few tunes to hum or sing that can help carry you through the ups and downs of public speaking.

Inspiration

different audiences. I was thrilled when she defeated the incumbent and was elected to office, fulfilling her lifelong dream.

You have a choice, as an expert, as a leader, to come forward and share what you know, or to stay in the background. I believe the world needs to hear your voice, too, or you would not be reading *Public Speaking for the GENIUS*! You would not be looking for ways to organize your expertise, to punch up your content, or to put yourself out there in a memorable, engaging way, if you did not have something worthwhile to say.

Your Success Is at Hand!

It's been my honor to be a part of your world for a little while, to shine some light on the ins and outs of public speaking, and to encourage you to try your hand.

Remember, while there are no shortcuts to being an outstanding public speaker. By following the guidelines I've shared, you're well on your way to the accolades and applause you so deserve.

Now, it's up to you to go out there and exceed expectations. Knock their socks off. Bring the house down! Rock and roll. Receive a standing ovation. Claim your place in the public speaking hall of fame. It's your turn!

To Summarize...

- The expression, #$%^&&* happens, applies to speakers far more often than we'd like. No matter how ready, and how many other things have happened before, expect more of the unexpected.

- Your know-how and your personality are equally in demand when you put yourself in the limelight.

- Developing your speaking skills rarely happens fast; for most of us it's a gradual, never-ending process.

- You bring your special gifts to the planet. Our world grows richer whenever you choose to share them through public speaking.

Developing Your Genius Message Checklist

Topic: _____   Date of Presentation: _____

Steps to Prepare Your Presentation	Start Date	First, Second Draft Dates	Ready
Prepare a set of possible titles for your message that will motivate people to attend, if an external speaking engagement. Prepare a short bio and photo as needed, with a catchy title for your talk.			
Get background on who's going to attend and their interests/needs.			
Establish how long you'll talk, where, when, and what a/v you'll need.			
Determine what your goals are for the speaking opportunity.			
Brainstorm your content and prioritize what you'll cover.			
Identify your main points—up to three or four maximum.			
Create a working outline with your three main points.			
Choose a body format by trying out your main ideas in it to see if they flow well. Try out at least two to three formats to determine which is best for your message.			
Classify and list other ideas, facts, examples, and stories as subpoints on your working outline.			
Write your closing summary and a call for action.			
Devise a prebody summary that promotes interest in your main points and message.			

Steps to Prepare Your Presentation	Start Date	First, Second Draft Dates	Ready
Identify stories and examples with emotional appeal that you can add strategically to your message.			
Review to be sure you've included pain points or problem-solving aspects of your message.			
Select an attention-grabbing opening. Be sure and try out several.			
Develop your visual support, i.e. slides, videos, posters.			
Anticipate and write down potentially hostile, difficult, or disruptive questions you may be asked.			
Check out your transitions between parts. Are they smooth? Awkward? Fix as needed.			
Schedule your rehearsals. Break your message into parts and practice out of order, at least nine times.			
Fix any parts that don't sound natural or are too hard for you to say comfortably.			
If possible, schedule a chance to present to a group that isn't your main target, for practice purposes. (Off-off-off-off Broadway.)			
Plan your outfit and emergency backup outfit in advance. Prepare your speaker introduction, if needed.			
Make extra copies of your notes and place in separate folders to bring with you. Put your presentation images and video on two flash drives in case there is no Internet access.			

Fill-in-the-Blank Outline for Your Presentation or Speech

Topic: _____ Date of Presentation: _____

Greeting. (See **Chapter 17**. Examples: Ladies and gentlemen, Good morning everyone, Members and guests of the XYZ Association, Hello y'all.) _____

_____

_____

_____

_____

_____

Optional gracious throwaway line. (See **Chapter 17** for examples.) _____

_____

_____

_____

_____

_____

Opening. (See **Chapter 11** for six types of openings and examples) _____

_____

_____

_____

_____

_____

Prebody. (See **Chapter 10** for explanation and examples) _____

_____

_____

_____

_____

_____

Body. (See **Chapter 12** for five formats and examples) _____

_____

_____

_____

_____

_____

Point 1. Choose an opening technique (see **Chapter 11**) to introduce your point then expand on your ideas and information. _____

_____

_____

_____

_____

_____

_____

_____

_____

Point 2. Choose an opening technique (see **Chapter 11**) to introduce your point then expand on your ideas and information. _____

_____

_____

_____

_____

_____

_____

_____

_____

Point 3. Choose an opening technique (see **Chapter 11**) to introduce your point then expand on your ideas and information. _____

_____

_____

_____

_____

_____

_____

_____

_____

Close. Include summary of your points and call for action, if any. _____

_____

_____

_____

_____

Index

For the GENIUS® Press is an imprint that produces books on just about any topic that people want to learn. *You don't have to be a genius to read a GENIUS book, but you'll sure be smarter once you do!*™ Here are some of our recently published titles.